W9-AOH-647

AMERICAN WOMEN FICTION WRITERS 1900-1960

VOLUME THREE

AMERICAN WOMEN FICTION WRITERS
1900–1960
VOLUME THREE

Edited and with an Introduction by

Harold Bloom

CHELSEA HOUSE PUBLISHERS

Philadelphia

ON THE COVER: Beatrice Whitney Van Ness (American, 1888–1981), *Summer Sunlight*, ca. 1936. Oil on canvas, 39″ x 49″. The National Museum of Women in the Arts, gift of Wallace and Wilhelmina Holladay.

CHELSEA HOUSE PUBLISHERS

EDITOR-IN-CHIEF   Stephen Reginald
PRODUCTION MANAGER   Pamela Loos
MANAGING EDITOR   James D. Gallagher
PICTURE EDITOR   Judy Hasday
ART DIRECTOR   Sara Davis
SENIOR PRODUCTION EDITOR   Lisa Chippendale

WOMEN WRITERS OF ENGLISH AND THEIR WORKS:
   American Women Fiction Writers, 1900–1960: Volume Three

PROJECT EDITOR   Robert Green
CONTRIBUTING EDITOR   Deborah Williams
SENIOR EDITOR   Therese De Angelis
INTERIOR AND COVER DESIGNER   Alison Burnside
EDITORIAL ASSISTANT   Anne Hill

The Chelsea House world wide web site address is
http://www.chelseahouse.com

3 5 7 9 8 6 4 2

Library of Congress Cataloging-in-Publication Data

American women fiction writers / edited and with an introduction by
   Harold Bloom.
      p.   cm. — (Women writers of English and their works)
   Includes bibliographical references and index.
   ISBN 0-7910-4652-4 (v. 3). — ISBN 0-7910-4653-2 (pbk. : v. 3)
   1. American fiction—Women authors—History and criticism.
2. American fiction—Women authors—Bio–bibliography. 3. Women and
literature—United States.   I. Bloom, Harold. II. Series.
PS374.W6A455 1997
813.009′ 9287—dc21
   [B]   97-6310
                                                                          CIP

CONTENTS

THE ANALYSIS OF WOMEN WRITERS

HAROLD BLOOM

I APPROACH THIS SERIES with a certain wariness, since so much of classical feminist literary criticism has founded itself upon arguments with that phase of my own work that began with *The Anxiety of Influence* (first published in January 1973). Someone who has been raised to that bad eminence—*The Patriarchal Critic*—is well advised that he trespasses upon sacred ground when he ventures to inquire whether indeed there are indisputable differences, imaginative and cognitive, between the literary works of women and those of men. If these differences are so substantial as pragmatically to make an authentic difference, does that in turn make necessary different aesthetic standards for judging the achievements of men and of women writers? Is Emily Dickinson to be read as though she has more in common with Elizabeth Barrett Browning than with Ralph Waldo Emerson?

Is Elizabeth Bishop a great poet because she triumphantly meets the same aesthetic criteria satisfied by Wallace Stevens, or should we evaluate her by criteria she shares with Marianne Moore, but not with Stevens? Are there crucial gender-based differences in the representations of Esther Summerson by Charles Dickens in *Bleak House*, and of Dorothea Brooke by George Eliot in *Middlemarch*? Does Samuel Richardson's Clarissa Harlowe convince us that her author was a male when we contrast her with Jane Austen's Elizabeth Bennet? Do women poets have a less agonistic relationship to female precursors than male poets have to their forerunners? Two eminent pioneers of feminist criticism, Sandra Gilbert and Susan Gubar, have suggested that women writers suffer more from an anxiety of authorship than they do from influence anxieties, while another important feminist critic, Elaine Showalter, has suggested that women writers, early and late, work together in a kind of quiltmaking, each doing her share while avoiding any contamination of creative envy in regard to other writers, provided that they be women. Can it be true that, in the aesthetic sphere, women do not beware women and do not suffer from the competitiveness and jealousy that alas do exist in the professional and sexual domains? Is there something in the area of literature, when practiced by women, that changes and purifies mere human nature?

I cannot answer any of these questions, yet I do think it is vital and clarifying to raise them. There is a current fashion, in many of our institutions of higher education, to insist that English Romantic poetry cannot be studied in the old way, with an exclusive emphasis upon the works of William Blake, William Wordsworth, Samuel Taylor Coleridge, Lord Byron, Percy Bysshe Shelley, John Keats, and John Clare. Instead, the Romantic poets are taken to include Felicia Hemans, Laetitia Landon, Charlotte Smith, and Mary Tighe, among others. It would be heartening if we could believe that these are unjustly neglected poets, but their current revival will be brief. Similarly, anthologies of 17th-century English literature now tend to include the Duchess of Newcastle as well as Aphra Behn, Lady Mary Chudleigh, Anne Killigrew, Anne Finch, Countess of Winchilsea, and others. Some of these— Anne Finch in particular—wrote well, but a situation in which they are more read and studied than John Milton is not one that is likely to endure forever. The consequences of making gender a criterion for aesthetic choice must finally destroy all serious study of imaginative literature as such.

In their *Norton Anthology of Literature by Women*, Sandra Gilbert and Susan Gubar conclude their introduction to Elizabeth Barrett Browning by saying that "she constantly tested herself against the highest standards of male-defined poetic genres," a true if ambiguous observation. They then print her famous "The Cry of the Children," an admirably passionate ode that protests the cruel employment of little children in British Victorian mines and factories. Unfortunately, this well-meant prophetic affirmation ends with this, doubtless its finest stanza:

XIII
They look up with their pale and sunken faces,
    And their look is dread to see,
For they mind you of their angels in high places,
    With eyes turned on Deity.
"How long," they say, "how long, O cruel nation,
    Will you stand, to move the world, on a child's heart,—
Stifle down with a mailèd heel its palpitation,
    And tread onward to your throne amid the mart?
Our blood splashes upward, O goldheaper,
    And your purple shows your path!
But the child's sob in the silence curses deeper
    Than the strong man in his wrath."

If you read this aloud, then you may find yourself uncomfortable, on a strictly aesthetic basis, which would not vary if you were told that this had been composed by a male Victorian poet. In their selections from Elizabeth Bishop, Gilbert and Gubar courageously reprint Bishop's superb statement explaining her refusal to permit her poems to be included in anthologies of women's writing:

> Undoubtedly gender does play an important part in the making of any art, but art is art and to separate writings, paintings, musical compositions, etc., into sexes is to emphasize values in them that are *not* art.

That credo of Elizabeth Bishop's is to me the Alpha and Omega of critical wisdom in regard to all feminist literary criticism. Gender studies are precisely that: they study gender, and not aesthetic value. If your priorities are historical, social, political, and ideological, then gender studies clearly are more than justified. Perhaps they are a way to justice, or at least to more justice than women have received throughout thousands of years of male domination and aggression. Yet that is a very different matter from the now vexed issue of aesthetic value. Biographical criticism, like the different modes of historicist and psychological criticism, always has relied upon a kind of implicit gender studies and doubtless will benefit, as other modes will, by a making explicit of such considerations, particularly in regard to women writers.

Each volume in this series contains copious refutations of, and replies to, the traditionally aesthetic stance that I have advocated here. These introductory remarks aspire only to a questioning, and not a challenging, of feminist literary criticism. There are no longer any Patriarchal Critics; they are all dinosaurs, fabulous beasts fit for revival only in horror films. Sometimes I sadly think of myself as Bloom Brontosaurus, amiably left behind by the fire and the flood. But more often I go on reading the great women writers, searching for the aesthetic difference that yet may prove to be there, but which has not yet been found.

Introduction

HISTORICALLY CONSIDERED, Gertrude Stein, Eudora Welty, and Edith Wharton are probably the most important writers considered in this book. I choose, however, to write this introduction on the stories of Katherine Anne Porter, because they have given me a particular delight since I first read them half a century ago. My favorite among her narratives remains "Flowering Judas," about which I wrote more than a decade ago, and which I have just reread, with renewed wonder and pleasure. I return to it here not so much to revise my earlier critical observations, but rather to offer testimony to the enduring nature of Porter's lyrical art as a storyteller. It surprises me that Porter seems to have fewer readers now, since her strengths as stylist and creator of characer endure. So powerful is her best work—the stories grouped as "The Old Order," and "Old Mortality" and "Noon Wine"—that I do not doubt her canonical survival, but perhaps I can send younger readers to her work by revisiting "Flowering Judas," a great narrative prose-poem, replete with the intensely evocative charm that is Porter's signature as a writer. I do not mean "charm" lightly or in the social sense, but in its archaic Old French meaning of "magic spell" from the Latin *carmen*, "incantation." Katherine Anne Porter's art is incantatory, and never more so than in "Flowering Judas":

> The tolling of the midnight bell is a signal, but what does it mean?
> Get up, Laura, and follow me: come out of your sleep, out of your
> bed, out of this strange house. What are you doing in this house?
> Without a word, without fear she rose and reached for Eugenio's
> hand, but he eluded her with a sharp sly smile and drifted away. This
> is not all, you shall see—Murderer, he said, follow me, I will show
> you a new country, but it is far away, and we must hurry. No, said
> Laura, not unless you take my hand, no; and she clung first to the
> stair rail and then to the topmost branch of the Judas tree that bent
> down slowly and set her upon the earth, and then to the rocky ledge
> of a cliff, and then to the jagged wave of a sea that was not water but
> a desert of crumbling stone. Where are you taking me, she asked in
> wonder but without fear. To death, and it is a long way off, and we
> must hurry, said Eugenio. No, said Laura, not unless you take my
> hand. Then eat these flowers, poor prisoner, said Eugenio in a voice
> of pity, take and eat: and from the Judas tree he stripped the warm
> bleeding flowers, and held them to her lips. She saw that his hand
> was fleshless, a cluster of small white petrified branches, and his eye
> sockets were without light, but she ate the flowers greedily for they
> satisfied both hunger and thirst. Murderer! said Eugenio, and
> Cannibal! This is my body and my blood. Laura cried No! and at
> the sound of her own voice, she awoke trembling, and was afraid to
> sleep again.

This is the concluding passage of the story, and is not exactly minimalist in its style, heightened even for Porter. Robert Penn Warren, celebrating Porter's prose, remarked that her "bright indicative poetry is, at long last, a literally metaphysical poetry, too. The luminosity is from inward." "Flowering Judas" is a great hymn to the healthiness of narcissistic self-regard, an observation in which I intend no irony whatsoever. Porter's Laura is wholly justified when she cries out "No" to the ghost of the young man to whom she has declined to sacrifice herself. Self-destruction is no more Laura's mode than it was Katherine Anne Porter's. When I first met her, in 1970, she was eighty and still formidably beautiful, a grand survivor in her life as in her art. Laura, her surrogate, is condemned by her beauty to a sorrow that afflicts rare but fated women: to be the involuntary catalyst for passions she herself does not suffer. That is part of the exquisite burden of "Flowering Judas"; the provocation for another's doom-eagerness remains innocent (though knowing) of what it is that is catastrophic for the other self. That sense of unanswered otherness is one of Porter's most original modes of sensibility, and is unlikely to meet much acceptance (or understanding) in what has been condemned as an Age of Narcissism. Porter both defines the narcissistic dilemma and celebrates it, without, however, making a moral judgment upon Laura, the incarnation of an enigmatic aesthete, a lyrical storyteller who will be her own *materia poetica*.

Eugenio's earlier manifestation in "Flowering Judas" prepares us for the conclusion:

> A brown, shock-haired youth came and stood in her patio one night
> and sang like a lost soul for two hours, but Laura could think of noth-
> ing to do about it. The moonlight spread a wash of gauzy silver over
> the clear spaces of the garden, and the shadows were cobalt blue.
> The scarlet blossoms of the Judas tree were dull purple, and the
> names of the colors repeated themselves automatically in her mind,
> while she watched not the boy, but his shadow, fallen like a dark gar-
> ment across the fountain rim, trailing in the water.

Here, as at the close, Porter may echo Eliot's "Gerontion," where "Christ the tiger" comes "In depraved May's dogwood and chestnut, flowering judas, / To be eaten, to be divided, to be drunk / among whispers." Porter, whose religion was eros, appropriates Eliot (and "Christ the tiger") for a purely erotic context. Freud prophesied Porter's natural stance in his wonderful paper, "On Narcissism" (1914):

> . . . there arises in the woman a certain self-sufficiency (especially
> when there is a ripening into beauty) which compensates her for the
> social restrictions upon her object-choice. Strictly speaking, such

women love only themselves with an intensity comparable to that of the man's love for them. Nor does their need lie in the direction of loving, but of being loved; and that man finds favour with them who fulfills this condition. The importance of this type of woman for the erotic life of mankind must be recognized as very great.

This is Laura's (as it was Porter's) special charm: a cool, childlike inaccessibility. The flowering Judas tree is her perfect emblem, because it is sufficient unto itself. Poor Eugenio is deluded when he cries out (in Laura's reverie) that the Judas tree is his body and his blood. Her outcry of "No!", which shocks her awake, is wholly accurate, for the flowers she eats are emblematic of her narcissistic self-passion. The artist's self establishes her ego only by further self-investment, and Laura crosses the threshold to become a storyteller, not at Eugenio's expense, but at her own.

SYLVIA PLATH

1932–1963

SYLVIA PLATH was born on October 27, 1932, in Jamaica Plain, Massachusetts. She was the eldest child of Otto and Aurelia Plath. Her father was a professor of German and entomology who specialized in bees, and her mother, who had been Otto's student, was a high school teacher. When Plath was eight her father died of complications following an operation; he would become the mythic and powerful presence of her poem "Daddy."

Plath was a talented student who won many honors and awards in high school, including a scholarship to attend Smith College. On the strength of her writing skills, she won a position on the College Board of *Mademoiselle* magazine in 1953. The experience of living and working in New York City provided the background of her autobiographical novel *The Bell Jar* (published in England under the pseudonym Victoria Lucas in 1965, but not released in the United States until after her death). *The Bell Jar* chronicles the adventures of Esther Greenwood from her arrival in New York to her subsequent breakdown, attempted suicide, and hospitalization. To some degree the popularity of *The Bell Jar* has overshadowed Plath's strong poetic gifts. She has become one of those literary figures whose life has achieved a legendary status (similar in this regard, perhaps, to Ernest Hemingway). The novel details the difficulties facing a talented and ambitious young woman whose desire to succeed is at odds with the social expectation that she marry, have children, and devote herself to her husband's career.

In her junior year at Smith, Plath suffered an emotional breakdown. In keeping with the conventional wisdom of the mid-1950s, Plath received electroshock therapy. This, in turn, probably led to her suicide attempt, in August 1953. After several months of intensive (non-electric) therapy, Plath recovered enough to finish her degree at Smith; she graduated summa cum laude and won a Fulbright to study at England's Cambridge University. In England she met and married the poet Ted Hughes. On the surface, their relationship seemed almost picture-perfect: two handsome young poets embarking on promising artistic careers. Four years after their marriage, Plath published her first volume of poetry, *The Colossus* (1960), and although it did not win the accolades that Hughes's first book, *The Hawk in the Rain*, did, the reviews were generally good.

During the last years of the '50s, Plath and Hughes lived in Boston, where Plath visited Robert Lowell's poetry seminar, a seminar also attended by Anne Sexton, with whom Plath maintained an uneasy friendship. Sexton's honest, confessional poetry inspired Plath, but she was also somewhat envious of the other woman's attractiveness and success. Both Plath and Sexton wrote poetry about previously "taboo" subjects: the terrible boredom of domesticity, the constraints of marriage and family life, and female sexuality.

Plath and Hughes moved back to England in 1960, when Plath was pregnant with their first child, Frieda. A year later they moved from London to the Devon countryside, where Plath was initially happy: she was writing, she had a lovely daughter (and in 1962, a son, Nicholas), and Hughes seemed to be a doting husband and father. Eventually, however, the isolation of the countryside, worries about money, and Plath's growing awareness of Hughes's infidelities combined to end the marriage. Plath moved back to London, where she found herself with little means of support and two small children to raise. It is one of the poignant ironies of Plath's short life that this difficult period, which ended on February 11, 1963, with her suicide, was also a period of intense artistic creativity. She was writing fiercely, sometimes three poems a day, and among these were some of her most important poems: "Lady Lazarus," "Daddy," "Fever 103," and "Ariel."

None of these poems was accepted for individual publication, however, despite their polish and incisiveness. When these poems were collected and published posthumously, in *Ariel* (1965), they were widely praised, particularly by women, who heard in the voice of the poems an articulation of their own frustration with a constrictive and patriarchal society. In 1982, Plath's *Collected Poems* was awarded a Pulitzer Prize for poetry, one of the few awards for poetry she ever received. Although today her poetry is sometimes criticized for being too dramatic, her work marks an important turning point in American letters: a moment when being a "woman poet" no longer meant emulating successful male poets but writing about female experiences with unflinching honesty and insight.

CRITICAL EXTRACTS

STAN SMITH

The material of Sylvia Plath's only novel, *The Bell Jar* (1963), is conspicuously autobiographical, as recent anecdotal memoirs have revealed. But the book is more than a case-history of the attempted suicide and psychiatric treatment of a sensitive girl with literary ambition. It is a highly and originally structured novel, which has transmuted its raw material in a manner consonant with Plath's own comments on the relationship between art and personal experience:

> I believe one should be able to control and manipulate experience,
> even the most terrifying—like madness, being tortured, this kind of
> experience—and one should be able to manipulate these experiences
> with an informed and intelligent mind. I think that personal
> experience shouldn't be a kind of shut box and mirror-looking
> narcissistic experience. I believe that it should be generally relevant.

The main principle of control in *The Bell Jar*, I wish to argue, lies precisely in the manipulation of a series of contrasts and analogies between "personal experience" and a variety of forms of "artifice." ⟨. . .⟩

In *The Bell Jar*, Sylvia Plath uses the psychological alienation of the heroine, Esther Greenwood, to reinforce this *aesthetic* alienation. Esther's "madness" offers her an increasingly "objective," exterior view of the "eating customs, jurisprudence, and love life" of the culture she has inherited. "Manners" provide an important motif of the book. Using the finger-bowl at a special lunch, Esther, for example, "thought what a long way [she] had come," and recalls that in her first encounter with a finger bowl, she drank the water and the cherry blossoms in it because "I thought it must be some clear sort of Japanese after-dinner soup." Esther's "oddity" is here revealed as, in origin, no more than a social disjunction, between her own learnt expectations and the codes of manners within which she comes increasingly to move. A clue to the process at work is revealed in her memory of a poet who in "do[ing] something incorrect at table with a certain arrogance," "made eating salad with your fingers seem to be the only natural and sensible thing to do." The poet, significantly, had been talking about "the antithesis of nature and art." Esther's perception of the fictive nature of "manners" spills over into an attitude which evacuated the world of all spontaneous content. There are no such things as "natural" responses, no intrinsic values in things, all are equally arbitrary and artificial, and all are viewed with the same cynical-naïve eye. Collapsing the "antithesis of nature and art," Esther comes to view her own life as an aesthetic construct, a perpetual self-manipulation, learning, like the babies she sees at the clinic, "all the little tricky things it takes to grow up, step by step, into an anxious and unsettling world." ⟨. . .⟩

The straightforward, callous prose is here undercut by currents of powerful irony which subvert the whole disinterested stance. For the aestheticism is redefined, implicitly, as the rationalized fear and insecurity of a pathological squeamishness, a social strategy that insulates one from feelings which expose and entrap. Omniscience is redefined as a pose assumed to evade the suspicion of callowness and ignorance.

This fastidious aesthetic distance extends, too, to the apparently "cured" and regenerate Esther who is the imputed author of *The Bell Jar*. The book itself supposedly fulfils that ambition to write a novel whose frustration contributed to the breakdown it records. If the younger Esther stands in schizoid relation to her own experiences, retrospectively analysing and interpreting them, endlessly turning them over in her mind in some kind of Proustian *recherche*, Esther the narrator assumes the same kind of stance to her past, seen as an initiation rite to be scrupulously and objectively tabulated. Plath, the actual author, seems to be manipulating a continuous and ironic parallel between the condition of schizophrenic self-alienation and the familiar devices of narrative technique. Esther's narrative distance from the recounted facts of her own previous life has a peculiar, antiseptic quality, presenting the most harrowing and intimate experiences with a dispassionateness which tends to endorse her own doubts about the extent of her cure. The hard-boiled narrative tone suggests a narrator herself numbed in some significant way, left cold by her own past. If the younger Esther once felt as if she were "sitting under the same glass bell jar, stewing in my own sour air," while the world "flashed by like an improbable postcard," Esther the narrator seems preoccupied with insulating her own past self under the bell jar of a retrospective fiction. Plath not only enables us to see the pathological honesty of vision which accompanies and in part causes the younger Esther's breakdown; she also suggests that the assurance embodied in the posture of the disinterested narrator may itself have more profound social significance, and closer analogies with the schizophrenic's experience, and with the self-alienation of a world that dismisses that experience as mere delusion, than we appreciate. This double "estrangement effect" acts as a critical, ironic dimension in the novel. ⟨. . .⟩

The book has abounded in images of ropes and cords and strings of various kinds that share this ambiguity—the telephone wire which connects and persecutes, the tramlines of New York, the ECT wires that purify and burn, the electric chair which kills the Rosenbergs, the rope-tow on the ski-slopes which offers security at the cost of dependence, the navel-string which gives life but can strangle. This ambiguity persists into the very last paragraph, when Esther faces the interviewing committee that is to decide on her release. The equivocal close opens a new putative future outside the bell jar of this story:

> The eyes and the faces all turned themselves towards me, and guiding myself by them, as if by a magical thread, I stepped into the room.

The thread could lead the redeemed heroine out of the "familiar labyrinth of shovelled asylum paths"; or it could be "the thread that might lead me back to my old, bright salesmanship" spoken of earlier, that makes the puppet dance in the eyes of others. For, if Esther seems at last in control of her own life, she is "guiding [her]self" back on to a public stage, where her future will be decided by the impression she makes on others. The novel closes on a deliberately unresolved upbeat note which never finally clarifies the tension between authentic selfhood and public image, between life as self-articulation and as ritual performance—between, ultimately, "life" itself, and those "attitudes," no matter how deeply assimilated and accredited, which merely counterfeit it.

—Stan Smith, "Attitudes Counterfeiting Life: The Irony of Artifice in Sylvia Plath's *The Bell Jar*," *The Critical Quarterly* 17, no. 3 (Autumn 1975), excerpted in *Sylvia Plath*, ed. Harold Bloom (New York: Chelsea House Publishers, 1989), 33–34, 36–37, 47–48

LYNDA K. BUNDTZEN

The structure of *The Bell Jar* is more like a Chinese box than a linear narrative with a distinct beginning, middle, and end in their proper order. Plath begins with the outward circumstances of Esther's depression—her reactions to New York City, the Rosenberg trial, new acquaintances, and her job as a college editor of *Mademoiselle* magazine—and then moves inward and backward in time, revealing incidents from the past that are presumably related to Esther's anxiety. This Chinese box mode of development is exemplified by Esther's progressive recognition of her isolation from other people and in her regression back to the time of her father's death. Her suicide attempt is a further regression; it is depicted as a retreat into the womb and nonentity. Where there is considerable overlap and interdependence of the social, artistic, and psychological allegories, their development is similarly like that of a Chinese box. Plath begins with social oppression—the limitations on Esther's future ambitions because she is a woman—moving to the specific threats against her creativity by friends and relatives, to, finally, the ways in which she victimizes herself. This multilayered, self-enclosed form works very well for allegory, each box as a separate episode with a lesson attached to it, and to articulate the movement of Esther's consciousness. In this movement, there are many missing links between episodes, but it is downward and inward to the single hope that the puzzle has been solved, the last box has been opened, and she may crawl in and extinguish her pain. After the suicide attempt, there is a reversal of this process. Esther reaches out first to an inmate at the asylum who is catatonic, and gradually ventures outward again. ⟨. . .⟩

From what she has seen, Esther fears that marriage will destroy her desire to write, that her artistic energies will be channelled into the humdrum activities of a housewife: "I also remembered Buddy Willard saying in a sinister, knowing way that after I had children I would feel differently, I wouldn't want to write poems anymore. So I began to think maybe it was true that when you married and had children it was like being brainwashed, and afterward you went about numb as a slave in some private, totalitarian state." Esther's fears are confirmed by Mrs. Willard's homely wisdom: "'What a man wants is a mate and what a woman wants is infinite security,' and 'What a man is is an arrow into the future and what a woman is is the place the arrow shoots off from.'" But Esther wants "to shoot in all directions myself, like the colored arrows from a Fourth of July rocket." Her mother, too, warns Esther that

> nobody wanted a plain English major. But an English major who knew shorthand was something else again. Everybody would want her. She would be in demand among all the up-and-coming young men and she would transcribe letter after thrilling letter.
> The trouble was, I hated the idea of serving men in any way. I wanted to dictate my own thrilling letters.

Servitude, brainwashing, numbness, drugs that wipe the mind clear, shock treatments—all of these are closely associated in Esther's mind with the connubial state and its threat to her creativity. Later, this victimization is made a part of her experience as a mental patient, and a bell jar that descends over all women, suspending them forever in a state of arrested development, like "the big glass bottles full of babies that had died before they were born" at Buddy's medical school. The women she meets at the mental asylum are analyzed and given insulin injections, shock treatments, or lobotomies, depending, it seems, on the degree of their rebelliousness. Mrs. Savage appears to have committed herself for no better reason than to "louse up" her daughters' debutante parties with the public shame of a crazy mother. As they get better, the women return to their old lives, filled with shopping and bridge, unfaithful husbands and catty chitchat. In fact, the society of women at Belsize reminds Esther of the "normal" girls in her college dormitory: "What was there about us, in Belsize, so different from the girls playing bridge and gossiping and studying in the college to which I would return? Those girls, too, sat under bell jars of a sort." The nurses and inmates respond with the same envy and excitement at the news of a male visitor and amuse themselves in the same ways. Their docility is symbolized by the lobotomized Valerie, who apparently passes her confinement in complete contentment, watching other women come and go, not so much as a mental patient but as a prim old "Girl Scout Leader" watching her "girls" grow up and leave childish things. Occasionally, there is a pathetic display of creativity and independent spirit: Dee Dee composes a tune on the piano and "everybody kept saying she ought to get it published, it would be a hit." But female society in *The Bell Jar*, whether it's the Amazon Hotel in New York City (an obvious, but clever transformation of the Barbizon for women), a college dormitory, or a mental asylum, is a state of waiting for the "right" man to come along and time is passed with "harem" activities.

Esther is surrounded by women like dolls, zombies, and mannequins. The epitome of this condition is Hilda, another guest editor in New York. She is a mindless mannequin for the stylish hats and other accessories she creates in accord with shifts in fashion (another example of female creative energy channeled into a socially acceptable, and absurdly insignificant, activity). Her narcissistic habit of gazing at herself in shop windows is compensation for nonentity: "she stared at her reflection in the glassed shop windows to make sure, moment by moment, that she continued to exist." Behind her "vacant, Slavic expression" is a "blind cave." She does not, in fact, exist, except for a cavernous voice that reminds Esther of a dybbuk when she responds to Esther's pity for the Rosenbergs: "It's awful such people should be alive. . . . I'm so glad they're going to die." As Esther falls deeper into depression, she comes to resemble Hilda. She is surprised by her reflection in mirrors, as if an unknown "other," flattened out and distorted by the mirror's flaws, stares back. She later sees her suicide like the Rosenbergs' trial and execution as a lurid newspaper headline, and similar to Hilda, is curiously detached from the human pain.

The electrocution of the Rosenbergs is at first simply a recognizable feature in the novel's American landscape. Eventually, Esther's obsession with their case is linked to the shock treatment she is given, which she does not see as therapy, but as a punishment for some terrible, unknown crime.

> Then something bent down and took hold of me and shook me like the end of the world. Whee-ee-ee-ee-ee, it shrilled, through an air crackling with blue light, and with each flash a great jolt drubbed me till I thought my bones would break and the sap fly out of me like a split plant.
> I wondered what terrible thing it was that I had done.

It is as if God bent down to smite her. Esther wants to confess to a priest, to be cleansed of her sins, and at one point, even thinks of entering a nunnery; but she has no idea of what her "sins" are. Later she tells her nervous Unitarian minister, who has come to call on her in the mental asylum, that she believes in hell. She must live in it before she dies, she says, "to make up for missing out on it after death," and this is a punishment, in turn, for not believing in a life after death.

This circular reasoning is symptomatic of Esther's anxiety and is similar to Freud's description of patients in "Analysis Terminal and Interminable," who, out of an unconscious sense of guilt, punish themselves by never getting well. It is an inner inhibition (i.e., they do not consciously reject health). Likewise, we begin to suspect that Esther's sudden halt after years of accomplishment is motivated by guilt, rather than the opposite cause-effect sequence. It is guilt that leads to failure, rather than, as we normally expect, failure that leads to guilt. And this unusual process of self-victimization casts doubt on both the allegories of the double standard and female creativity as the sole explanations for Esther's depression and her feelings of inadequacy.

—Lynda K. Bundtzen, "Women in *The Bell Jar*: Two Allegories," *Plath's Incarnations: Women and the Creative Process* (1983), excerpted in *Sylvia Plath*, ed. Harold Bloom (New York: Chelsea House Publishers, 1989), 121–22, 129–31

MELODY ZAJDEL

Although Sylvia Plath wrote approximately seventy short stories, only ten were published in her lifetime. Since her death, three appeared in popular magazines and an additional seven stories were printed in the recently published volume *Johnny Panic and the Bible of Dreams*. What is interesting to the reader of these twenty stories is the consistency with which Plath dealt with the same materials and themes throughout her fiction. Although her prose works span over ten years, much of that time seems spent in writing and rewriting the same story, the story which reaches its fruition in *The Bell Jar*. This is particularly obvious in several of the short stories published after her death ("Tongues of Stone," "Sweetie Pie and the Gutter Men," and "Johnny Panic and the Bible of Dreams"). These stories, along with "In the Mountains" (published in the *Smith Review*, 1954), serve almost as apprentice pieces for key scenes in *The Bell Jar*, containing episodes with the same actions, characters, images, sometimes even the same words. Beyond these apprentice pieces, however, a reader discovers that not only do Plath's stories stylistically show her direct movement into the writing of *The Bell Jar*, but they also mirror her continued thematic concern with two interrelated ideas: first, the idea of living and sustaining a life of the imagination, and second, the socio-mythic form of this theme, what Josephine Donovan has called "the sexual politics of Sylvia Plath." Although Plath's short stories will probably not change her reputation from poet to proficient popular fiction writer (an epithet that Hughes suggests she desired), they are markers to understanding Plath's skill in her finished fictional effort, *The Bell Jar*, just as *The Colossus* stands as a necessary apprenticeship to the final poems of *Ariel*.

Hughes indicates that Plath "launched herself into *The Bell Jar* in 1960." But at least the four stories mentioned above, written between 1954 and 1959, deal with some of the same material. One in particular, "Tongues of Stone" (1955), uses the experience of a young girl's nervous breakdown much as Plath uses it in *The Bell Jar*. At least six key incidents appear first in this story, before being transformed and interpolated into the novel. The start of the breakdown is the same in both pieces. The main character is suffering from extreme apathy, anxiety and insomnia. In *The Bell Jar*, Esther enters the first clinic, Walton, after three weeks of not sleeping; in "Tongues of Stone," the character is at the end of two months of sleeplessness. In setting the scene, the "Tongues of Stone" narrator explains, "It was sometime in October; she had long ago lost track of all the days and it really didn't matter because one was like another and there were no nights to separate them because she never slept anymore." Both young women try to forestall their depression by looking for intellectual occupations to, literally, kill time. Each tries particularly hard to read, only to find the print on the pages of their books indecipherable, "dead black hieroglyphs" and "fantastic, untranslatable shapes, like Arabic and Chinese." Both are denied solace by their alienation from the dead intellectual world represented by the printed books. But more obvious in their similarities than these parallels of general circumstances are the active steps in their attempted suicides and their subsequent treatments. Looking at these steps, the reader can see Plath's movement from a rather flat narrative to the evocative and powerful personal voice of the novel. The apprentice piece has all the isolated units but doesn't have the developed style, theme or political focus of *The Bell Jar*. ⟨. . .⟩

Obviously, Plath is using the same material, even some of the same phrases and images, in this early story and *The Bell Jar*. Equally obviously, there are some significant differences in her presentations, many of which seem caused by an increased thematic awareness on Plath's part in the novel. In "Tongues of Stone," we have a description more than a clearly delineated conflict. The causes of the breakdown, the fears for the future, the active resistance of the girl to both medical help and her surroundings, are never presented. It seems doubtful that the girl herself is aware of all the factors surrounding her previous actions. We are given a third-person, limited view of the events. All conflicts and conditions leading to the suicide attempt are cloaked. In the expanded scope of *The Bell Jar*, on the other hand, the older Esther, the narrator, has moved to a recognition, frequently frustrated and angry, of the social and familial forces which lead to her breakdown. Her mother is seen in sharply critical relief. Her male doctor is at best indifferent to Esther's struggle; at worst he denies its value. It is a world of stultified options and intellectual sterility which places Esther under the bell jar. It is this thematic awareness even more than a stylistic change which gives *The Bell Jar* a power lacking in the earlier story. This same factor accounts for much of the difference between the other apprentice pieces and the novel. ⟨. . .⟩

Plath's short stories show her development as a fiction writer. Stylistically and thematically they prefigure and serve as her apprenticeship for *The Bell Jar*. Without them as test grounds, *The Bell Jar* could not have been so rapidly produced, so strongly presented. After all the pre-tellings and thinking, in *The Bell Jar* Plath is able to move into her own narrative voice and pace. Her well-wrought and hard wrung apprenticeship yielded to a haunting powerful craftsmanship.

—Melody Zajdel, "Apprenticed in a Bible of Dreams: Sylvia Plath's Short Stories," *Critical Essays on Sylvia Plath*, ed. Linda W. Wagner (1984), excerpted in *Sylvia Plath*, ed. Harold Bloom (New York: Chelsea House Publishers, 1989), 149–50, 155–56, 161

HOWARD MOSS

Between the original and the second publications of *The Bell Jar* in England, Sylvia Plath's second, and posthumous, volume of poems, *Ariel*, was printed. Some of the poems had appeared in magazines, but no one was prepared for their cumulative effect. Murderous experiences of the mind and the body, stripped of all protection, they were total exposures, and chilling. They made clear almost instantly that someone who had been taken for a gifted writer might well be one of genius, whose work—intense, luxurious, barbarous, and worldly—was unlike anything ever seen before. Although the extraordinary quality of the poems made her death the more lamentable, that death gave her work certain immediate values it might not otherwise have had. Death cannot change a single word written down on paper, but in this case who the poet was and what had been lost became apparent almost at the same time, as if the poems had been given and the poet taken away in one breath. An instantaneous immortality followed. Sylvia Plath also became an extra-literary figure to many people, a heroine of contradictions—someone who had faced horror and made something of it as well as someone who had been destroyed by it. I don't think morbid fascination accounts for her special position. The energy and violence of the late poems were acted out. What their author threatened she performed, and her work gained an extra status of truth. The connection between art and life, so often merely rhetorical, became all too visible. The tragic irony is that in a world of public-relations liars Sylvia Plath seemed a truth-dealer in life by the very act of taking it.

The Bell Jar lacks the coruscating magnificence of the late poems. Something girlish in its manner betrays the hand of the amateur novelist. Its material, after all, is what has been transcended. It is a frightening book, and if it ends on too optimistic a note as both fiction and postdated fact, its real terror lies elsewhere. Though we share every shade of feeling that leads to Esther's attempts at suicide, there is not the slightest insight in *The Bell Jar* into suicide itself. That may be why it bears the stamp of authority. Reading it, we are up against the raw experience of nightmare, not the analysis or under-standing of it.

—Howard Moss, "Dying: An Introduction," *Ariel Ascending*, ed. Paul Alexander (New York: Harper & Row, 1985), 128–29

ROBERT SCHOLES

On the surface *The Bell Jar* is about the events of Sylvia Plath's twentieth year: about how she tried to die, and how they stuck her back together with glue. It is a fine novel, as bitter and remorseless as her last poems—the kind of book Salinger's Franny might have written about herself ten years later, if she had spent those ten years in Hell. It is very much a story of the Fifties, but written in the early Sixties, and, after being effectively suppressed in this country for eight years, was published in the Seventies.

F. Scott Fitzgerald used to claim that he wrote with "the authority of fail-ure," and he did. It was a source of power in his later work. But the authority of failure is but a pale shadow of the authority of suicide, as we feel it in *Ariel* and in *The Bell Jar*. This is not so much because Sylvia Plath, in taking her own life, gave her readers a certain ghoulish interest they could not bring to most poems and novels, though this is no doubt partly true. It is because she knew that she was "Lady Lazarus." Her works did not only come to us posthumously. They were written posthumously: between suicides. She wrote her novel and her *Ariel* poems feverishly, like a person "stuck together with glue" and aware that the glue was melting. Should we be grateful for such things? Can we accept the price she paid for what she has given us? Is dying really an art?

There are no easy answers for such questions, maybe no answers at all. We are all dying, of course, banker and bum alike, spending our limited allotment of days, hours, and minutes at the same rate. But we don't like to think about it. And those men and women who take the matter into their own hands, and spend all at once with prodigal disdain, seem frighteningly different from you and me. Sylvia Plath is one of those others, and to them our gratitude and our dismay are equally impertinent. When an oracle speaks it is not for us to say thanks but to attend to the message. ⟨. . .⟩

In *The Bell Jar*, Sylvia Plath has used superbly the most important technical device of realism—what the Russian critic Viktor Shklovsky called "defamiliarization." True realism defamiliarizes our world so that it emerges from the dust of habitual acceptance and becomes visible once again. This is quite the opposite of that comforting false realism that presents the world in terms of clichés that we are all too ready to accept.

Sylvia Plath's technique of defamiliarization ranges from tiny verbal witticisms that bite, to images that are deeply troubling. When she calls the hotel for women that Esther inhabits in New York the "Amazon," she is not merely enjoying the closeness of the sound of that word to "Barbizon," she is forcing us to rethink the entire concept of a hotel for women: "mostly girls of my age with wealthy parents who wanted to be sure that their daughters would be living where men couldn't get at them and deceive them." And she is announcing a major theme in her work, the hostility between men and women.

—Robert Scholes, "Esther Came Back Like a Retreaded Tire," *Ariel Ascending*, ed. Paul Alexander (New York: Harper & Row, 1985), 130–32

VANCE BOURJAILY

What happens to the way we read and estimate *The Bell Jar* if we really go along with Sylvia Plath, taking it as the first novel of the young American writer, Victoria Lucas, then living in England, otherwise unknown? Under the Lucas pseudonym it was published, in January 1963, the month before the poet's death, by Heinemann of London—published, locally reviewed, modestly promoted, and briefly sold. With which, as most books do, it disappeared. It was pretty much unheard of, at least in this country, until eight years later, in February 1971, when it was ready to become a major item in a tragic legend, and Harper & Row had the business-wit to bring it out. ⟨. . .⟩

The Bell Jar, by Victoria Lucas, though not so-divided by its author, is nevertheless a novel in three parts. In the first, Esther Greenwood is an academically brilliant, socially insecure, and constantly introspective college junior. She has won, along with eleven others, a fashion magazine contest "by writing essays and stories and poems and fashion blurbs and as prizes they gave us jobs in New York for a month, expenses paid" (p. 2). ⟨. . .⟩

The flaws of execution in *The Bell Jar* are not many and not serious. They are outnumbered by examples of felicity by a margin of, say, fifty to one. There is, however, a flaw of intention to consider, though the effects of it are hard to measure. We must leave the text, for now, but not for good, and deal with Victoria Lucas as a mask.

Victoria Lucas was not supposed to be a totally serious writer. She was to write best-sellers. There is plenty of evidence for this in memoirs like Lois

Ames's (*The Bell Jar*, p. 203), and in the entry for Monday, March 4, 1957, on page 156 of *The Journals of Sylvia Plath*.

Victoria Lucas, as I've tried to show, was pretty good. She had her limits. Sometimes she fell beow them, more often she exceeded them. In general, she was a necessary fiction through which Sylvia Plath could hold back a really reckless commitment of talent, thought, and feeling at the depths where they are too nearly inexpressible to make for easy reading. I'll need to return to this at the end of my piece, but for now I hope you'll accept it as one of my reasons for not wanting to treat *The Bell Jar* as an autobiographical effort, in which Sylvia Plath demeans herself as Esther Greenwood. The book is something better than a document. It is a work of fiction in which, to sum up, an unhappy, intelligent schizoid, Esther Greenwood, sinks into the lesser of her two selves, becomes Elly Higginbottom—in which Elly must die so that Esther may be reborn.

If I may so describe it, then, *The Bell Jar* is a brave try at a minor work of art, rarely undercut by the inexperience and light intention permitted Victoria Lucas, instead of a nervously clever piece of confession and catharsis. It stands, supported by the poet's reputation but not really in need of it, as a small, rather haunting, American youth-book. Exit Victoria. She has served, and disserved, but not so much. Leave her to Heinemann.

—Vance Bourjaily, "Victoria Lucas and Elly Higginbottom," *Ariel Ascending*, ed. Paul
Alexander (New York: Harper & Row, 1985), 134–35, 144–45

TED HUGHES

Sylvia Plath's journals exist as an assortment of notebooks and bunches of loose sheets, and the selection just published here contains about a third of the whole bulk. Two other notebooks survived for a while after her death. They continued from where the surviving record breaks off in late 1959 and covered the last three years of her life. The second of these two books her husband destroyed, because he did not want her children to have to read it (in those days he regarded forgetfulness as an essential part of survival). The earlier one disappeared more recently (and may, presumably, still turn up).

The motive in publishing these journals will be questioned. The argument against is still strong. A decisive factor has been certain evident confusions, provoked in the minds of many of her readers by her later poetry. *Ariel* is dramatic speech of a kind. But to what persona and to what drama is it to be fitted? The poems don't seem to supply enough evidence of the definitive sort. This might have been no bad thing, if a riddle fertile in hypotheses is a good one. But the circumstances of her death, it seems, multiplied every one of her statements by a wild, unknown quantity. The results, among her interpreters, have hardly been steadied by the account she gave of herself in her letters to her mother, or by the errant versions supplied by her biographers. So the question grows: how do we find our way through this accompaniment, which has now become almost a part of the opus? Would we be helped if we had more firsthand testimony, a more intimately assured image, of what she was really like? In answer to this, these papers, which contain the nearest thing to a living portrait of her, are offered in the hope of providing some ballast for our idea of the reality behind the poems. Maybe they will do more.

Looking over this curtailed journal, we cannot help wondering whether the lost entries for her last three years were not the more important section of it. Those years, after all, produced the work that made her name. And we certainly have lost a valuable appendix to all that later writing. Yet these surviving diaries contain something that cannot be less valuable. If we read them with understanding, they can give us the key to the most intriguing mystery about her, the key to our biggest difficulty in our approach to her poetry.

That difficulty is the extreme peculiarity in kind of her poetic gift. And the difficulty is not lessened by the fact that she left behind two completely different kinds of poetry.

Few poets have disclosed in any way the birth circumstances of their poetic gift, or the necessary purpose these serve in their psychic economy. It is not easy to name one. As if the first concern of poetry were to cover its own tracks. When a deliberate attempt to reveal all has been made, by a Pasternak or a Wordsworth, the result is discursive autobiography—illuminating enough, but not an X ray. Otherwise poets are very properly bent on exploring subject matter, themes, intellectual possibilities and modifications, evolving the foliage and blossoms and fruit of a natural cultural organism whose roots are hidden, and whose birth and private purpose are no part of the crop. Sylvia Plath's poetry, like a species on its own, exists in little else but the revelation of that birth and purpose. Though her whole considerable ambition was fixed on becoming the normal flowering and fruiting kind of writer, her work was roots only. Almost as if her entire oeuvre were enclosed within those processes and transformations that happen in other poets before they can even begin, before the muse can hold out a leaf. Or as if all poetry were made up of the feats and shows performed by the poetic spirit Ariel. Whereas her poetry is the biology of Ariel, the ontology of Ariel—the story of Ariel's imprisonment in the pine, before Prospero opened it. And it continued to be so even after the end of *The Colossus*, which fell, as it happens, in the last entries of this surviving bulk of her journal, where the opening of the pine took place and was recorded.

—Ted Hughes, "Sylvia Plath and Her Journals," *Ariel Ascending*, ed. Paul Alexander (New York: Harper & Row, 1985), 152–54

DIANE S. BONDS

As Paula Bennett has written, Sylvia Plath's *The Bell Jar* offers a brilliant evocation of "the oppressive atmosphere of the 1950s and the soul-destroying effect this atmosphere could have on ambitious, high-minded young women like Plath." It has not been widely recognized, however, that the "soul-destroying effect" of Plath's social context is dramatized as vividly by the putative recovery of the heroine as by her breakdown and attempted suicide. The novel presents the transformation of Esther Greenwood from a young woman who hates the idea of serving men in any way to one who appears to earn her exit from the asylum by committing herself, albeit unwittingly, precisely to that project. In the first half of the novel, the pervasive imagery of dismemberment conveys the alienation and self-alienation leading to Esther's breakdown and suicide attempt. In the second half of the novel a pattern of symbolic rebirth is superimposed on a narrative which in its detail suggests that Esther purchases her "new" self by the discontinuance of any relations that might threaten by means of intimacy or tenderness the boundaries of a self conceived as an autonomous entity, as a separate and "separative" self.

Contemporary feminist theory has questioned the validity of this model of the self. Catherine Keller, for example, has recently drawn on theology, philosophy, psychology (including the work of Nancy Chodorow and Carol Gilligan), and literature, to demonstrate in impressive detail the historic collusion between the notion of a separate subject or bounded, autonomous self and the cultural forces that have oppressed women. *The Bell Jar* vividly illustrates that collusion by proposing, through its representation of Esther's recovery, an ideal of a self uncontaminated by others. But such a conception of the self denies the undeniable: the relationality of selfhood. The recovery which Plath constructs for her heroine reenacts the dismemberments obsessively imaged in the first half of the novel; I would argue that it merely leaves Esther prey to defining herself unwittingly and unwillingly in relation to all that remains to her: culturally-ingrained stereotypes of women. Critics for the most part seem to have brought to the novel the same assumptions about the self which inform Plath's book, assumptions deriving from a separative model of the self. Thus they have failed to recognize what the novel has to teach about the effects of our cultural commitment to that model. ⟨. . .⟩

⟨. . .⟩ Esther embraces relations with most of the women in the novel only to cast them off, as if they constituted a foreign presence within the purity of her own identity, some threat to her integrity. Doreen, for example, speaks to her with a voice "like a secret voice speaking straight out of [her] own bones" (6), but after the evening in Lenny's apartment, Esther decides to have nothing to do with her. A similar pattern is repeated with every female character in the novel, including Dr. Nolan, the psychiatrist who brings about Esther's recovery, and Esther's mother.

Esther's aversion from her mother is obvious, ascending in stridency from the mild understatement, "My own mother wasn't much help" (32) to the murderous fantasy inspired by sharing a room with her mother: one sleepless night, after staring at "the pin curls on her [mother's] head glittering like a row of little bayonets" (100), Esther comes to feel that the only way she can escape the annoying sound of her mother's faint snore "would be to take the column of skin and sinew from which it rose and twist it to silence between [her] hands" (101). Even though Esther at one point wishes that she had a mother like Jay Cee, the editor for whom she works at *Ladies' Day*, her ambivalence toward Jay Cee and other women who have nurtured her talents is profound— and it appears to derive, quite simply, from their supposed unattractiveness to men. Of Jay Cee, Esther says ". . . I liked her a lot. . . . [She] had brains, so her plug-ugly looks didn't seem to matter" (5); but sentences later, after admitting that she cannot imagine Jay Cee in bed with her husband, Esther changes her attitude abruptly: "Jay Cee wanted to teach me something, all the old ladies I ever knew wanted to teach me something, but I suddenly didn't think they had anything to teach me" (5). A similar reflection recurs near the end of the novel in a scene where the lesbian Joan Gilling lounges on Esther's bed in the asylum and Esther's revery seems to lump the unattractive, the manless, and the woman-loving together. She remembers:

> . . . the famous woman poet at my college [who] lived with another woman—a stumpy old Classical scholar with a cropped Dutch cut. When I told the poet that I might well get married and have a pack of children someday, she stared at me in horror. "But what about your *career*?" she had cried.
> My head ached. Why did I attract these weird old women? There was the famous poet, and Philomena Guinea, and Jay Cee, and the Christian Science lady, and lord knows who, and they all wanted to adopt me in some way, and, for the price of their care and influence, have me resemble them. (180)

This passage focuses our attention on the immersion of Plath/Esther in what Adrienne Rich has called the "compulsive heterosexuality," the pervasive heterosexism, of our culture. It also reinforces our awareness that despite her intelligence, imagination and professional ambition, Esther's sense of identity as a woman is predicated on finding "the right man." ⟨. . .⟩

Thus, at the end of the novel, far from having moved in the direction of an "authentic self," Esther has been systematically separated from the very means by which such a self might be constituted: relationships with others. Her high heels and "red wool suit flamboyant as [her] plans" (199) clearly signal a renewed and energized willingness to enter the sexual hunt that so dispirited her during her summer in New York. Esther's seeming preparation to reenter the hunt for "the right man" is accompanied by the strong suggestion that the right man is one with whom she may avoid emotional attachment. Esther says gleefully, after realizing that Irwin's voice on the phone means nothing to her and that he has no way of getting in touch with her again, "I was perfectly free" [198].) In other words, Esther's identity, the boundary of her self, has been secured by her isolation.

The Bell Jar makes apparent the oppressive force (at least for women) of the model of separative selfhood which dominates patriarchal culture. The novel dramatizes a double bind for women in which, on the one hand, an authentic self is one that is presumed to be autonomous and whole, entire to itself and clearly bounded, and yet in which, on the other hand, women have their identity primarily through relationship to a man. It is the increasing tension of this double bind for Esther which results in her breakdown; her release from the asylum, I have argued, is marked by a restoration of the double bind at a different and tolerable level of tension. The experiences of both Esther and Joan suggest that escape is not possible through conscious rejection of the expectation that a woman find herself in a man; in my reading, Plath's novel hints that the expectation is, in that instance, likely to be heeded at a more deeply unconscious level. (This would be a possible explanation of Joan's unexpected suicide, and the idea is supported by the imagery of the closing episode as I have analyzed it.) Yet the other alternative, to reject the model of separative selfhood and embrace a relational model, involves—in the cultural context portrayed by Plath—the restoration of the traditional plight of women: subservience to or submersion in others.

    —Diane S. Bonds, "The Separative Self in Sylvia Plath's *The Bell Jar*," *Women's Studies* 18 (1990): 49–50, 55–56, 61–62

TED HUGHES

Her breakthrough came—by the backdoor. Spring 1959, in a moment of seemingly no importance, like a gambler, playful and reckless, out of the blue she wrote her short story "Johnny Panic and the Bible of Dreams." This first-person narrative is composed in a voice that approximates the one she would find for *The Bell Jar*—a voice, that is, rather than a style. It whirls in a high-trapeze glitter of circus daring around one of her most serious terrors: her experience of the electroconvulsive shock treatment that jumped her out of the torpor in which her attempted suicide had left her.

Perhaps "Johnny Panic" was the divining work that located and opened the blocked spring. Change of home and travel prevented her from writing anything more till late fall. Then almost at once, with a place and a few brief weeks to concentrate, she made the first big breakthrough in her poetry. "Poem for a Birthday" returns to that stony source, but now lifts the shattered soul reborn from the "quarry of silences" where "men are mended," and where her "mendings itch." And the voice of Ariel can be heard clearing its throat.

Immediately after that, her writing was once again disrupted by physical upheavals: change of country, home-building, birth and infancy of her first child, all these interposed a full year, during which time that new voice, with the story it had to tell, stayed incommunicado. But in the spring of 1961 by good luck circumstances cooperated, giving her time and place to work uninterruptedly. Then at top speed and with very little revision from start to finish she wrote *The Bell Jar*.

In this narrative the voice has perfected itself. And what it has to tell is the author's psychic autobiography, the creation-myth of the person that had emerged in the "Poem for a Birthday" and that would go on in full cry through Ariel.

The Bell Jar is the story, in other words, from behind the electroconvulsive shock treatment. It dramatizes the decisive event of her adult life, which was her attempted suicide and accidental survival, and reveals how this attempt to annihilate herself had grown from the decisive event in her childhood, which was the death of her father when she was eight. Taken separately, each episode of the plot is a close-to-documentary account of something that did happen in the author's life. But the great and it might be said profoundly disturbing effect of this brisk assemblage is determined by two separate and contradictory elements. One of these operates on what could be called an upper level, the other on a lower.

The first, on the upper level, is the author's clearly recognizable purpose in the way she manipulates her materials. Her long-nursed ambition to write an objective novel about "life" was swept aside by a more urgent need. Fully aware of what she was doing, she modeled the sequence of episodes, and the various characters, into a ritual scenario for the heroine's symbolic death and rebirth. To her, this became the crucial aspect of the work. That mythic schema of violent initiation, in which the old self dies and the new self is born, or the false dies and the true is born, or the child dies and the adult is born, or the base animal dies and the spiritual self is born, which is fundamental to the major works of Lawrence and Dostoyevski, as well as to Christianity, can be said to have preoccupied her. Obviously, it preoccupied her in particular for very good reasons. She saw it as something other than one of imaginative literature's more important ideas. As far as she was concerned, her escape from her past and her conquest of the future, or in more immediate, real terms her well-being from day to day and even her very survival, depended absolutely on just how effectively she could impose this reinterpretation on her own history, within her own mind, and how potently her homemade version of the rite could give sustaining shape and positive direction to her psychological life. Her novel had to work as both the ranking of the mythic event and the liturgy, so to speak, of her own salvation.

The very writing of *The Bell Jar* did seem to succeed in performing this higher function, for the author, with astounding immediacy and power. And the role of each episode and character, as they operate on this level in the book, has been a good deal discussed.

The main movement of the action is the shift of the heroine, the "I," from artificial ego to authentic self—through a painful "death." The artificial ego is identified with the presiding moral regime of the widowed mother. The inner falsity and inadequacy of this complex induces the suicidal crisis. With the attempted suicide it is successfully dislodged, scapegoated into the heroine's double, Joan Gilling, and finally, at the end of the book, physically annihilated when Joan Gilling hangs herself. Simultaneously, the authentic self emerges into fierce rebellion against everything associated with the old ego. Her decisive act (the "positive" replay of her "negative" suicide) takes the form of a sanguinary defloration, carefully stage-managed by the heroine, which liberates her authentic self into independence. On this plane, the novel is tightly related to the mythos visible in the plots and situations of the poems, which here and there share a good deal of its ritualized purpose. It can be read, in fact, as the logbook of their superficial mechanisms and meanings. To a degree, the novel is an image of the matrix in which the poems grew and from which they still draw life.

—Ted Hughes, "On Sylvia Plath," *Raritan* 14, no. 2 (1994): 2–4

CAROL MUSKE

There's a moment that has always intrigued me in the journals of Sylvia Plath. The moment when the twenty-six year-old Sylvia meets a fellow poet, Adrienne Rich, whose work she has been following with admiration. The year is 1958, a rainy evening just after Ted Hughes's reading at Radcliffe College. Plath, ever watchful of competitors, homes in, deftly sketching Rich for her purposes—she is "round," with black shining hair, black eyes, an "honest, forthright" manner and a red "tulip-like" umbrella. Then the *coup de grace*: Plath, from behind her spy's veil of cocktail decorum, judges Rich a trifle "opinionated."

I allude to this historic meeting (and Plath's unconsciously funny aside) not just because (beyond the set piece of Literary Legend) the encounter begs for the kind of enlightened guesswork of which biographies are made. Here they are, of course, two as-yet-unveiled literary colossae, sizing each other up through the post-reading chat. But what is bizarre about the meeting, glimpsing it from the future, is the near-comical aura of tamped-down power in the room—that is to say, in the room of Plath's inhibited prose. The heady breeze of things to come riffles those glimmering, hesitant observations. A forthright little Adrienne Rich and a shy courteous Plath. Side by side for a few moments, smiling. Do we think we know them in this little grey interlude? Better than they know themselves?

I had forgotten that Plath and Rich were such contemporaries. (Adrienne Rich was born in 1929, Sylvia Plath in 1932.) I'd somehow thought of Plath as part of an earlier generation of poets, when in fact at the time of their meeting, Rich was decidedly her senior, not just in age, but in accomplishment. Rich had won the Yale Younger Poets Series in 1951 with *A Change of World* and had published a second book, *The Diamond Cutters*, in 1955. Plath's poems were printed in magazines; it would not be until 1960 that she signed a contract for *The Colossus*, her first book of poems.

Neither had started any literary bonfires, though Rich had shed a few sparks. The Literary Establishment had patted them on the head, or not. Plath had managed some too-obvious imitations of Roethke; her book manuscript, recently submitted to the Yale Younger Poets Prize, had lost "by a whisper," according to Dudley Fitts (then editor of the Series), due to its "lack of technical finish," just as Rich's *A Change of World* had been cheerfully condescended to by W. H. Auden (who'd selected her work for the prize) who praised her poems in the book's introduction as: "neatly and modestly dressed, [they] speak quietly but do not mumble, respect their elders . . . and do not tell fibs."

Through the clouds of that grey rainy evening in 1958, they glow portentously and we are reminded how *like* they appeared: bright-faced daughters of the middle class—each apparently happily wed (though in 1970 Rich's husband would commit suicide, Hughes and Plath would split and by 1963 Plath would end her life). Wives and future mothers, sipping bourbon or sherry, discussing "The Thought-Fox"—when just "a whisper" below the surface of their late-twenties sangfroid, the rapids (where we later watched them rising, cresting) swirled over their lives.

The background: a dying decade, the Fifties, that methodically-mortared brick edifice, mortgaged repression. Up on the roof each poet's doppelgänger is poised, on tiptoe. This is the precipice from which each will leap into She (or the third person "I"), into the dramatic persona of Adrienne Rich or Sylvia Plath, each name henceforth undifferentiated from the poet's individual life.

But on that rainy night, neither Plath's nor Rich's identity as a woman was a matter of literary urgency, a matter to be addressed directly in poetry. The passionate vindication of women's lot that would seize the imagination of the reading public, the high voltage wired in the infrastructures of their poems, had not yet been activated. In 1963, Rich would publish *Snapshots of a Daughter-in-Law* and not long after, Plath's posthumous *Ariel* would begin to appear in the bookstores.

Plath's journal entry inadvertently reminds us that not too long hence an evolved image of the "woman poet" would begin to take shape in consciousness. One could say that the day Rich and Plath met was the day the phrase "woman poet" kicked in the womb. Red tulip umbrellas aside, these were *not* poet-ingenues. But, again, I am "reading into" the moment, I am *inventing* what I absolutely believe to be the truth.

Woman poet—the term might appear, on the face of it, condescending, nevertheless it came to exist in the 1960s and '70s as less a descriptive than an unconscious prescriptive: the distinction made between one version of history and another. Gazing at Plath's "snapshot": two remarkable twentieth-century poets tugging on their dress gloves, smiling, you smile yourself. You know that each is going to have it out with history, as Rich said later about Dickinson, "on her own premises."

They were (along with Anne Sexton) the beginning of an era. Prior to this era, the categories were set well apart. Women. Poets. Of course there was the Über-frau-ish "poetess," a dread diminutive with an arched eyebrow over every syllable. "Woman poet" *was* used, but with about the same degree of gravity as poetess. But there were always women who wrote poetry. Some major voices, some not. There were also wives, mistresses, girlfriends, secretaries. Muses. Sometimes women poets got mixed up with a few of the above. How to tell them apart? ⟨. . .⟩

The "she" of *Ariel*, on the other hand—fiery, dark, death-obsessed, explosively self-destructive—was conflated with Plath's personal desperation. This was an alternative vision of a future that liberated the suffering consciousness from its painful constraints but destroyed the physical self in the process. Plath captured the collective imagination with her challenge to an unjust past. Rich too summoned history and held it to account, but simultaneously beamed it forward in time; Rich offered the possibility of turning, transformed, from the ruins of the past and in true Sixties and post-Wordsworthian style dreamed of a common language, a relocation of feminism, outside the "phallo-centered, written-out" vulgate. Plath's vision (or the vision of *Ariel*) occurred at the bloody intersection of the personal and historical—and Plath, like a well-trained terrorist, blew herself up with the corrupt installation.

—Carol Muske, "Women and Poetry," *Michigan Quarterly Review*, 35, no. 4 (Fall 1996): 586–88, 592

BIBLIOGRAPHY

The Colossus. 1960.
The Bell Jar. 1963 England, 1965 America.
Ariel. 1965.
Wreath for a Bridal. 1970.
Crossing the Water. 1971.
Crystal Gazer and Other Poems. 1971.
Lyonnesse. 1971.
Million Dollar Month. 1971.
Winter Trees. 1971.
Letters Home: Correspondence, 1950–1963 (edited by Aurelia Plath). 1975.
Johnny Panic and the Bible of Dreams, Short Stories, Prose and Diary Excerpts (edited by Ted Hughes). 1977.
Collected Poems. 1981.
The Journals of Sylvia Plath (edited by Ted Hughes and Frances McCollough). 1982.
Stings (drafts). 1983.

KATHERINE ANNE PORTER

1890-1980

KATHERINE ANNE PORTER was born on May 15, 1890, in Indian Creek, Texas. She was educated at a southern convent and at private schools before working as a newspaperwoman in Chicago and Denver. In 1920, she left for Mexico, which would become the scene of several of her stories, including her first published story, "Maria Concepcion" (1922). Porter would travel widely in Mexico, Germany, and France. She was in Mexico when the revolution ended in 1920; in New York City throughout the 1920s; in the company of other American expatriates in Paris during the 1930s; in Germany as the Nazis began to rise; in Washington, D.C., during World War II and again during the Kennedy and Johnson administrations. Only France failed to provide a setting for her writing. She did, however, translate a French song book in 1933.

Porter's first book of stories, *Flowering Judas*, which included "Maria Concepcion," was not published until 1930, although she had been writing for many years. The book was an immediate critical and popular success and was expanded and reissued in 1935. Her subtle and penetrating psychological portraits are drawn in an economical, clear style; her long stories achieve a complexity usually found in novels. In *Pale Horse, Pale Rider: Three Short Novels* (1939), the title story is a tale of youthful love ended brutally by the influenza epidemic of 1919. The heroine of the story is Miranda, a strong, independent, and questioning figure who appears also in "The Grave" and "Old Mortality." In the title story of Porter's collection *The Leaning Tower* (1944), a young Texas artist in Berlin responds to the rise of Nazism.

Porter's only full-length novel was published when she was 72 years old and after much critical anticipation: *Ship of Fools* (1962) also addresses the spectre of Nazism. In this moral allegory, a group of international passengers are on a voyage of life from Mexico to Germany on the eve of Hitler's political triumph in 1931. During the 27-day journey, Porter's characters support her argument that "evil is always done with the collusion of good." The book was a best-seller and adapted to film, but critics preferred her short stories.

Her *Collected Stories* (1965) won both the National Book Award and the Pulitzer Prize for fiction in 1966. *The Days Before*, published in 1952, revised in 1970, and reissued as *The Collected Essays and Occasional Writings of Katherine Anne Porter*, is a collection of essays, articles, book reviews, poetry, and a brief journalistic memoir.

From 1969 until her death, Porter lived outside Washington, D.C., near the University of Maryland, which became the recipient of her papers and awarded her an honorary degree in 1966. Her final book, *The Never-Ending Wrong* (1977), is a memoir of her protests during the notorious 1920–27 murder trial of Sacco and Vanzetti. Katherine Anne Porter suffered a disabling stroke in 1977 and died in Silver Spring, Maryland, on September 18, 1980.

CRITICAL EXTRACTS

EDMUND WILSON

Miss Porter is baffling because one cannot take hold of her work in any of the obvious ways. She makes none of the melodramatic or ironic points that are the stock in trade of the ordinary short story writers; she falls into none of the usual patterns and she does not show anyone's influence. She does not exploit her personality either inside or outside her work, and her writing itself makes a surface so smooth that the critic has little opportunity to point out peculiarities of color or weave. If he is tempted to say that the effect is pale, he is prevented by the realization that Miss Porter writes English of a purity and precision almost unique in contemporary American fiction. If he tries to demur that some given piece fails to mount with the accelerating pace or arrive at the final intensity that he is in the habit of expecting in short stories, he is deterred by a nibbling suspicion that he may not have grasped its meaning and have it hit him with a sudden impact some minutes after he has closed his book.

Not that this meaning is simple to formulate even after one has felt its emotional force. The limpidity of the sentence, the exactitude of the phrase, are deceptive in that the thing they convey continues to seem elusive even after it has been communicated. These stories are not illustrations of anything that is reducible to a moral law or political or social analysis or even a principle of human behavior. What they show us are human relations in their constantly shifting phases and in the moments of which their existence is made. There is no place for general reflections; you are to live through the experience as the characters do. And yet the writer has managed to say something about the values involved in the experience. But what is it? I shall try to suggest, though I am afraid I shall land in ineptitude.

Miss Porter's short stories lend themselves to being sorted into three fairly distinct groups. There are the studies of family life in working-class or middle-class households (there are two of these in *The Leaning Tower*), which, in spite of the fact that the author is technically sympathetic with her people, tend to be rather bitter and bleak, and, remarkable though they are, seem to me less satisfactory than the best of her other stories. The impression we get from these pieces is that the qualities that are most amiable in human life are being gradually done to death in the milieux she is presenting; but Miss Porter does not really much like these people or feel comfortable in their dismal homes, and so we, in turn, don't really much care. Another section of her work, however, contains what may be called pictures of foreign parts, and here Miss Porter is much more successful. The story which gives its name to her new collection and which takes up two-fifths of the volume belongs to this category. It is a study of Germany between the two wars in terms of a travelling American and his landlady and fellow-lodgers in a Berlin rooming house. By its material and its point of view, it rather recalls Christopher Isherwood's *Goodbye to Berlin*, but it is more poetic in treatment and more general in implication. The little plaster leaning tower of Pisa which has been cherished by the Viennese landlady but gets broken by her American tenant stands for something in the destruction of which not merely the Germans but also the Americans have somehow a criminal part (though the American is himself an artist, he finds that he can mean nothing to the Germans but the power of American money). So, in a fine earlier story, "Hacienda," a Mexican peon is somehow destroyed—with no direct responsibility on the part of any of the elements concerned—by a combination of Soviet Russians intent on making a Communist movie, their American business manager, and a family of Mexican landowners.

In both cases, we are left with the feeling that, caught in the meshes of interwoven forces, some important human value has been crushed. These stories especially, one gathers, are examples of what Miss Porter means when she says, in her foreword to *Flowering Judas* in the Modern Library edition, that most of her "energies of mind and spirit have been spent in the effort to grasp the meaning" of the threats of world catastrophe in her time, "to trace them to their sources and to understand the logic of this majestic and terrible failure of the life of man in the Western world."

But perhaps that most interesting section of Katherine Anne Porter's work is composed of her stories about women—particularly her heroine Miranda, who figured in two of the three novelettes that made up her previous volume, *Pale Horse, Pale Rider*. The first six pieces of *The Leaning Tower* deal with Miranda's childhood and her family background of Louisianians living in southern Texas. This is the setting in which Miss Porter is most at home, and one finds in it the origins of that spirit of which the starvation and violation elsewhere make the subjects of her other stories. One recognizes it in the firm little sketches that show the relations between Miranda's grandmother and her lifelong colored companion, the relations between the members of the family, and the relations between the family and the Negro servants in general. Somewhere behind Miss Porter's stories there is a conception of a natural human spirit in terms of their bearing on which all the other forces of society are appraised. This spirit is never really idealized, it is not even sentimentalized; it can be generous and loving and charming, but it can also be indifferent and careless, inconsequent, irresponsible, and silly. If the meaning of these stories is elusive, it is because this essential spirit is so hard to isolate or pin down. It is peculiar to Louisianians in Texas, yet one misses it in a boarding house in Berlin. It is the special personality of a woman, yet it is involved with international issues. It evades all the most admirable moralities, it escapes through the social net, and it resists the tremendous oppressions of national bankruptcies and national wars. It is outlawed, driven underground, exiled; it becomes rather unsure of itself and may be able, as in "Pale Horse, Pale Rider," to assert itself only in the delirium that lights up at the edge of death to save Miranda from extinction by war flu. It suffers often from a guilty conscience, knowing too well its moral weakness; but it can also rally bravely if vaguely in vindication of some instinct of its being which seems to point toward justice and truth.

But I said that this review would be clumsy. I am spoiling Miss Porter's stories by attempting to find a formula for them when I ought simply to be telling you to read them (and not merely the last volume but also its two predecessors). She is absolutely a first-rate artist, and what she wants other people to know she imparts to them by creating an object, the self-developing organism of a work of prose.

—Edmund Wilson, "Katherine Anne Porter" (1944), *Classics and Commercials* (1950), reprinted in *Twentieth-Century American Literature*, ed. Harold Bloom (New York: Chelsea House Publishers, 1987), 3127

V. S. PRITCHETT

Katherine Anne Porter's stories have rightly had the highest reputation in America since they first appeared in the early Thirties. Her scene changes often, a good sign. Her subjects bear out O'Connor's theory: Mexico, but in revolution; life in the decaying American South, in rootless New York, in hysterical post-1914 Berlin. Where she settles she writes from the inside. Her singularity is truthfulness: it comes out in the portrait of Laura, the virginal but reckless American schoolteacher in 'Flowering Judas' who has ventured her political and personal chastity among the vanities and squalors of the Mexican revolution, perhaps as a religious exercise. She is a good old Calvinist-Catholic:

> But she cannot help feeling that she has been betrayed irresponsibly
> by the disunion between her way of living and her feeling of what
> life should be, and at times she is almost contented to rest in this
> sense of grievance as a private consolation. Sometimes she wishes to
> run away but she stays.

Laura wishes to live near enough to violent passion to be singed by it and is willing to pay for the experience in terrifying dreams. The Mexicans appeal to her because of their boundless vanity, their violence, their ability to forget and their indifference: Miss Porter austerely tests her characters against things that are elemental or ineluctable—a classical writer. There is a point at which life or circumstance does not give: when human beings come to this point she is ready for them. Braggioni, the Stalin-like Mexican revolutionary leader, is at this point: he is identified in a frightening, yet slightly fatuous and amicable way with the shady needs of revolution.

In the tale 'Maria Concepcion' it is the respectable churchwoman, with her classical Christian sense of the rights of jealousy and vengeance, who murders and who is backed up by the villagers. Her husband will punish her: she accepts that. In 'Noon Wine' we have an incompetent poor white farmer whose fortunes are saved by a Swedish hired hand down from Dakota. The hand speaks to no one, slaves night and day and consoles himself only by playing the harmonica. Years pass and then a blackmailer comes down from Dakota to reveal that the Swede is a murderous escaped lunatic. The farmer, faced with losing his saviour, kills the blackmailer. The Swede runs away, consoled by his harmonica. The poor farmer has nothing but a sense of social injustice. He kills himself out of self-pity.

Katherine Anne Porter does not find her tests only in these Verga-like subjects. The girl reporter and the soldier-boy in New York 'dig in' in spiritual self-defence against the hysteria of the 1914 war. The choice is between reality and illusion and the reality is harder to bear. It is no reward. It is the same in the comic tale of the Depression: the domestic war between the out-of-work Irishman turned windbag and drunk and his avaricious and scornful wife who keeps him and ends by beating him up with a knotted towel. Violent: these classical heroes and heroines are always that. Again, in the comical sad history of the old Southern aunts and cousins one sees that Aunt Amy was wild, amusing, cruel and destructive because she knew she would soon die; she had inner knowledge of Fate. Killed, she could be a killer. Old Granny Weatherall fights to the last drop of consciousness on her death-bed because her pride will not really accept, even now, that she was once jilted as a girl. And that is not funny, it is terrifying. To every human being there eventually comes—Miss Porter seems to say—the shock of perception of something violent or rock-like in themselves, in others, or in circumstance. We awaken to primitive knowledge and become impersonal in our tragedies. There will arise a terrible moment of crisis, a kind of illness, when, for Laura, there will be *no* disunion between her way of living and her feeling for what life should be. She will discover what life is. It is something out of one's control, scarcely belonging to one, and that has to be borne as if one were a stone.

Miss Porter's singularity as a writer is in her truthful explorations of a complete consciousness of life. Her prose is severe and exact; here ironies are subtle but hard. If she is arbitrary it is because she identifies as a conservative with a classical view of human nature. Laura listens to Braggioni with 'pitiless courtesy' because she dare not smile at his bad performance on the guitar:

> He is so vain of his talents and so sensitive to slights that it would require a cruelty and vanity greater than his own to lay a finger on the vast careless world of his self-esteem.

Miss Porter has a fine power of nervous observation. Her picture of Berlin in the Isherwood period is eerie and searching. She sees everything that disturbs. She notices peculiar local things that one realises afterwards are true: how often, for example, the Berliners' eyes filled with tears when they were suddenly faced with small dilemmas. Hysteria is near to the surface. Yet the tears were a kind of mannerism. Her power to make a landscape, a room, a group of people, thinkingly alive is not the vague, brutal talent of the post-Hemingway reporter but belongs to the explicit Jamesian period and suggests the whole rather than the surface of a life. Her stories are thoroughly planted. It is true that she is chastely on the edge of her subjects, that one catches the wild look of the runaway in her eye; but if her manner is astringent it is not precious. She is an important writer in the genre because she solves the essential problem: how to satisfy exhaustively in writing briefly.

—V. S. Pritchett, "Stones and Stories," *New Statesman* (10 January 1964): 47–48

EUDORA WELTY

In "Old Mortality" how stirring the horse race is! At the finish the crowd breaks into its long roar "like the falling walls of Jericho." This we hear, and it is almost like seeing, and we know Miss Lucy has won. But beyond a fleeting glimpse—the "mahogany streak" of Miss Lucy on the track—we never get much sight of the race with our eyes. What we see comes afterward. Then we have it up close: Miss Lucy bleeding at the nose. For Miranda has got to say "That's winning too." The race would never have got into the story except that Miranda's heart is being prepared to reject victory, to reject the glamour of the race and the cheering grandstand; to distrust from now on all evidence except what she, out of her own experience, can testify to. By the time we *see* Miss Lucy, she is a sight for Miranda's eyes alone: as much symbol as horse.

Most good stories are about the interior of our lives, but Katherine Anne Porter's stories (in *The Collected Stories of Katherine Anne Porter*) take place there; they show surface only at her choosing. Her use of the physical world is enough to meet her needs and no more; she is not wasteful with anything. This artist, writing her stories with a power that stamps them to their last detail on the memory, does so to an extraordinary degree without sensory imagery.

I have the most common type of mind, the visual, and when first I began to read her stories it stood in the way of my trust in my own certainty of what was there that, for all my being bowled over by them, I couldn't see them happening. This was a very good thing for me. As her work has done in many other respects, it has shown me a thing or two about the eye of fiction, about fiction's visibility and invisibility, about its clarity, its radiance.

Heaven knows she can see. Katherine Anne Porter has seen all her life, sees today, most intimately, most specifically, and down to the bones, and she could date the bones. There is, above all, "Noon Wine" to establish it forever that when she wants a story to be visible, it is. "Noon Wine" is visible all the way through, full of scenes charged with dramatic energy; everything is brought forth into movement, dialogue; the title itself is Mr. Helton's tune on the harmonica. "Noon Wine" is the most beautifully objective work she has done. And nothing has been sacrificed to its being so (or she wouldn't have done it); to the contrary. I find Mr. Hatch the scariest character she ever made, and he's just set down there in Texas like a chair. There he stands, part of the everyday furniture of living. He's opaque, and he's the devil. Walking in at Mr. Thompson's gate—the same gate by which his tracked-down victim walked in first—he is that much more horrifying, almost too solid to the eyes to be countenanced. (So much for the visual mind.)

Katherine Anne Porter has not in general chosen to cast her stories in scenes. Her sense of human encounter is profound, is fundamental to her work, I believe, but she has not often allowed it the dramatic character it takes in "Noon Wine." We may not see the significant moment happen within the story's present; we may not watch it occur between the two characters it joins. Instead, a silent blow falls while one character is alone—the most alone in his life, perhaps. (And this is the case in "Noon Wine" too.) Often the revelation that pierces a character's mind and heart and shows him his life or his death comes in a dream, in retrospect, in illness or in utter defeat, the moment of vanishing hope, the moment of dying. What Miss Porter makes us see are those subjective worlds of hallucination, obsession, fever, guilt. The presence of death hovering about Granny Weatherall she makes as real and brings as near as Granny's own familiar room that stands about her bed—realer, nearer, for we recognize not only death's presence but the character death has come in for Granny Weatherall.

The flash of revelation is revelation but is unshared. But how unsuspecting we are to imagine so for a moment—it *is* shared, and by ourselves, her readers, who must share it feeling the doubled anguish of knowing this fact, doubled still again when it is borne in upon us how close to life this is, to *our* lives.

It is to be remembered that the world of fiction is not of itself visible. A story may or may not be born in sensory images in a given writer's mind. Experience itself is stored in no telling how many ways in a writer's memory. (It was "the sound of the sea, and Beryl fanning her hair at the window" that years later and thousands of miles away brought Katherine Mansfield to writing "At the Bay.") But if the physical world *is* visible or audible in the story, it has to be made so. Its materialization is as much a created thing as are the story's characters and what they think or do or say.

Katherine Anne Porter shows us that we do not have to see a story happen to know what is taking place. For all we are to know, she is not looking at it happen herself when she writes it; for her eyes are always looking through the gauze of the passing scene, not distracted by the immediate and transitory; her vision is reflective.

Her imagery is as likely as not to belong to a time other than the story's present, and beyond that it always differs from it in nature; it is *memory* imagery, coming into the story from memory's remove. It is a distilled, re-formed imagery, for it is part of a language made to speak directly of premonition, warning, surmise, anger, despair.

It was soon borne in upon me that Katherine Anne Porter's moral convictions have given her readers another way to see. Surely these convictions represent the fixed points about which her work has turned, and not only that, but they govern her stories down to the smallest detail. Her work has formed a constellation, with its own North Star.

Is the writer who does not give us the pictures and bring us the sounds of a story as it unfolds shutting out part of life? In Katherine Anne Porter's stories the effect has surely been never to diminish life but always to intensify life in the part significant to her story. It is a darkening of the house as the curtain goes up on this stage of her own.

Her stories of Mexico, Germany, Texas all happen there: where love and hate, trust and betrayal happen. And so their author's gaze is turned not outward but inward, and has confronted the mysterious dark from her work's beginning.

—Eudora Welty, "Katherine Anne Porter: The Eye of the Story" (1965), *The Eye of the Story* (1978), excerpted in *Twentieth-Century American Literature*, ed. Harold Bloom (New York: Chelsea House Publishers, 1987), 3128–29

CLEANTH BROOKS

If I had to choose a particular short story of Katherine Anne Porter's to illustrate her genius as a writer—the choice is not an easy one—I think that I should choose "The Grave." I did choose it some months ago for a lecture in Athens, where the special nature of the audience, whose English ranged from excellent to moderately competent, provided a severe test. The ability of such an audience to understand and appreciate this story underlines some of Miss Porter's special virtues as a writer. Hers is an art of apparent simplicity, with nothing forced or mannered, and yet the simplicity is rich, not thin, full of subtleties and sensitive insights. Her work is compact and almost unbelievably economical.

The story has to do with a young brother and sister on a Texas farm in the year 1903. Their grandmother, who in some sense had dominated the family, had survived her husband for many years. He had died in the neighboring state of Louisiana, but she had removed his body to Texas. Later, when her Texas farm was sold and with it the small family cemetery, she had once more moved her husband's body, and those of the other members of her family, to a plot in the big new public cemetery. One day the two grandchildren, out rabbit hunting with their small rifles, find themselves in the old abandoned family cemetery.

> Miranda leaped into the pit that had held her grandfather's bones. Scratching round aimlessly and pleasurably as any young animal, she scooped up a lump of earth and weighed it in her palm. It has a pleasantly sweet, corrupt smell, being mixed with cedar needles and small leaves, and as the crumbs fell apart, she saw a silver dove no larger than a hazel nut, with spread wings and a neat fan-shaped tail.

Miranda's brother recognizes what the curious little ornament is—the screwhead for a coffin. Paul has found something too—a small gold ring—and the children soon make an exchange of their treasures, Miranda fitting the gold ring onto her thumb.

Paul soon becomes interested in hunting again, and looks about for rabbits, but the ring,

> shining with the serene purity of fine gold on [the little girl's] rather
> grubby thumb, turned her feelings against her overalls and sockless
> feet. . . . She wanted to go back to the farm house, take a good cold
> bath, dust herself with plenty of Maria's violet talcum powder . . . put
> on the thinnest, most becoming dress she ever owned, with a big
> sash, and sit in the wicker chair under the trees.

The little girl is thoroughly feminine, and though she has enjoyed knocking about with her brother, wearing her summer roughing outfit, the world of boys and sports and hunting and all that goes with it is beginning to pall.

Then something happens. Paul starts up a rabbit, kills it with one shot, and skins it expertly as Miranda watches admiringly. "Brother lifted the oddly bloated belly. 'Look,' he said, in a low amazed voice. 'It was going to have young ones.'" Seeing the baby rabbits in all their perfection, "their sleek wet down lying in minute even ripples like a baby's head just washed, their unbelievably small delicate ears folded close," Miranda is "excited but not frightened." Then she touches one of them, and exclaims, "Ah, there's blood running over them!" and begins to tremble. "She had wanted most deeply to see and to know. Having seen, she felt at once as if she had known all along."

The meaning of life and fertility and of her own body begin to take shape in the little girl's mind as she sees the tiny creatures just taken from their mother's womb. The little boy says to her "cautiously, as if he were talking about something forbidden: 'They were just about ready to be born.' 'I know,' said Miranda, 'like kittens. I know, like babies.' She was quietly and terribly agitated, standing again with her rifle under her arm, looking down at the bloody heap." Paul buries the rabbits and cautions his sister "with an eager friendliness, a confidential tone quite unusual in him, as if he were taking her into an important secret on equal terms: Listen now. . . . Don't tell a soul."

The story ends with one more paragraph ⟨describing a scene 20 years later in a Mexican marketplace⟩ ⟨. . . .⟩

The story is so rich, it has so many meanings that bear close and subtle relations to each other, that a brief summary of what the story means will oversimplify it and fail to do justice to its depth, but I shall venture a few comments.

Obviously the story is about growing up and going through a kind of initiation into the mysteries of adult life. It is thus the story of the discovery of truth. Miranda learns about birth and her own destiny as a woman; she learns these things suddenly, unexpectedly, in circumstances that connect birth with death. Extending this comment a little further, one might say that the story is about the paradoxical nature of truth: truth wears a double face—it is not simple but complex. The secret of birth is revealed in the place of death and through a kind of bloody sacrifice. If there is beauty in the discovery, there is also awe and even terror.

These meanings are dramatized by their presentation through a particular action, which takes place in a particular setting. Something more than illustration of a statement is involved—something more than mere vividness or the presentation of a generalization in a form to catch the reader's eye. One notices, for example, how important is the fact of the grandmother's anxiety to keep the family together, even the bodies of the family dead. And the grandmother's solicitude is not mentioned merely to account for the physical fact of the abandoned cemetery in which Miranda makes her discovery about life and death. Throughout this story, birth and death are seen through a family perspective.

Miranda is, for example, thoroughly conscious of how her family is regarded in the community. We are told that her father had been criticized for letting his girls dress like boys and career "around astride barebacked horses." Miranda herself had encountered such criticism from old women whom she met on the road—women who smoked corncob pipes. They had always "treated her grandmother with most sincere respect," but they ask her "What yo Pappy thinkin about?" This matter of clothes, and the social sense, and the role of women in the society are brought into the story unobtrusively, but they powerfully influence its meaning. For if the story is about a rite of initiation, an initiation into the meaning of sex, the subject is not treated in a doctrinaire polemical way. In this story sex is considered in a much larger context, in a social and even a philosophical context.

How important the special context is will become apparent if we ask ourselves why the story ends as it does. Years later, in the hot tropical sunlight of a Mexican city, Miranda sees a tray of dyed sugar sweets, moulded in the form of baby pigs and baby rabbits. They smell of vanilla, but this smell mingles with the other odors of the marketplace, including that of raw flesh, and Miranda is suddenly reminded of the "sweetness and corruption" that she had smelled long before as she stood in the empty grave in the family burial plot. What is it that makes the experience not finally horrifying or nauseating? What steadies Miranda and redeems the experience for her? I quote again the concluding sentence:

> Instantly upon this thought the dreadful vision faded, and she saw
> clearly her brother, whose childhood face she had forgotten, standing
> again in the blazing sunshine, again twelve years old, a pleased sober
> smile in his eyes, turning the silver dove over and over in his hands.

I mentioned earlier the richness and subtlety of this beautiful story. It needs no further illustration; yet one can hardly forbear reminding oneself how skilfully, and apparently almost effortlessly, the author has rendered the physical and social context that gives point to Miranda's discovery of truth and has effected the modulation of her shifting attitudes—toward the grave, the buried ring, her hunting clothes, the dead rabbit—reconciling these various and conflicting attitudes and, in the closing sentences, bringing into precise focus the underlying theme.

—Cleanth Brooks, "On 'The Grave,'" *Yale Review* (Winter 1966), reprinted in *Twentieth-Century American Literature*, ed. Harold Bloom (New York: Chelsea House Publishers, 1987), 3135–36

JOSEPH WIESENFARTH

Ship of Fools, twenty years in the writing, is Katherine Anne Porter's most thorough exploration of her perennial theme of the restless and frustrating search of human being for the order of human love. The reader is invited to watch two different couples make two different kinds of love in the presence of an English bulldog. He is invited to contrast the lust of Arne Hansen and that of William Denny, the one open-handed, liberal, and satisfied by the love he buys, the other close-fisted, brooding, and eminently thwarted. He is invited to compare the gentle kiss of Dr. Schumann and the sleeping Condesa with the brutal kiss of the young officer and Mrs. Treadwell. He is invited to contrast the violence of Pepe and Amparo's usual vigorous love-making with the new and searching love of Johnny and Concha. In short, the reader is invited to the spectacle of the world making love.

Lovemaking is the most important of the many daily activities of man aboard the *Vera*, the ship of fools. People eat and drink, dress and undress, talk and read, as well as love and hate. The reader is spectator to a life of order that seems as meaningless as the daily promenade around the ship's deck. In short, the reader is spectator to life's order in its ultimate disorder. Through a pattern of fixed and repeated actions, Porter examines the eternal in man through his daily activities.

The captain of the *Vera* is a megalomaniac named Thiele who is concerned about the good order of his ship alone. He is so blind and rigid that he can take a knife away from a woodcarver and at the same time ignore the Zarzuela dance troop, which turns the last night of the ship's voyage into a *Walpurgisnacht* during which the patterns of established order disintegrate and the mad pursuit of lovers ends variously in sexual satisfaction or brutal frustration. At this point in the novel everything collapses according to plan because each person seems more intent than usual on acting the way he always acts. Thus the captain dissociates himself from the passengers and goes to the bridge where clicking heels and saluting officers allow him to pretend the ship is in order. Meanwhile the Zarzuelas have so taken over the ship that disorder and debauchery are rampant: the drunken Denny is drunker than ever, the frustrating actions of David and Jenny are more frustrating than ever, the frigidity of Mrs. Treadwell culminates in the savage beating of Denny, who is more savagely in pursuit of Pastora than ever before. In this manner the established patterns of action end in the disorder that they continuously hinted at throughout the novel. One night out of Bremerhaven is the focal point toward which all lives converge to produce a symmetrical picture of disorder in which lust is the closest a person can come to love.

Standing outside this pattern and measuring it are Dr. Schumann and La Condesa. The man, though sentimental, actually good and noble; the woman, though a criminal, actually saintly. The doctor gives her what he considers a guilty kiss and the Condesa accepts it as the most innocent love of her life. But she sends no answer to his note which offers her the continuing solicitude of his affection, and her silence proves to be this noisy novel's most magnificent gesture. Both end their affair before the *Walpurgisnacht* and both establish their generosity as the anti-model to the selfishness that stands as cause to effect in the disorderly and loveless lives of so many on the *Vera*.

In the *Ship of Fools* Katherine Anne Porter writes her constant theme: "It is hardly possible to exaggerate the lovelessness in which most people live, men or women: wanting love, unable to give it, or inspire it, unable to keep it if they get it, not knowing how to treat it, lacking the humility, or the very love itself that could teach them how to love: it is the painfullest thing in human life." The reason that Porter names her ship of fools *Vera* is to indicate that she believes that only by seeing the truth about themselves will people have a chance to change. Truth for her is a prelude to love.

⟨Porter's stories⟩ repeat some truths that must be recognized. Sexual frustration is part of them all. Stephen and He are unwanted children. Ellen Weatherall's children substitute for those she might have had by George who jilted her. The woman in "Theft" has substituted a "baseless and general faith" in humanity for her love for Eddie. Ninette's sex is a commodity that men miss. Mrs. Thompson refuses to sleep with her husband, and his sons threaten his life. Thwarted sexual desire turns to aggression in "The Downward Path to Wisdom." The last six whacks Mrs. Halloran gives her husband with the wet knotted towel are "for your daughter and your part in her." Mrs. Treadwell beats Denny bloody with her spiked-heel shoe in *Ship of Fools*, where varieties of frustration and aggression are set in kaleidoscopic patterns.

The usual escape from the sexual self is the embracing of some external form of order. The family ideal and moral rectitude are celebrated in "A Downward Path" and "The Jilting of Granny Weatherall." Social recognition in "He" and "Noon Wine." Law and order in "Magic" and "Noon Wine." Humanity in "Theft." Religion in "Granny Weatherall" and "A Day's Work." And all of these are upheld by Captain Thiele in *Ship of Fools*, where the cap-

tain himself is projected as the image of a modern God who wants the floating planet shipshape even if the crew itself is a hopeless wreck. As long as
there is some external order to distinguish virtuous from vicious, Porter suggests, those who do but slenderly know themselves and those who do but slenderly love others can always fill themselves up with self-righteousness.

—Joseph Wiesenfarth, "Negatives of Hope: A Reading of Katherine Anne Porter," *Renascence*
25, no. 2 (Winter 1973), reprinted in *American Fiction 1914 to 1945*, ed. Harold Bloom (New
York: Chelsea House Publishers, 1987), 132–33

Barbara Harrell Carson

Perhaps the best internal evidence that the way Miranda will claim her "honest self" is through art lies in the title *Pale Horse, Pale Rider*. It comes from the
song that Miranda, sick with influenza, sings with Adam, the man she has
known for ten days and is falling in love with. In the old spiritual, Miranda
says, the pale horse of death takes away lover, mother, father, brother, sister,
the whole family, but is always implored to "leave one singer to mourn."
Miranda is left, after multiple remembered deaths of family members and after
the death of Adam, as the one who will sing of the others. As she once wrote
about the theater of the stage, she will now write of the theater of life. This
interpretation is supported by the frequent comparisons of life to plays or to
movies, occurring throughout the story. Bill, the city editor of the Blue
Mountain *News*, behaves "exactly like city editors in the moving pictures, even
to the chewed cigar"; Chuck, the tubercular sportswriter, dresses his part from
turtlenecked sweater to tan hobnailed boots; the restaurant next door to the
newspaper, like all its cinematic counterparts, it seems, is nicknamed "The
Greasy Spoon"; Miranda finds Liberty Bond salesmen in her office and on the
stage of the theater; she and Adam talk to each other in the prescribed flip-
pancies of the day as if they are role-playing; even the vision that comes to her
when she is near death is couched in imagery of the theater: she sees that
"words like oblivion and eternity are curtains hung before nothing at all."

Just as it took a war to release the Grandmother's true, subjective self in
action (in "The Old Order"), so it takes a war to free Miranda's to art. In her
case, however, the war is clearly internal as well as external. As surely as
Miranda fights against death from influenza at the end of World War I, she
also fights—as a woman struggling for psychological and creative independence—against the death that comes from intellectual passivity, from the failure to act or to create, from the surrender of one's honest self. The story opens,
significantly, with a description of an almost totally motionless Miranda, just
beginning to feel the symptoms of her disease. She is half in a coma ⟨. . . .⟩
Only through a stubborn act of will, conscious refusal to die, will Miranda

make it to the other side. In *Old Mortality* the child Miranda dreamed of being a jockey when she grew up, envisioning the day "she would ride out . . . and win a great race, and surprise everybody, her family most of all." Her victory will, like Miss Lucy's, be filled with suffering, but this is her day to ride. Although her pulse lags and her heart is almost lifeless, in her mind there is still action: she dreams of mounting her horse and riding to escape death—physical death and that other death, that sacrifice of self, associated with the spider web, or tangled fishing lines, of family.

But if the family was, in her past, the major source of temptations to passivity, other lures have presented themselves in her new life, calling on her to deny her integrity. Even though she believes the war "filthy," it takes all the strength she can muster to resist the intimidations of the men selling Liberty Bonds (the pun is perfect), who assert that she is the lone holdout in all the businesses in the entire city. She surrenders at least momentarily to social pressure when she puts in her time visiting hospitalized soldiers ⟨. . . .⟩ Even Adam and the love she feels for him seem a threat to her free will—Adam who keeps her "on the inside of the walk in good American style," who helps her "across street corners as if she were a cripple," who would have carried her over mud puddles had they come across any, and whom she does not want to love, not now, but whom she feels forced to love *now*, because their time seems so short.

With Adam's death and her own delirious vision of oblivion, Miranda gives up all illusions, all hopes, all love. She is left with what Nannie had found only at the end of her life: that reduction to the very core of selfhood, that "hard unwinking angry point of light" that Miranda saw in her death sleep and heard say, " 'Trust me. I stay.' " She is left with the awareness of the power of her own will (strong enough to conquer death); of her ability to survive alone; and of an identity, a reality that is hers without dependence on any one else. But unlike Nannie, Miranda has the time and the emotional and practical equipment to make this center a starting point instead of a final station. As she returns from her race with death, she is not only a Lazarus come forth, but a "seer" in another sense now, a *vates*, who has looked into the depths and will, no doubt, be compelled to tell about it in certain seasons to come, when Pegasus replaces that other pale horse. "The Grave" in "The Old Order" had revealed to Miranda that treasure can come from a tomb; her art will be another proof of the truth of this promise.

The likelihood that Miranda will express her selfhood in art may also suggest her superiority to her Grandmother in Porter's view. Porter once indicated her agreement with E. M. Forster's belief that "there are only two possibilities for any real order: art and religion." The essential difference is significant: religion, the Grandmother's source of order in old age, has its anchor outside the self, in institutions, rules, dogmas. Art, on the other hand, has an interior source; the self becomes creator. Religion, as the Grandmother practiced it, means limitation of the self; art, expression of the self. For Porter it is the center that will hold.

—Barbara Harrell Carson, "Winning: Katherine Anne Porter's Women," in *The Authority of Experience: Essays in Feminist Criticism*, ed. Arlyn Diamond and Lee R. Edwards (Amherst: University of Massachusetts Press, 1977), 252–56

JOAN GIVNER

The shift of Porter's attention from the villian to the saintly heroine (in the early 20s) was not a temporary change of focus but a permanent one, and her attitude toward the virtuous heroine eventually formed the cornerstone of her moral philosophy. The main tenet of this philosophy is that the evildoers are not the most reprehensible people in the world, because they at least have the courage of their convictions. Nor are they the most dangerous people, since they can be easily recognized. The people who really need to be watched are the so-called innocents who stand by and allow others to perpetrate evil. Porter was to express repeatedly the opinion that the innocent bystanders allow the activity of evildoers, not merely because of fear and indifference, but because they gain vicarious pleasure from seeing others perform the wicked deeds which they themselves wish but fear to perform. She came eventually to see the passive virtuous people as guilty of promoting evil even when they do not consciously do so.

This theory about the relationship between saints and evildoers and their collusion in evil became her lifelong gospel, the subject of numerous informal talks, the message she preached from political platforms, and the basis of her interpretation of current events. After the publication of *Ship of Fools* she gave this account of some of the events of the twentieth century:

> . . . . the collusion in evil that allows creatures like Mussolini, or Hitler, or Huey Long or McCarthy—you can make your own list, petty and great,—to gain hold of things, who permits it? Oh, we're convinced we're not evil. We don't believe in that sort of thing, do we? And the strange thing is that if these agents of evil are all clowns, why do we put up with them? God knows, such men are evil, without sense—forces of pure ambition and will—but they enjoy our tacit consent. (James Ruoff and Del Smith, "Katherine Anne Porter on *Ship of Fools*," *College English* 24 (February 1963))

Her judgments in literary criticism were influenced by the same point of view. She praised Eudora Welty's stories because she depicted villains pure and unmitigated and with none of the sympathy and understanding which Porter believed amounted to criminal collusion in evil between author and character.

Consistently, when Robert Penn Warren published *All the King's Men* she wrote to various friends of her shock and horror that he should have explored carefully the motivation of the character based on Huey Long. She felt that he should have portrayed the character as a villain, and she condemned the book as a sentimental apology for the worst kind of fascist demagogue.

The same theory informed all her fiction. An early spare version of her theme appears in the short story "Magic." Here a maid, hoping to relax her mistress as she brushes her hair, tells a story of a villainous madam who cheats and bullies the prostitutes in a New Orleans brothel. The point of the story is that the madam's activity is made possible by those around her—the male clients, the police, and the cook—who do nothing. Not only are these people as guilty as the one who perpetrates the violence, but so too are the woman and the maid who relish the story. The woman sniffs scent (a detail which suggest her desire to hide the unpleasant realities), stares at her blameless reflection in the mirror, and urges the storyteller to continue whenever she pauses. Lest there be any doubt about the equation of guilt between both madams and both maids, they resemble each other so closely as to invite confusion. When the storyteller describes the cook of the brothel she might be describing herself: "she was a woman, colored like myself with much French blood all the same, like myself always among people who worked spells. But she had a very hard heart, she helped the madam in everything, she liked to watch all that happen" ⟨*The Collected Stories of Katherine Anne Porter*, 1965, 41⟩. The theme of the story echoes Porter's words that the evil of our time is not an accident but a total consent.

A fuller version of the theme appears in "Flowering Judas," which, like many of Porter's stories, has a triangular arrangement of characters, consisting of villain, victim, and "heroine." Braggioni, like all Porter's villains, is pure caricature and looms in the story like a grotesque Easter egg in shades of mauve and purple and yellow. A hideous creature with the eyes of a cat and the paunch of a pig, he embodies each of the seven deadly sins.

The implication of the story is that if Braggioni is a self-serving, self-indulgent villain, he has not always been so. Once he was a young idealist in both politics and love. It is Laura and people like her who have caused him to change from idealist to opportunist, and the main focus of the story is upon her and upon her motivation. She neither loves nor opposes Braggioni, because she is basically indifferent to him as she is to most people. She has trained herself to remain uncommitted in her relationships with others and has developed a principle of rejection: ". . . . the very cells of her flesh reject knowledge and kinship in one monotonous word. No. No. No. She draws her strength from this one holy talismanic word which does not suffer her to be led into evil. Denying everything she may walk anywhere in safety, she looks at everything without amazement" ⟨97⟩. It is the death of Eugenio in which she has conspired with Braggioni that causes her finally to become aware of her guilt, and then only in a dream. As she falls asleep she receives a message from her own depths which warns her of motives and the meaning of her acts.

Porter's longest treatment of her theme is, of course, *Ship of Fools*. She described her intentions in the novel in a 1946 letter to Josephine Herbst. She said that her book was about the constant endless collusion between good and evil. She said that she believed human beings to be capable of total evil but thought that no one had ever been totally good, and that gave the edge to evil. She intended not to present any solution, but simply to show the principle at work and why none of us had an alibi in the world. She said that her plan and conclusion had been worked out ten years before and that nothing had happened since to change her mind—indeed, everything confirmed her old opinion.

—Joan Givner, "Katherine Anne Porter, Journalist," *Southwest Review* (Autumn 1979), excerpted in *Twentieth-Century American Literature*, ed. Harold Bloom (New York: Chelsea House Publishers, 1987), 3136–37

ROBERT PENN WARREN

In my view, the final importance of Katherine Anne Porter is not merely that she has written a number of fictions remarkable for both grace and strength, a number of fictions which have enlarged and deepened the nature of the story, both short and long, in our time, but that she has created an *oeuvre*—a body of work including fiction, essays, letters, and journals—that bears the stamp of a personality distinctive, delicately perceptive, keenly aware of the depth and darkness of human experience, delighted by the beauty of the world and the triumphs of human kindness and warmth, and thoroughly committed to a quest for meaning in the midst of the ironic complexities of man's lot ⟨. . . .⟩ A review of her *oeuvre* reveals that, in spite of its sharp impression of immediacy, it is drenched in historical awareness.

Most obviously, we have the story of Miranda—a sharply defined person, but also a sort of alter ego of the author. In *Old Mortality*, Miranda, first as a child, then as a young woman with a broken marriage returning to a family funeral, grows into an awareness of the meaning of myth and time. In the beginning of the story Miranda inspects the myth of the beautiful Aunt Amy, doomed to an early and perhaps disgraceful death. The romantic story is first subjected to a child's realistic scrutiny, then to an old-fashioned moral judgment, and finally to the modern judgment of Marx and Freud (although these names never appear). Miranda, at the end, swears that she will be done with all old tales, old romance, that she will live her own life, will know the truth "about what happens to me." This is a promise she makes to herself, and this would be the end of a certain kind of story. But this story ends with three simple phrases: ". . . making a promise to herself, in her hopefulness, her ignorance." And indeed, these three phrases *are* the story. What kind of truth can we know about our own being, our own fate?

Later, in *Pale Horse, Pale Rider*, we see Miranda again, she and her lover set against the hysteria of war, the lover dying, she herself dying into a new order of life—the life of the great ruthless machine of the modern world.

This question is always present in the work of Katherine Anne Porter: What does our history—of the individual or in the mass—mean? World War II is only one episode in that long question, with the horror of Nazism only an anguishing footnote to a great process in which we are all involved. In the face of the great, pitiless, and dehumanizing mechanism of the modern world, what her work celebrates is the toughness and integrity of the individual. And the great virtue is to recognize complicity with evil in the self. We may be foolishly hopeful, or ignorant, as young Miranda making her promise to herself. But even in the face of the savage irony of history, could she otherwise affirm her integrity?

—Robert Penn Warren, "The Genius of Katherine Anne Porter," *Saturday Review* 7, no. 16 (December 1980): 10–11

BIBLIOGRAPHY

Flowering Judas and Other Stories. 1930, 1935.
Pale Horse, Pale Rider: Three Short Novels. 1939.
The Leaning Tower and Other Stories. 1944.
The Days Before. 1952.
Ship of Fools. 1962.
The Collected Stories of Katherine Anne Porter. 1965.
The Collected Essays and Occasional Writings of Katherine Anne Porter. 1970.
The Never-Ending Wrong. 1977.
The Letters of Katherine Anne Porter. 1990.

AYN RAND

1905-1982

AYN RAND was born Alyssa (Alissa) Rosenbaum in St. Petersburg, Russia, on February 2, 1905. In Russia, the Rosenbaum family was well-to-do, and Alyssa had a comfortable childhood and an excellent education. When she was thirteen, the Russian Revolution broke out and her father's business was nationalized. The Revolution's impact on her family contributed to her life-long hatred of communism or any other collectivist ideology. In 1921, Rand began to study philosophy in Leningrad. After leaving the university, she received an invitation to visit from relatives in the United States, and when her passport visa was actually granted, she left Russia for good. En route from Russia to the United States, she changed her name to Ayn (rhymes with "mine") Rand and eventually made her way from Berlin, to New York, to Chicago, and finally, to Hollywood.

In Hollywood, she worked for Cecil B. DeMille's studio as a junior screenwriter and occasionally as an extra in crowd scenes. In 1929 she married an American, Frank O'Connor, and two years later she became an American citizen. Although she sold a screenplay, "Red Pawn," in 1932, she did not publish her first novel until 1936, by which time she and O'Connor were living in New York City. She did, however, write a successful dramatic script that, under the title "January the 16th," became a Broadway hit.

Her first novel, *We the Living* (1936), received mixed reviews, and sales were mediocre. Nevertheless, it provided the impetus for Rand to begin work on one of her most well-known novels, *The Fountainhead* (1943). This novel illustrates one of Rand's most central beliefs: the superiority of the individual over the collective, an idea that she also expresses in one of her shortest novels, *Anthem* (1938, in Britain). After writing the screenplay for the movie version of *The Fountainhead* (starring Gary Cooper and Patricia Neal), Rand turned again to fiction and began work on *Atlas Shrugged* (1957). The novel sold extraordinarily well despite negative reviews but proved to be Rand's last work of fiction. She abandoned writing fiction to devote herself to philosophy.

Rand's philosophy, called objectivism, has been described as antialtruist, procapitalist, anticollectivist, and proindividualist. Its teachings were spread through the *Objectivist Newsletter* and through Rand's own speaking engagements, interviews, and essays. To some degree, Rand's ideas were publicized by Nathaniel Branden, whom Rand had met in 1950, and who for almost ten years was Rand's intellectual heir apparent. Branden convinced Rand to allow him to start the Nathaniel Branden Institute, which existed until Rand and Branden had a much publicized falling-out (which Branden claimed was caused in part by the fact that he had recently ended their affair, an explanation supported by several people, but denied by Rand). Rand insisted that Branden had betrayed her and the movement. During this period, Rand published only nonfiction, including *The Virtue of Selfishness* (1964), *Capitalism: The Unknown Ideal* (1966), and *Philosophy: Who Needs It?* (1982).

Although Rand's newsletter at one time claimed a subscription list of over twenty thousand, her ideas have never been taken seriously by the academic establishment. Many libertarian politicians, however, credit her work as influential, and a Book-of-the-Month Club survey, done in 1991, found that *Atlas Shrugged* was second only to the Bible in a list of books that most influenced people's lives. Today her work has equally ardent supporters and detractors. Her supporters suggest that sexism may be a reason her work is discredited; America, they claim, is simply not ready to take a female philosopher seriously. Ayn Rand died on March 6, 1982.

CRITICAL EXTRACTS

LEONARD PEIKOFF

In a journal entry written at the time (dated April 9, 1934), Miss Rand ⟨states⟩:

> I believe—and I want to gather all the facts to illustrate this—that the worst curse on mankind is the ability to consider ideals as something quite abstract and detached from one's everyday life. The ability of *living* and *thinking* quite differently, in other words eliminating thinking from your actual life. This applied not to deliberate and conscious hypocrites, but to those more dangerous and hopeless ones who, alone with themselves and to themselves, tolerate a complete break between their convictions and their lives, and still believe that they have convictions. To them—either their ideals or their lives are worthless—and usually both.

Such "dangerous and hopeless ones" may betray their ideal in the name of "social respectability" (the small businessman in this story) or in the name of the welfare of the masses (the Communist) or the will of God (the evangelist) or the pleasure of the moment (the playboy Count)—or they may do it for the license of claiming that the good is impossible and therefore the struggle for it unnecessary (the painter). *Ideal* captures eloquently the essence of each of these diverse types and demonstrates their common denominator. In this regard, it is an intellectual tour de force. It is a philosophical guide to hypocrisy, a dramatized inventory of the kinds of ideas and attitudes that lead to the impotence of ideals—that is, to their detachment from life.

(The inventory, however, is not offered in the form of a developed plot structure. In the body of the play, there is no progression of events, no necessary connection between one encounter and the next. It is a series of evocative vignettes, often illuminating and ingenious, but as theater, I think, unavoidably somewhat static.)

Dwight Langley, the painter, is the pure exponent of the evil the play is attacking; he is, in effect, the spokesman for Platonism, who explicitly preaches that beauty is unreachable in this world and perfection unattainable. Since he insists that ideals are impossible on earth, he cannot, logically enough, believe in the reality of any ideal, even when it actually confronts him. Thus, although he knows every facet of Kay Gonda's face, he (alone among the characters) does not recognize her when she appears in his life. This philosophically induced blindness, which motivates his betrayal of her, is a particularly brilliant concretization of the play's theme, and makes a dramatic Act I curtain.

In her journal of the period, Miss Rand singles out religion as the main cause of men's lack of integrity. The worst of the characters, accordingly, the one who evokes her greatest indignation, is Hix, the evangelist, who preaches earthly suffering as a means to heavenly happiness. In an excellently worked-out scene, we see that it is not his vices, but his religion, including his definition of virtue, that brings him to demand the betrayal of Kay Gonda, her deliberate sacrifice to the lowest of creatures. By gaining a stranglehold on ethics, then preaching sacrifice as an ideal, religion, no matter what its intentions, systematically inculcates hypocrisy: it teaches men that achieving values is low ("selfish"), but that giving them up is noble. "Giving them up," in practice, means betraying them.

"None of us," one of the characters complains, "ever chooses the bleak, hopeless life he is forced to lead." Yet, as the play demonstrates, all these men do choose the lives they lead. When confronted by the ideal they profess to desire, they do not want it. Their vaunted "idealism" is largely a form of self-deception, enabling them to pretend to themselves and others that they aspire to something higher. In fact and in reality, however, they don't.

Kay Gonda, by contrast, is a passionate valuer; like Irene in "The Husband I Bought," she cannot accept anything less than the ideal. Her exalted sense of life cannot accept the ugliness, the pain, the "dismal little pleasures" that she sees all around her, and she feels a desperate need to know that she is not alone in this regard. There is no doubt that Ayn Rand herself shared Kay Gonda's sense of life, and often her loneliness, too—and that Kay's cry in the play is her own:

> I want to see, real, living, and in the hours of my own days, that
> glory I create as an illusion! I want it real! I want to know that there is
> someone, somewhere, who wants it, too! Or else what is the use of
> seeing it, and working, and burning oneself for an impossible vision?
> A spirit, too, needs fuel. It can run dry.

Emotionally, *Ideal* is unique among Ayn Rand's works. It is the polar opposite of "Good Copy." "Good Copy" was based on the premise of the impotence and insignificance of evil. But *Ideal* focuses almost exclusively on evil or mediocrity (in a way that even *We the Living* does not); it is pervaded by Kay Gonda's feeling of alienation from mankind, the feeling, tinged by bitterness, that the true idealist is in a minuscule minority amid an earthful of value-betrayers with whom no communication is possible. In accordance with this perspective, the hero, Johnny Dawes, is not a characteristic Ayn Rand figure, but a misfit utterly estranged from the world, a man whose virtue is that he does not know how to live today (and has often wanted to die). If Leo feels this in Soviet Russia, the explanation is political, not metaphysical. But Johnny feels it in the United States.

In her other works, Ayn Rand herself gave the answer to such a "malevolent universe" viewpoint, as she called it. Dominique Francon in *The Fountainhead*, for instance, strikingly resembles Kay and Johnny in her idealistic alienation from the world, yet she eventually discovers how to reconcile evil with the "benevolent universe" approach. "You must learn," Roark tells her, "not to be afraid of the world. Not to be held by it as you are now. Never to be hurt by it as you were in that courtroom." Dominique does learn it; but Kay and Johnny do not, or at least not fully. The effect is untypical Ayn Rand: a story written *approvingly* from Dominique's initial viewpoint.

Undoubtedly, the intensity of Miss Rand's personal struggle at the time—her intellectual and professional struggle against a seemingly deaf, even hostile culture—helps to account for the play's approach. Dominique, Miss Rand has said, is "myself in a bad mood." The same may be said of this aspect of *Ideal*.

Despite its somber essence, however, *Ideal* is not entirely a malevolent story. The play does have its lighter, even humorous side, such as its witty satire of Chuck Fink, the "selfless" radical, and of the Elmer Gantry–like Sister Essie Twomey, with her Service Station of the Spirit. The ending, moreover, however unhappy, is certainly not intended as tragedy or defeat. Johnny's final action is *action*—that is the whole point—action to protect the ideal, as against

empty words or dreams. *His* idealism, therefore, is genuine, and Kay Gonda's search ends on a positive note. In this respect, even *Ideal* may be regarded as an affirmation (albeit in an unusual form) of the benevolent universe.
—Leonard Peikoff, *The Early Ayn Rand* (New York: New American Library, 1984), 182–84

BARBARA BRANDEN

As she first conceived of ⟨*Atlas Shrugged*⟩, Ayn had thought that her theme, "the mind on strike," would not require the presentation of new philosophical ideas. It would demonstrate the application of the theme of *The Fountainhead*, individualism, to the political-economic arena. The action, with a minimum of comment, would carry the philosophical message, it would demonstrate that capitalism rests on the mind and the freedom of the mind. It was when she began to concretize more specifically what her theme required, to outline the means by which she would show the role and importance of the mind in human society, that she began to have the first glimmering of the philosophical dimensions of what she had undertaken. One day, while she was working on the final movie script for *The Fountainhead*, a young Associated Press reporter came to the studio to interview her. He asked her about the new novel she was planning. She told him, "it will combine metaphysics, morality, economics, politics, and sex—and it will show the tie between metaphysics and economics." Ayn beamed like a young girl when she later told the story, adding, "I'll never forget his look. He said helplessly, 'I can't see how you'll manage it . . . but I guess you know what you're doing.' And he released the story exactly as I'd stated it."

In order to achieve full conceptual clarity before beginning to write the novel, Ayn made extensive notes on the ideas that were explicitly or implicitly to be involved. In these early notes, one sees the scope of the novel begin to grow and broaden.

"My most important job," she wrote, "is the formulation of a rational morality of and for man, of and for his life, of and for this earth."

While projecting what would happen if the men of the mind went on strike, while defining how and why civilization would collapse, she was led to a crucial question. If it is the men of the mind who carry the world on their shoulders and make civilization possible—why have they never recognized their own power? Why have they never challenged their torturers and expropriators? When she grasped the answer, she knew it was to be one of the most important moral concepts in the novel: the concept of "the sanction of the victim." She saw that it is the *victims*, the men of virtue and ability, who make the triumph of evil possible by their willingness to let their virtues be used against them: their willingness to bear injustice, to sacrifice their own interests, *to concede moral validity to the claims of their own destroyers.*

Her identification of the disastrous consequences of the soul-body dichotomy was another contributing element to the growth of the novel's scale; it would become a central philosophical issue. In her notes, she described the way in which this dichotomy has served as sanction and excuse for the persecution of industrialists and for the scorn directed against those who create the physical means of man's survival. She wrote: "Show that the real sources, key spots, spark plugs of material production (the inventors and industrialists) are creators in the same way, in the same sense, with the same heroic virtues, of the same high *spiritual* order, as the men usually thought of as creators—the artists. Show that *any* original rational idea, in any sphere of man's activity, is an act of creation and creativeness. *Vindicate* the industrialist—the author of material production."

She added, "It would be interesting to show how the same principle operates in relation to sex." She believed that just as men do not understand that the source of the production of wealth is man's mind, so they do not understand that the source of a man's sexual desires and choices is his philosophical values: both production and sex are scorned for the same reason, as mindless, animalistic activities that have no relation to man's spirit. The meaning of the soul-body dichotomy as applied to sex became a crucial part of the story. The manner in which it is tied, through the character and life of Hank Rearden, to the same dichotomy in the realm of economics and politics, constitutes one of the most brilliant feats of integration in *Atlas Shrugged.* ⟨. . .⟩

In *Atlas Shrugged,* Dagny Taggart would ask John Galt what he had told the inventors, the artists, the industrialists, the scientists, the men of the mind in every field of activity who had joined his strike, leaving behind their work and their lives—what he told them to convince them to abandon everything and to join him. Galt answers, "I told them they were right. . . . I gave them the pride they did not know they had. I gave them the words to identify it. I gave them that priceless possession which they had missed, had longed for, yet had not known they needed: a moral sanction."

This was to be Ayn's gift to America. A moral sanction. The philosophical demonstration that to live for one's own rational self-interest, to pursue one's own selfish, personal goals, to use one's mind in the service of one's own life and happiness, is the noblest, the highest, *the most moral* of human activities. Speaking of his strikers, Galt would say: "I have given them the weapon they had lacked: the knowledge of their own moral value. They, the great victims who had produced all the wonders of humanity's brief summer . . . had not discovered the nature of their right. They had known that theirs was the power.

I taught them that theirs was the glory." Speaking to the unnamed, unchampi-
oned, beating heart of her new land, Ayn was to say: "Yours is the glory."
—Barbara Branden, *The Passion of Ayn Rand* (New York: Doubleday, 1986), 220–21, 230–31

NATHANIEL BRANDEN

Atlas Shrugged is most certainly a philosophical novel, expressing all of the
author's key ideas in dramatic form. As Ayn herself said at one point, it has all
the elements of a mystery, which keeps building as the story progresses.
Initially we are presented with a series of events that appear inexplicable. We
see these events chiefly through the eyes of the heroine, Dagny Taggart, Vice-
President in Charge of Operation of Taggart Transcontinental, the nation's
largest and most powerful railroad. The world seems to be moving toward
destruction, in a manner neither Dagny nor anyone else can understand. A
brilliant industrialist, Francisco d'Anconia, the first man Dagny ever loved,
appears to have abandoned all purpose, as well as every character trait that
Dagny had admired in him; he becomes a worthless playboy. A great composer, Richard Halley, renounces his career, after years of struggle, on the very
night of his triumph. Businessmen who have been single-tracked in their devotion to their work—Midas Mulligan, Ellis Wyatt, and Ken Danagger—retire
without explanation, and disappear. A pirate, Ragnar Danneskjöld, once a brilliant student of physics and philosophy, is loose on the high seas, attacking
and robbing government relief ships. The world's most distinguished philosopher, Hugh Akston, once Francisco and Ragnar's teacher, leaves his university
position to work as a cook in a diner. The remnant of a new type of motor that
could have revolutionized the economy is abandoned on a scrap heap in the
ruins of a factory. And in the growing darkness of a crumbling civilization, in
moments of hopelessness, bewilderment, and despair, people are crying, "Who
is John Galt?"—without knowing what the question means or where it came
from. ⟨. . .⟩

"Dagny is a man-worshiper," Ayn remarked, "as any heroine of mine would
have to be. For Dagny, Dominique, and Kira, man is the ultimate, just as he is
for me—and I don't have to tell you how important my work is to me or how
important Dagny's work is to her."

On another occasion Ayn stated, "Dagny is myself, with any possible flaws
eliminated. She is myself without my tiredness, without my chronic, slightly
antimaterial feeling, without that which I consider the ivory tower element in
me, or the theoretician versus the man of action." I thought it typical that she
did not say *woman* of action. I also thought it typical that she spoke of tiredness as a flaw. "Dagny is myself without a moment of exhaustion."

Ayn would make statements of this kind quite often and I was always surprised in that, as a total human being, I thought her Dagny's superior. Dagny

was beautiful; Ayn was not. But Ayn was a genius, a cosmic force so powerful that thoughts of physical beauty rarely entered my mind in regard to her. The only exception were those infrequent moments when I thought how Russian-Jewish she looked; she could have been a family relative, a cousin, say, of my parents; but this was a thought I quickly dismissed because it did not fit my vision of her. No, she did not have Dagny's appearance, nor Dagny's ease with the material world, nor Dagny's tireless energy—although I never thought of Ayn's energy as less than awesome—but she was Dagny's creator, she was the source from which Dagny and Francisco and Rearden and all the characters flowed, and in my eyes that placed her above them all.

When I attempted to convey this perspective to her, she became strangely modest, almost humble, as if she did not *want* to think herself superior to her own characters because as long as she could look up to them she felt relief from her aloneness. She said, "A man, conceivably, could adjust to the knowl-edge that he was at a higher level than those around him, although no ratio-nal man could possibly enjoy that perspective; but to a woman it would be unbearable."

Ayn did have two striking physical attributes: dark, enormous eyes, alive with consciousness and passion, and beautiful legs, in scale with her height, which was about five two or three. She was very proud of both these features, but apart from that she did not like her appearance. Dagny was the incarna-tion of Ayn's physical ideal and frustrated yearnings: tall, slender, with long legs and a sculptured face. "I see Dagny more or less as Katharine Hepburn looked in her thirties," Ayn told me.

To see a woman in heroic terms seemed very natural to me—I had never been impressed by conventional notions of femininity like passivity or weak-ness—and Dagny did strike me as an exciting projection of woman at her highest possibility, in effect as a kind of goddess of the industrial revolution, a supremely American kind of woman. ⟨. . .⟩

She believed her most important task, as a novelist, was the development of an all-encompassing "rational morality." I remarked that by the time she had written this she must have gone beyond her original notion of simply writing an action novel to dramatize the importance of political and economic free-dom to the creative mind. She agreed and said that she had seen that in order to tell the story properly she was obliged to work out her moral philosophy in comprehensive detail on the one hand, and on the other, to create a plot-structure that would probably dramatize it.

In a novel, she said, nothing is more important than the plot, and in a philosophical novel nothing is more important than the way ideas and actions are integrated. "I despise novels like Thomas Mann's *The Magic Mountain*, in which characters merely sit around and philosophize about life. And that's why I admire Dostoevsky so much, in spite of his mysticism and his malevolence: he's a master of integrating philosophy, psychology, and action. There's no one better at it. Read *The Possessed;* it's a masterpiece. If you want to write philosophical novels, your events have to really dramatize and illustrate your ideas—integration is everything—just as a rational human being is integrated, just as mind and body, theory and practice, need to be integrated in a proper existence."

I had not yet identified the fact that one of the characteristics of nineteenth-century Russian novelists was that they tended to create characters on the basis of an individual's ideas—in contrast, for instance, with English novelists, who tended to characterize on the basis of social class considerations. And so I did not yet recognize how typically Russian Ayn was in this aspect of her literary approach. She told me explicitly that she created characters out of philosophical abstractions, and neither of us was aware of the psychological limitations this imposed. But I was aware of her animus against treating her heroes from a developmental perspective when I read her notes for the character of John Galt:

> No progression here. . . . He is what he is from the beginning—
> integrated . . . and perfect. No change in him, because *he has no
> intellectual contradictions and, therefore, no inner conflict.* . . . His important
> qualities (to bring out): *Joy in living*—the peculiar, deeply natural,
> serene, all-pervading joy in living which he alone possesses so
> completely in the story (the other strikers have it in lesser degree,
> almost as reflections of that which, in him, is the source); all-
> pervading in the sense that it underlies all his actions and emotions,
> it is an intrinsic, inseparable part of his nature . . . it is present *even
> when* he suffers . . . [I want to show] the worship of joy as against
> the worship of suffering, [and his] magnificent innocence—the
> untroubled purity—a pride which is serene, not aggressive—"the
> first man of ability who refused to feel guilty."

—Nathaniel Branden, *Judgement Day: My Years with Ayn Rand* (Boston: Houghton Mifflin, 1989), 80, 82–83, 88–89

NATHANIEL BRANDEN

A few months before the publication of *Atlas*, Bennett Cerf invited Ayn to speak at a Random House sales conference. Everyone's expectations for the book were high and the room was alive with excitement. A salesman asked her, jokingly, if she could summarize her philosophy while standing on one foot. This was the kind of challenge to which Ayn responded with glee. She lifted one foot in the air, and answered, "Metaphysics—objective reality; Epistemology—reason; Ethics—self-interest; Politics—capitalism." She was

proud of the instant rapport she could establish in such situations. The salesmen applauded her.

When Ayn recounted the incident, I recall thinking how exciting it was
that something as explosive as *Atlas Shrugged* should be involved with a sales
conference and all the other routine business of publishing; I enjoyed the
sense of connection to "ordinary reality."

I did not think it strange that Ayn should choose to present to the world
a new philosophical vision by means of a novel. She had said to me, "All of the
world's major religions have, in effect, their own mythology—tales, parables,
stories of various kinds, that are intended to dramatize and illustrate abstract
values and precepts. Although that is not how the novel started out in my
mind, that is what it developed into: a mythology that concretizes, by means
of the actions of its characters, the meaning of my philosophy."

To Barbara and me she said, "I know I am challenging the cultural tradition of two and a half thousand years." She said it to the whole Collective and
to Bennett Cerf and Donald Klopfer. She warned them that they should not
expect—should not count on—any favorable reviews. I did not think they
fully believed her; I do not think she fully believed it herself.

The *New York Times* assigned *Atlas Shrugged* to Granville Hicks, an ex-
member of the Communist party and an ex-apologist for Stalinism—the same
editor who, years earlier at Macmillan, had opposed the publication of *We the
Living*.

The article appeared in the October 13 issue of the Sunday *Book Review*.
When I saw Hicks's name I was shocked; I did not yet know how typical this
was of the *Times*; I thought that such a choice was the depth of irrationality and
injustice. Few reviewers feel morally obliged to communicate clearly what a
book is about before proceeding to their evaluation. I did not know that at the
time, either.

"This Gargantuan book," wrote Hicks, "comes among us as a demonstra-
tive rather than as a literary work. . . . Not in any literary sense a serious novel
. . . this book is written out of hate." The review attacked the novel on every
possible level. I recall, as clearly as if it were ten minutes ago, my stunned
inability to grasp how anyone, even a Granville Hicks, could permit himself
such dishonesty and lack of intellectual scruples.

—Nathaniel Branden, *Judgement Day: My Years with Ayn Rand* (Boston: Houghton Mifflin,
1989), 229–30

RONALD E. MERRILL

Judged purely as a piece of literature, *The Fountainhead* is Ayn Rand's best work.
Although it lacks the enormous philosophical scope and the intricate multi-

level organization of plot and theme that we find in *Atlas Shrugged*, the earlier book presents a fascinating and subtle interplay of ethical and psychological themes.

On one level, *The Fountainhead* is a treatment of Rand's professed theme: the ideal man, Howard Roark. She set out initially to portray the ideal man. It is no coincidence, one may suspect, that the book begins and ends with the words, "Howard Roark".

But she did not get far into the construction of the novel before encountering two serious problems. First, she simply was not ready to portray the ideal man; her ideas, her ideals, were in a state of flux at that time and she was far from having developed them sufficiently to accomplish her self-assigned task.

Second, from the point of view of literary technique, problems arise in writing a story about an 'ideal' person. To use a central character who is morally perfect makes it difficult to center the story on internal moral conflict. Adopting a hero who has no psychological problems rules out centering the story on psychological conflict. Thus when we encounter an 'ideal' hero, the story usually involves a basic dilemma of some less fundamental sort, such as a physical challenge.

Rand resolved this problem in *The Fountainhead* by removing Roark from the lead role. In the novel as it exists, Roark is 'off stage' for over half of the book. Instead, Dominique Francon becomes the real protagonist. The plot-theme of the book now becomes something different: 'How would imperfect people react to the ideal man?' This makes it possible to center the plot on a moral conflict within Dominique—and, later in the book, Gail Wynand.

For, on this level, *The Fountainhead* is a novel about the sin of despair. Though Rand would no doubt have been horrified to hear it thus described, the book has a theme prominent in Christian theology. Hope (as in "faith, hope, and charity") is a virtue in Christian doctrine because its antithesis, despair, leads one to feel that it is permissible to sin. If evil is destined to inevitable triumph, why struggle to achieve virtue? This is precisely the fundamental premise of Dominique and Wynand. Having despaired, not believing that good can triumph, they permit themselves to do evil. Wynand uses his 'power' to exalt the banal in human existence, and to crush men who show signs of integrity. Dominique wastes her talents and, like Wynand, leaves a trail of agony behind her, as she does her best to destroy that which she most values, from statues, to Roark, to her own soul.

On still another level, *The Fountainhead* deals with the twin issues of independence and integrity. Rand's unification of these two virtues is not sufficiently appreciated. One of her objectives in the novel is to show that independence, in the end, must mean intellectual independence. The man who allows others to tell him what to think, thereby allows others to tell him what to do. Rand provides numerous examples of this principle, culminating in the illuminating scene where Peter Keating is reduced to abject slavery by Ellsworth Toohey. Rand goes on to show that integrity can exist only in the man who possesses intellectual independence. For the 'second-hander,' dependent on others for his beliefs, can never resist their sway.

On still another level, Rand in *The Fountainhead* returns to her perennial theme: How can the good man live in an evil society? As we shall see, she still could not find a satisfactory answer to this riddle. ⟨. . .⟩

The novelette *Anthem* was produced during ⟨an⟩ interruption of Rand's work on *The Fountainhead*. This short but powerful story provides a further premonition of *Atlas Shrugged*, particularly in stylistic matters. The narrative makes scarcely a pretense of 'romantic realism'; the style is that of fantasy, sometimes more like poem than prose, quite unique among Rand's works. The stylistic influence of Nietzsche is evident, particularly in the eleventh chapter, which is strikingly similar to the opening of *Thus Spoke Zarathustra*. The actual events of the story range from improbable to impossible; it is the ideas that count.

Rand adopts a literary technique popular in the eighteenth and nineteenth centuries, the diary-narrative. The story supposedly is an account written by the hero. The text thus consists solely of a sequence of flashbacks; each chapter jumps ahead in the story, maintaining a high level of suspense until the narrative explains what led up to the new situation. Though old-fashioned, this technique can be highly effective and it is still used (for instance, in Kubrick's *2001: A Space Odyssey*).

The story employs a classically Randian gimmick: In a collectivist, totalitarian world of the future, the very word 'I' has been eliminated from the language. The conflict between individualism and collectivism is thereby reduced to its ultimate fundamentals.

Rand uses this story to illuminate an issue also basic to *The Fountainhead*: the individual as the source of human knowledge and progress. *Anthem*, in contrast to other collectivist dystopias, forecasts no universal electronic surveillance networks, no manipulative biotechnologies, no domed cities or spaceships. Instead, we are shown a collectivist government that has just accomplished, with no small difficulty, the transition from torches to candles. Rand drives home the point by making her hero a self-made scientist, who rediscovers electricity and uses it to make light. The symbolism is effective.

Indeed, Rand may have intended *Anthem* as a response to the influential Russian dystopia *We*, written by Yevgeny Zamiatin in 1920–1921. Like *We*, *Anthem* uses the device of a naive narrator in a world in which names have been replaced by numbers. But here the similarity ends. Zamiatin's hero, like those of *Nineteen Eighty-Four* and *Brave New World*, revolts against an allegedly scientific and logical society in the name of love, poetry, and emotion. D-503, a scientist of the One State, is led into rebellion under the sexual domination of a female mystic. His evident masochism makes his final submission to authority plausible.

Rand, on the other hand, champions reason and science as the enemies of totalitarianism. Her hero, assigned as a streetsweeper, makes himself into a scientist. He is a leader, not a follower, in his rebellion, and his love interest is an adoring and submissive young girl.

The story begins with a superb hook ("It is a sin to write this.") and never drags for an instant. Its inspirational and often poetic narrative is interspersed with just the right amount of Rand's distinctive humor (as for instance the heroine's behavior on her first encounter with a mirror).

In *Anthem*, Rand's concept of the importance of evil is enhanced and expanded. The men of evil now are seen as almost comically helpless and incompetent, fleeing like roaches from the light created by the book's hero. Like John Galt, *Anthem*'s hero is a scientist and inventor who develops a new source of energy. And the climax, in which he establishes a remote mountain refuge of reason, looks ahead to Galt's Gulch.

—Ronald E. Merrill, *The Ideas of Ayn Rand* (La Salle, IL: Open Court Publishing, 1991), 45–47, 56–57

GEORGE H. SMITH

Ayn Rand was one of the most intriguing and dynamic figures in twentieth-century thought. She had enormous power to inspire or to frustrate, to engage one's sympathies or to enrage them. While primarily a novelist, Ayn Rand constructed a philosophic system, which, although sketchy at times, is integrated, coherent, and compelling.

Many modern libertarians came to their present views by reading Ayn Rand. Whether they now favor limited government or some form of anarchism, it was Rand who first fired their imaginations and impressed upon them the crucial role of principles in thought and action.

Possibly because of the fierce emotions, pro and con, that Rand evokes, there has appeared relatively little in the way of competent reflection on Ayn Rand as philosopher. Accounts of Objectivism written by Rand's admirers are frequently eulogistic and uncritical, whereas accounts written by her antagonists are often hostile and, what is worse, embarrassingly inaccurate.

Evaluations of Rand in the academic community vary widely. On one extreme, the head of a philosophy department at a major university once called Rand "the worst philosopher in the history of Western Civilization." On the other extreme, the late Hiram Hadyn, an accomplished scholar who disagreed with Rand, remarked that Rand had constructed the most impressive philosophic edifice since Thomas Aquinas in the thirteenth century.

How, then, are we to evaluate the work of Ayn Rand as philosopher? How are we to judge the work of this astonishing woman who wrote with such intellectual passion?

I shall not attempt to analyze or criticize Rand's theories; this complex task would require far more than a single essay. Nor shall I assess Rand's influence on the climate of opinion, for this requires a perspective that can come only with the passage of time.

Another approach to Rand's ideas, and the one I shall adopt here, is to examine Objectivism for points of similarity to other philosophies. As I shall demonstrate, many features of Objectivism can be found elsewhere. In epistemology and ethics, some of Rand's arguments are strikingly similar to the arguments of Aristotelians, especially to those modern followers of Thomas Aquinas known as Thomists. In political philosophy, Rand's approach to natural rights and limited government falls squarely in the tradition known as Classical Liberalism.

Although Rand is often represented as a philosophic maverick, she actually represents a throwback to philosophy in the classical sense. The true mavericks are found in logical positivism, ordinary language philosophy, existentialism, and other schools that (until recently, perhaps) dominated much of modern philosophy. Unlike many of her contemporaries, Rand addressed the same basic questions that have vexed philosophers for centuries: What is the nature of existence? How do we acquire knowledge? What are concepts? What is ethics, and why do we need this discipline? What is the proper role of government?

Uncovering precedents and parallels to Rand's philosophy is not a popular enterprise among her more ardent disciples. For these true believers, it is not enough for Rand to be totally right; she must also be totally *original*. The problem here, of course, is what we mean when we call a philosopher "original."

Ayn Rand was not especially well-read in philosophy, and this fueled some of her originality. If previous philosophers anticipated some of her arguments or if some of her contemporaries made similar points, Rand seemed largely oblivious to those facts. Thus, in citing precedents and parallels, I don't wish to suggest that Rand borrowed from other philosophers without acknowledgment (although this does seem likely in a few instances). Rather, I believe that Rand originated most of her ideas; that is, she worked them out for herself, unaware that they had been previously worked out by others. She reinvented a number of wheels, so to speak. Whether this kind of originality is especially praiseworthy is an open question, but it at least demonstrates a remarkable ingenuity.

I do think that Rand was original in a more fundamental sense. A philosophy is (or should be) more than unconnected theories and arguments bundled together by a common name. A philosophy is an integrated and organized system of theories and arguments. Therefore, even if many elements of Objectivism can be found in other philosophers, this does not mean that Objectivism, considered as a philosophical system, is unoriginal.

In the final analysis, originality may or may not be admirable. A new method of torture may be original, but this does not recommend it. Conversely, to say that torture is wrong may be unoriginal but important nonetheless. It is always better to reaffirm old truths than to originate new falsehoods.

Another problem haunts Ayn Rand's philosophy. Rand was a sharp polemicist who gave no quarter to her adversaries. Many philosophers have retaliated by exiling her beyond the pale of respectable discussion. This is a mistake. Whether you like the woman or not, her brilliance and influence cannot be gainsaid. If Rand is to be excluded from serious consideration because of her polemicism, then why not exclude other polemical philosophers as well?

—George H. Smith, *Atheism, Ayn Rand, and Other Heresies* (Buffalo, NY: Prometheus Books, 1991), 193–95

JEFF WALKER

To Rand, the Declaration of Independence was flawed in its contamination by Christianity, euphemistically called "mysticism," which subordinates self-interest to sacrifice of self to God, God's spokesmen, and the godly community. Atheistic communism merely capitalizes on that mentality and substitutes statist ideology for God. Thus atheism guaranteed nothing and was for Rand barely a consideration. Her only critique of theism per se was that it was unworthy of her critique, hardly a humanist perspective.

However, she thought that were we committed to facing reality and coping with it by 100 percent dedication to "reason" and 100 percent rejection of mysticism, this would inexorably imply a society dedicated to rational selfishness, the supremacy of individual rights, and prosperous laissez-faire capitalism. To this end she cobbled together a philosophy incorporating bits of Aristotle and Aquinas; Locke, Adam Smith, other Enlightenment thinkers, and the American Founding Fathers; Gilded Age economic history, Nietzsche, and Austrian School economics.

The gist of that philosophy is as follows: humans must rely on their unique and practical smarts in order to make the choices that will keep them alive—the process of which generates distinctively human satisfactions—so reality calls for the maximum cultivation and use of brains. It would be self-destructive for any individual using practical smarts to join a group favoring physical force over brains because force negates brains. She would though enhance her chances of survival and well-being by initiating a group that respects smarts and thus shuns first use of force. She could then benefit from the division of labor and trade. Such a group, thereby enjoying the fruits of production and commerce (in ideas as well as goods and services), would eventually outlaw initiatory force by enshrining individual rights and restricting retaliatory force to government. This would deter enviers of those fruits within and outside the group from stealing them or destroying those who produce them. Because those with less practical intelligence but impressive impractical intelligence (mystics, many intellectuals) chip away at individual rights so as to claim fruits earned by others, it becomes necessary for everyone's survival that someone elaborate a convincing justification for the practical values of free commerce. And it would have to be a moral justification, one more convincing than any spun by those with impractical smarts, who favor shaking the tree to painstakingly cultivating it. That someone is Ayn Rand and once her prescription for saving humanity at its best from humanity at its worst has been proclaimed, its dissemination and implementation must swiftly follow lest barbarians topple the fruit-bearing tree and plunge the world into another dark age. Those who critique Ayn Rand's justification thereby lend credence to the destructive philosophies it alone can replace and are thus enemies, not just of Objectivism, but of reason and all human values. Objectivism's truths, necessitated as they are by the reality of human life on earth, are absolute, final, and all-encompassing, and invite only understanding and application rather than critique and revision. 〈. . .〉

Rand's reputation as a guru depends on the worth of *Atlas Shrugged* as a novel of ideas. The book is read mainly by senior high school students. While loyalists maintain that the reason adults fail to appreciate her is either their loss of ideals since adolescence or their opposition to Rand's ideology, the truth is that Rand's admitted "stunt novel" is a painfully resounding belly flop. While one can admire her ability to come up with and illustrate a "new" philosophy in action, her inability to make her characters anything but ventriloquist puppets mouthing either Objectivist philosophy or caricatures of opposing views is a literary disaster. Furthermore, the book is a gusher of hatred and contempt for the 99.9 percent of humanity who fall short of the Randian ideal man. This is a philosopher who loves not real human beings as they are or could reasonably be but only embodiments of her abstractions as they must but never will be. In *The Fountainhead*, Rand's best outing, the subordination of character and plot to ideological polemic is less glaring. Too bad the movie version for which Rand wrote the screenplay was as kitschy a clunker as *Atlas*.

For most if not all Objectivists, *Atlas* is not just the greatest novel of all time but the greatest human achievement of all time. Her work towers over that of Plato, Shakespeare, Galileo, Mozart, Dostoevsky, Einstein—to continue the list would merely lend to their grotesque aesthetic a dignity it self-evidently does not merit. Yet it forms the basis of Rand's guruhood and her followers' abject sycophancy—all in the name of, incredibly, reason and individualism. To paraphrase Voltaire: "Every sensible man, every honorable man, must hold the Randian sect in horror."

—Jeff Walker, "Was Ayn Rand a Humanist?" *Free Inquiry* 14, no. 3 (Summer 1994): 51

BIBLIOGRAPHY

Night of January 16th (drama, originally titled *Penthouse Legend*). 1935.
We the Living. 1936.
Anthem. 1938.
The Fountainhead. 1943.
Atlas Shrugged. 1957.
For the New Intellectual: The Philosophy of Ayn Rand. 1961.
The Virtue of Selfishness. 1964.
Capitalism: The Unknown Ideal. 1966.
Introduction to Objectivist Epistemology. 1967.
The Romantic Manifesto: A Philosophy of Literature. 1969.
Philosophy: Who Needs It? 1971.
see also: *The Objectivist Newsletter* (published throughout the 1960s) and
     The Ayn Rand Letter (published irregularly until 1976)

MARJORIE KINNAN RAWLINGS
1896-1953

MARJORIE KINNAN RAWLINGS was born to Arthur Frank and Ida May Kinnan on August 8, 1896, in Washington, D.C. She attended the University of Wisconsin, from which she graduated in 1918. At the university she met Charles Rawlings and the couple married in 1919. They moved to Rochester, New York, where Marjorie wrote a column, "Songs of the Housewife," for the local paper; the column was eventually syndicated in about fifty newspapers. In 1928, after visiting northern Florida with Charles's brothers, they decided to buy land in Florida and relocate there. That piece of land in Cross Creek, Florida, would provide the setting for *The Yearling* and much of Rawlings' other work, both fiction and nonfiction.

Although Marjorie loved rural life, her husband did not, and in 1933 they divorced. She stayed on the farm and continued to pursue a literary career, publishing her first novel, *South Moon Under*, the same year as her divorce. The novel was greeted with great acclaim, praised for details about life on the "scrub," which she learned by spending several months with swamp hunters, moonshiners, and the few families that populated that area of wilderness, about twenty miles from Rawlings' farm.

It was about this time when Rawlings was taken under the wing of the editor Maxwell Perkins, who also worked with F. Scott Fitzgerald, Ernest Hemingway, and Thomas Wolfe. Although Perkins was initially dubious that a book about a boy and a deer would be a success, Rawlings' enthusiasm for this project was contagious, and he helped her trim sentimental excess from *The Yearling*, which was awarded a Pulitzer in 1938. Perkins was also excited about Rawlings' next project, *Cross Creek* (1940), which has been described as a Florida version of *On Walden Pond. Cross Creek* records Rawlings' observations and comments on her Florida neighbors, whom she admired for their independence and work ethic. While working on *Cross Creek*, Rawlings finally accepted the marriage proposal of her longtime friend Norton Baskin, although she kept Rawlings as her professional name.

After *Cross Creek* was published, to favorable reviews, Rawlings was sued by one of her neighbors, Zelma Cason, for libel and invasion of privacy, claiming that Rawlings used her name without permission. When the suit was tried, in 1946, many writers rallied to support Rawlings, as did many of her Cross Creek neighbors. The court found for Rawlings, but the Florida Supreme Court overturned the ruling and awarded Cason a nominal amount for damages. Although this case was a landmark for the right to privacy in Florida, it has not been used as a precedent in similar cases.

Despite the legal uproar surrounding *Cross Creek*, the book was tremendously popular, leading Rawlings to publish *Cross Creek Cookery* in 1942. During the rest of the forties, however, she published very little due to a combination of ill health and legal battles. Her love for the Cross Creek area seemed undiminished by the lawsuit, and she continued to use it as the settings for her work. The sense of place in her work led reviewers to call Rawlings a regionalist or local-color writer, labels she found demeaning and limiting, as did her close friend Ellen Glasgow. Local colorist, in Rawlings' opinion, seemed to preclude any possibility that her work could have universal themes. Glasgow and Rawlings shared a long correspondence and an interest in one another's work; Rawlings was in fact at work on a biography of Glasgow when she died, on December 14, 1953, of a cerebral hemorrhage. Although Rawlings' work does not criticize patriarchal society the way Glasgow's novels do, her best work offers a clear and unvarnished portrait of a rural community that would all but vanish in the face of the ever-expanding Florida tourist industry, an industry that Rawlings vigorously opposed.

CRITICAL EXTRACTS

GORDON E. BIGELOW

One reason for *The Yearling*'s excellence as fiction is that in this book the characters were conceived of as people first and as crackers second. All the main characters are almost entirely fictional, though many of their particular traits and many of the incidents in their lives were suggested from real life. Penny Baxter bears little resemblance to Reuben Long, his real-life counterpart who first homesteaded Pat's Island in the scrub, and Jody Baxter has no specific resemblance to either of Reuben's sons, Mel or Cal, from whom Marjorie had much information about early life in the scrub. The Forresters in the novel were based upon a family of Sullivans who lived (as depicted in the book) about four miles west of Pat's Island at a place which is now called Hughes Island. The Sullivans, like the Forresters, farmed very little, but lived from their cattle, from hunting, fishing, and horsetrading, and from moonshining.

Grandma Hutto and her sailor son Oliver had no real-life counterparts and came close to being the kind of romantic cliché which often resulted from Marjorie's attempts to create character wholly from imagination.

At times Marjorie was quite aware of her own limitations as a creator of character, and once wrote in a letter to Fitzgerald, "You have what must actually be a painful insight into people, especially complicated people. I don't understand people like us—and what little I do understand, terrifies me. That's why I write, gratefully, of the very simple people whose problems are only the most fundamental and primitive ones. I have probably been more cowardly than I'd admit, in sinking my interests in the Florida backwoods, for the peace and beauty I've found there have been definitely an escape from the confusion of our generation. You have faced the music and it is a symphony of discord" [MKR to FSF n.d. (October ?) 1936]. Of course, rural people, including crackers in the scrub, are not necessarily any more "simple" than anyone else, but her tendency to see them in this fashion explains why so few of her fictional characters are convincing human beings. Penny Baxter and Jody are two notable exceptions, possibly because both are to an important degree projections of her own character and thus acquire a psychological depth and complexity not to be found in her other characters.

She told Perkins, after reading Henry James' *The Art of the Novel*, "My writing is too personal a thing. The artist like de Maupassant or James can do a good job with any subject, any 'germ' as James calls it. I can only work with something that is of intense personal interest" [MKR to MEP November 17, 1934]. Undoubtedly this is one reason why *The Yearling* succeeded so well. According to her own statement, the book had its ultimate origins in her own childhood. In a piece she wrote to be broadcast overseas in a Voice of America series entitled "In This I Believe," she had this to say about the book's beginnings: "I remember a very special sort of April day, the day I describe in the first chapter of *The Yearling*. I remember the delirious excitement I felt. And at the height of my delight, a sadness came over me, and I understood suddenly that I should not always be a child, and that beyond this carefree moment life was waiting with its responsibilities. The feeling was so strong that I never forgot it. As I became a writer, I thought back often to that April day and that emotion, and I said to myself, 'Sometime I shall write a story about the job of childhood, and the strange foreknowledge of maturity.'"

She had the same intense personal commitment to the subject matter of *Cross Creek*. When she said in court at the "Cross Creek Trial" that the book was a love song, of her love for Florida, she meant it quite literally. By the time she began writing this book in 1940 her apprenticeship was entirely behind her and she wrote as a first-rate literary craftsman, a true professional in full command of a significant talent. The measure of her growth as artist can be had by comparing this book with "Cracker Chidlings" where she was using almost identical materials. If the early piece was journalism, *Cross Creek* is literary art which bears comparison with Thoreau's *Walden*. In this book as in *The Yearling* circumstances combined to release her finest powers. She was dealing with material which she knew and loved deeply, but she had also learned the necessity for the right degree of artifice, the necessity to dominate "the facts" with imagination. She started with copious notes and sketches and she wrote in the vein of personal anecdote, lyric nature description, and earnest meditation in which she felt most at home. Her basic problem was to find a way to homogenize these materials into some kind of artistic whole. She wrote four drafts of the book over a period of nearly two years trying to discover the proper key.

Though it started out to be a book about a place, before she was done it had become quite as much a book about people. She wrote about real people whom she knew well, and whom she therefore did not conceive of as "characters" to be looked at as either simple or complicated. But she shaded her account of each of these people so that in effect she presents a large number of unusually vivid personalities who are based on real people but who are also quite as much fictive creations.

—Gordon E. Bigelow, *Frontier Eden: The Literary Career of Marjorie Kinnan Rawlings* (Tallahassee: University of Florida Press, 1966), 137–39

SAMUEL IRVING BELLMAN

Despite all the nerve-racking toil and care involved in writing her second novel, *Golden Apples*, Mrs. Rawlings was dissatisfied with the result. "'I don't blame anyone but myself for *Golden Apples* being interesting trash instead of literature,'" she wrote to her Scribner's editor, Maxwell Perkins, on October 15, 1935. "'But you should have bullied and shamed me further. I can do better than that and you know it.'" To the anonymous reviewer in *The Nation*, *Golden Apples* was "given over to the staples of petty fiction," it was "trite and quite harmless." "The people are disappointing," complained *The New Republic*, but *The New York Times Book Review* was somewhat more favorable. Mrs. Rawlings' literary executor, Julia Scribner Bigham, commented two decades later that *Golden Apples* was less successful than *South Moon Under*, "perhaps because the author had not the same distinctive sympathy with the main character, a young Englishman, that she had with the country itself and the Crackers." Mrs. Rawlings' biographer, Gordon Bigelow, is generally disparaging in his remarks about the novel: "an ill-starred book from the beginning," "unity is so conspicuously lacking," etc. Yet oddly enough, while she was revising the book for publication, the serial rights were sold to *Cosmopolitan* magazine, which wanted a shortened, four-installment version of the story. And, during

World War II, when the paper shortage was acute, the World Publishing Company published a hard-cover edition of the novel in its Forum Books series; this edition went through three printings between February, 1944, and April, 1946. ⟨. . .⟩

Golden Apples, for all of its merits as a story of Florida life at the end of the nineteenth century, generally fails to capture our imagination. We miss such conventional literary devices as in-depth character analysis and the "iceberg effect"—revealing only a little and letting the reader discern the vast bulk of hidden meaning—so widely used by Hemingway.

There are in the book, however, some very fine artistic touches that offset in part the noticeable deficiencies. For example, Luke Brinley's remarkable sermon on love (spoken to the aloof and indifferent Tordell, who has made Luke's sister Allie pregnant): "'I been studyin'. A man kin love a woman a heap o' ways. He kin love her the way he love a drink o' likker on a cold evenin'. He kin love her hateful-like, the way a man that loves the taste o' quail-meat'll kill 'em in the nestin' season, jest so he gits the good of 'em hisself. Or he kin love her the way I'd be proud to figger you done loved Allie—gentle-like and lookin' out for her'" (260). There is also a beautiful passage about the bereaved Luke's grieving for his dead sister. Suddenly Luke is pricked by a thorn on the "small holly tree he had left to grow for Allie's pleasure. A hot hand seized his vitals. For an instant it was past bearing, that spring should be here, and the holly growing, and the sweet orange grove, and Allie gone past knowing (351–52)."

And, near the end of the book, there is a wonderful piece of uproarious humor worthy of comparison with the comic portion of William Faulkner's *As I Lay Dying*. Not long after Allie has died during pregnancy, Luke realizes that he must have a woman around to help with the chores and to do for him and Tordell, so he decides to get himself a wife right away. Whom does he choose but the mentally retarded daughter of a long-time acquaintance, a widow with a large brood of children. There is much comic dialogue here, as Luke woos the girl through her mother. (The point is made that love is not an issue in this business; Luke has no time for love now, especially after his beloved sister's death.) The widow Raynes expostulates with this Cracker Touchstone who is seeking his Audrey: "'I mean, you figgered on it shore! I'll swear, Luke, this ain't decent. Courtin' and askin' and marryin' all in one day'" (334). But Luke will be served, and soon he and his "intended" and her mother ride off to the general store where the circuit riding preacher is expected to be (and, it is assumed, the storekeeper will stand treat).

Perhaps the author was mixing her modes somewhat too freely here: to describe Luke's sister's death, the story had just been pitched in a pathetic, poignant key. But it is hard to resist laughing at Mrs. Rawlings' graphic picture—sketched with flawlessly appropriate dialogue—of the hurry-up, back-woods wedding and the honeymoon in the kitchen. Luke doesn't want to waste a moment, there is so much work to do. His newly wedded wife explains that she has her best clothes on; Luke tells her bluntly, "'It ain't goin' to hurt 'em none to wash the dishes and scrub the floor'" (337). ⟨. . .⟩

Golden Apples treats at length and in many different ways a very important subject of concern for Mrs. Rawlings: the overriding importance of love and the seeming unavoidability of betrayal, after one gives oneself to love. Thus, Tordell says to Doctor Albury, who is nursing him back to health after his beating, "'You didn't agree with me once, Doctor, when I insisted that love was beastly, because it carried with it always, in one way or another, betrayal.'" Albury replies, "'I've had a great deal of love in my life, and sooner or later it's been a means of hurting me. I loved the woman who bore me, and she died. I loved the father who sired me, and he died. I loved the mother of my son, and she died, bearing him. I loved a woman again, and she went away and would have no more of me. All of it ended in pain.'" He concludes, "'I still say, I wouldn't have been without it. Not even to avoid the bitterness of death and betrayal, would I have done without the love'" (210).

—Samuel Irving Bellman, *Marjorie Kinnan Rawlings* (Boston: Twayne, 1974), 42–45, 48

SAMUEL IRVING BELLMAN

⟨*Cross Creek*⟩ is a record of Mrs. Rawlings' experiences of about a thirteen-year period spent in and around Cross Creek. As the book makes clear, the affinity she felt with the region reshaped her being in a way that must appeal to the most urbanized sensibility. In a much earlier society, she might well have considered changing her name to express this new self more accurately: *The Northern Lady Who Found a New Home in Cross Creek*, perhaps. The title of her first chapter tells the story: "For this is an enchanted land."

Because *Cross Creek* is so intensely personal, it is difficult to summarize it in any systematic fashion. Mrs. Rawlings wrote as an amateur naturalist, and her frequent detailing of flora and fauna places her firmly within a given, meaningful space, while her occasional vagueness about time gives an odd impression of existential drift. ⟨. . .⟩

⟨. . .⟩ *Cross Creek* may be seen as a repudiation of one kind of sophistication in favor of another kind of sophistication. "Having left cities behind her," Mrs. Rawlings transferred her cultivated, reflective sensibility to the North Florida woods where she could, for all her occasional loneliness and frustration, make the best of two worlds. Far above the other inhabitants of the Creek area in education and refinement, she was a kind of reportorial visitor from another planet. A great deal of time, she wrote or attempted to write, enjoying the status of one of Scribner's important authors. Celebrities visited her at the Creek and enjoyed her gourmet meals. On occasion she traveled to New York for an editorial conference or left the Creek far behind to get a change of scenery. For all its pastoral quality, *Cross Creek* reflects a wider range of experience than the bucolic or even the bucolic seen through urban eyes; there is the dimension of privilege that gives the book its particular character.

But the pastoral quality of *Cross Creek* (and *Walden*) calls up a related matter, the agrarian mythos, the mystique of the "field," the virtue of self-reliant cultivation of the land. "Insofar," ⟨Larry E.⟩ Taylor points out ⟨in *Pastoral and Anti-Pastoral Patterns in John Updike's Fiction*, 1971⟩, "as elements of the pastoral and anti-pastoral traditions exist in twentieth-century American fiction, they exist in some relation to a 'return to nature' motif, or a 'nature myth,' or an 'agrarian mystique.'" And, when he uses the last term, Taylor means "a generalized American attitude toward nature, the land, and rural life—an attitude historically traceable and still current in large segments of American culture."

Bigelow in *Frontier Eden* relates both the pastoral and the agrarian traditions to the backwoods way of life Mrs. Rawlings made famous. Penny Baxter (Jody's father in *The Yearling*), according to Bigelow, "falls squarely into the image of the idealized agrarian freeholder, which has been pervasive in American culture since the eighteenth century." Penny, "an independent, self-reliant yeoman farmer living in a great forest," represents "a frontier condition midway between the savagery of the mountain men and the corruptions of sophisticated society, that agrarian middle ground esteemed by Crèvecoeur and Jefferson as the ideal condition for human happiness."

Mrs. Rawlings' "use of this middle ground in her stories" leads Bigelow to identify "her with an important American pastoral tradition which has begun to be explored by scholars only in recent years"; by Henry Nash Smith in *Virgin Land* (1950), for example, and by Leo Marx in *The Machine in the Garden* (1964). Marx, extending Smith's earlier formulations, has demonstrated "the presence in American culture of a pastoral tradition deriving ultimately from Virgil." In *The Machine in the Garden*, Marx makes it clear that numerous writers in this country have made use of "'the syntax of the middle landscape'—a symbolic setting or background for their stories which they locate somewhere between the corruption of effete civilization and the barbarism of the howling wilderness. . . . Among the major authors who have written American versions of the pastoral, utilizing this symbolic middle landscape, Marx discusses Jefferson, Thoreau, Twain, Hemingway, Frost, and Fitzgerald." Mrs. Rawlings "clearly belongs to this company."

There can no longer be any doubt that it is high time for Mrs. Rawlings to be carefully reconsidered by American literary historians, most of whom have been almost entirely unaware of her contributions to our cultural heritage and her affinity with our more important homegrown naturalists of fact and fancy.

—Samuel Irving Bellman, *Marjorie Kinnan Rawlings* (Boston: Twayne, 1974), 106, 114–16

MARJORIE KINNAN RAWLINGS

⟨A letter to Maxwell Perkins from Marjorie Kinnan Rawlings, July 31, 1936.⟩

Dear Max:

I can see that you're disturbed about my feeling that I had better take a full-length for the boy's book. ⟨*The Yearling*⟩

It will positively be as we both first conceived of it. I have in front of me your letter of October 27, 1933. You say, "I am thinking of a book about a boy.—A book about a boy and the life of the scrub is the thing we want.—It is those wonderful river trips and the hunting and the dogs and guns and the companionship of simple people who care about the same things which were included in 'South Moon Under'—"

Until lately, I have had in mind one incident, almost, that would make a complete long-story in itself, about a boy. I wanted a bear-hunt in the story, for it fitted in with the other, and I have been prowling all over trying to find somebody who was actually bear-hunting, for I felt I had to see one to get what I want from it. By the merest accident, I met, and was taken into the confidence of, a perfectly marvelous old pioneer [Barney Dillard] living on the St. Johns river—the beautiful broad river I took the trip on, and which borders the scrub on the east side. This old man, a famous "bad man," but honorable and respected and at one time prosperous, too, took me bear-hunting twice, and in a few days I am going over to live a while with him and his wife and go hunting and fishing with him. So much material has come from my contact with him, and there is so much more there—anecdotes, hunting incidents, people—that I realized before I went to North Carolina that I had at hand a mass of stuff—and as always, the facts have suggested imaginary characters to me who fit in with the true ones—that couldn't possibly go in the simple 50,000 word narrative that I was ready to do. I had to resist constantly the thought of all these other things. . . . ⟨. . .⟩

It will be absolutely all told through the boy's eyes. He will be about twelve, and the period will not be a long one—not more than two years. I want it through his eyes before the age of puberty brings in any of the other factors to confuse the simplicity of viewpoint. It will be a book boys will love, and if it is done well enough otherwise, the people who liked *South Moon* will like it too. It is only since *Golden Apples* that I realize what it is about my writing that people like. I don't mean that I am writing *for* anyone, but now I feel free to luxuriate in the simple details that interest me, and that I have been so amazed to find interested other people—probably just from the element of sincerity given by my own interest and sympathy. . . .

I have a mass of animal material that will be fascinating to anyone at all interested. I have to laugh at Carl Brandt. I have told him again and again that the short thing I was ready to do was not for any magazine. I wrote him that the short thing would have to be full-length. He wrote back blandly, "Such good news. *Cosmo* will be delighted." I refuse to tell Carl what I have in mind, but what a shock it will be when all the stuff about bear-hunts and so on comes before him! ⟨. . .⟩

⟨A letter to Maxwell Perkins from Marjorie Kinnan Rawlings, May 14, 1938.⟩

Dear Max:

My secret fear about "The Yearling" has just been allayed. I was so afraid the old-guard hunters and woodsmen would find flaws. I know you think I put too much emphasis on the importance of fact in fiction, but it seems to me that this type of work is not valid if the nature lore behind it is not scientifically true in every detail. I saw a letter to the old man who told me so much, from the hunter who was with us on several of our hunts and prowls, and who knows his lore backward and forward. He wrote the old man that the book was a masterpiece, and that he not only read it but studied it. He said it made him so hungry for the scrub that he was ready to throw over his job and get back to it; that he could almost see old Slewfoot's tracks beside the branch. So now everything's all right.

People's response to the book amazes me. I am getting the most wonderful and touching letters. Readers themselves, I think, contribute to a book. They add their own imaginations, and it is as though the writer only gave them something to work on, and they did the rest.

—Gordon E. Bigelow and Laura Monti, eds., *Selected Letters of Marjorie Kinnan Rawlings* (Gainesville: University Presses of Florida, 1983), 112–14, 151–52

PATRICIA NASSIF ACTON

Marjorie had come to Cross Creek in 1928. She was tired of life in large northern cities and discouraged by her prospects as a writer. The isolation and lush beauty of the half-wild Florida countryside stirred her imagination. She was moved by the quiet dignity and friendliness of her modest neighbors. Here, she decided, she would write something good or admit finally that she was no writer at all.

Marjorie abandoned her former literary efforts and began to write stories inspired by her cracker neighbors. The books emerged in quick succession, and Marjorie became world-famous. In 1939 she won a Pulitzer Prize for *The*

Yearling, a novel about a boy's coming of age in the lonely Florida scrub country. In 1942 she published the highly acclaimed *Cross Creek*, an introspective, often hilarious sketchbook of life in her adopted community. Marjorie described the book as "a love story."

One of the characters in *Cross Creek* was Zelma Cason, a feisty and controversial inhabitant of nearby Island Grove. Marjorie met Zelma the first day she arrived in Florida, and they became close friends. Marjorie once accompanied Zelma on horseback to take the local census. She wrote about their adventures in the chapter "The Census," which began with a colorful description of Zelma:

> Zelma is an ageless spinster resembling an angry and efficient canary.
> She manages her orange grove and as much of the village and county
> as needs management or will submit to it. I cannot decide whether
> she should have been a man or a mother. She combines the more
> violent characteristics of both and those who ask for or accept her
> manifold ministrations think nothing of being cursed loudly at the
> very instant of being tenderly fed, clothed, nursed or guided through
> their troubles.

Zelma Cason was furious when she read this. She complained to friends that she had never consented to be in the book, and she was humiliated by Marjorie's description. When Marjorie visited her with an autographed copy of *Cross Creek*, Zelma burst into an angry tirade. "You have made a hussy out of me," she fumed. Marjorie apologized, and the two women talked. Marjorie left, satisfied that their friendship was restored.

She was wrong. Within a few months of this meeting, Zelma Cason filed a lawsuit against the celebrated author for invasion of her "right of privacy." The suit was a shock in more ways than one. Marjorie couldn't believe that her old friend had turned against her. And she was even more surprised at the nature of the lawsuit. Never before had a disgruntled literary subject claimed invasion of a "right of privacy" in a suit against the author of an autobiographical work. The state of Florida hadn't even recognized the existence of such a right. But Zelma was determined to defend her privacy, even if it meant a long legal battle. ⟨. . .⟩

Marjorie worked steadily on *Cross Creek* through most of 1940 and 1941. For Marjorie writing was "a peculiar anguish," but this book was a labor of love. She later explained her feelings at the trial: "To me 'Cross Creek' is a love story. It is a story of my love for the land, and for that particular portion of the land where I have felt that I belonged, which is Cross Creek."

Cross Creek was an immediate hit. The first of many trade editions was published in February of 1942. It was chosen as a Book-of-the-Month Club selection and was also published in a special armed forces edition, read by thousands of servicemen during World War II. Four years later the acclaim of critics and the glow of public approval would become an integral part of Marjorie's defense at the trial.

Although *Cross Creek* sprang from the same soil as Marjorie's other writings, it was a work that defied conventional literary description. Uproarious as well as introspective, the book has no specific chronology or plot structure. Instead, it is a loosely woven fabric of sketches, impressions, and narrative description, the warp and woof of life at Cross Creek. At the trial Marjorie explained that her purpose in writing *Cross Creek* was to "interpret . . . this lovely country and these people as they appealed to me." Consequently, the book revealed more of Marjorie's heart and soul than her personal history.

The precise character of *Cross Creek* became an issue in the lawsuit, with Zelma Cason claiming that the book "was advertised for sale and sold as a true account of the life and sojourn of the said Marjorie Kinnan Rawlings in the Florida backwoods, but was, as a matter of fact, in large part devoted to gossipy and scandalous tales and accounts . . . of the private lives of her friends." Marjorie's lawyers responded that the book was "purely an autobiography," but Marjorie undoubtedly came closer to the truth when she testified that *Cross Creek* was a "limited selective autobiography." In fact, she had confided to Perkins shortly before the book's publication: "I did not want anything like an autobiography of these past thirteen years. I wanted the thing objective, the only subjectivity consisting of my personal reaction to the Creek, its natural aspects and its people."

This element of "subjectivity" made Marjorie vulnerable at the trial to the charge that she fictionalized certain events, distorting a purportedly factual picture of her neighbors. All this was irrelevant to Zelma's claim of invasion of privacy, as the Florida Supreme Court would eventually rule, but it was the stuff of which good cross-examination was made. Zelma's lawyer questioned Marjorie vigorously about a passage in *Cross Creek* where she wrote: "I have used a factual background for most of my tales, and of actual people a blend of the true and the imagined. I myself cannot quite tell where the one ends and the other begins." How then could Marjorie discern fact from fiction in *Cross Creek*, particularly the passages concerning Zelma Cason? Marjorie admitted that she had "rearranged" several stories, but she insisted that "there is as little fiction in it as you could possibly have in a book of that type." As to the chapter on Zelma, "nothing is imagined."

—Patricia Nassif Acton, *Invasion of Privacy: The Cross Creek Trial of Marjorie Kinnan Rawlings* (Gainesville: University Presses of Florida, 1988), 1–3, 11–13

ELIZABETH SILVERTHORNE

The Yearling received an abundance of rave reviews.

One Florida reviewer said she would give ten years of her life to have written the book. The *Saturday Review of Literature* said, "Mrs. Rawlings has written a wise and moving book informed with a love of all living kind." The Philadelphia *Inquirer* called it "truly American and deeply human." William Soskin in the New York *Herald Tribune* maintained, "With Tom Sawyer and Huckleberry Finn well in mind it is quite possible to maintain that Jody Baxter . . . is the most charming boy in the entire national gallery." William Lyon Phelps called it "tremendously interesting and wholly charming." *Time* said that the book "stands a good chance, when adults have finished with it, of finding a permanent place in adolescent libraries." Others found it a "leisurely, beautifully composed record of a year's living" and a book with the same "irresistible appeal" as *The Swiss Family Robinson*.

The warm praise of reviewers for the book she had once been tempted to chunk into Mrs. Grinnell's canal was gratifying, but among all the comments there were a few less agreeable to Marjorie. Clifton Fadiman in the *New Yorker* advised his readers to "Take note of *The Yearling* by Marjorie Kinnan Rawlings, who writes the kind of regional novel that makes sense." The word "regional" always made Marjorie's blood boil. She thought it was a misleading and limiting term that ignored the fact that a writer uses his art to transform his regional material into something universal. She appreciated the closing sentences of the laudatory review by Edith Walton in the New York *Times*: "*The Yearling*—and this is the best tribute one can pay it—is nothing so narrowly limited as a 'local-color' novel. Rather, it recasts with unusual beauty the old, timeless story of youth's growth to maturity." Likewise, the *North American Review* thought the label "regionalist" obscured the major import of her work. Calling her "a new classicist," the *Review* compared her work to that of Willa Cather and Edith Wharton (both of whom Marjorie admired).

Edward Weeks, editor of the *Atlantic Monthly*, called *The Yearling* the "best and most endearing" book of the year and the London *Times* said the book was "bound to please everybody," a statement that seemed valid as praise for the book continued to pour in. Marjorie's meticulous care with the details of her descriptions of the country, the animals, and the hunting episodes was rewarded. She wrote Max ⟨Perkins⟩ on May 14 that her secret fear that old-guard hunters and woodsmen would find flaws had been allayed. One old hunter told a friend, who had passed it on to Marjorie, that the book made him so hungry for the Scrub that he was ready to throw over his job and get back to it. And Hubert Lyman Clark, the curator of the Museum of Comparative Zoology in Cambridge, Massachusetts, wrote to thank her for writing the book. He marveled at her ability to depict a boy's mind and emotions so per-fectly. He was equally amazed at the accuracy of her natural history. Birds and snakes, he told her, had been his lifelong hobbies, and not once in reading *The Yearling* did he detect a careless or an inaccurate statement. "Your descrip-tion of animal, bird life, scenery and the boy's reaction to them are simply delightful."

She did not accept criticism of her nature lore by those who did not know what they were talking about. She was tempted to jump on Lewis Gannett for questioning her *"provable"* nature incidents in his otherwise generous review, she told Max. But she had grown wise in dealing with critics, for she added she didn't think a writer ever got anywhere with any sort of protest "no matter how right he is."

Max told Marjorie he had never known a book to be so universally liked, and the sales figures bore him out. Fourteen days after publication *The Yearling* was on most lists of best sellers. It quickly moved upward and reached the top of the lists, where it remained for ninety-three weeks. During the first two months, sixty thousand copies were sold and during the first year, the total reached two hundred and forty thousand.

—Elizabeth Silverthorne, *Marjorie Kinnan Rawlings: Sojourner at Cross Creek* (Woodstock, NY: The Overlook Press, 1988), 149–51

B I B L I O G R A P H Y

South Moon Under. 1933.
Golden Apples. 1935.
The Yearling. 1938.
When the Whippoorwill. 1940.
Cross Creek. 1942.
Cross Creek Cookery. 1942.
Jacob's Ladder. 1950.
The Sojourner. 1953.
The Secret River. 1955.
The Marjorie Rawlings Reader. 1956.

MARY ROBERTS RINEHART
1876-1958

MARY ROBERTS RINEHART, the mother of the detective novel in America, was born in 1876 in Pennsylvania. After graduating from high school, she trained as a nurse and married a doctor, Stanley Rinehart, with whom she had three sons. She began writing mystery stories in secret (embarrassed because her husband and their friends did not read "cheap thrillers") in the early 1900s, while also working in her husband's medical office. Her short stories led an editor at *Munsey's Magazine* to suggest that she try her hand at a novel that would combine mystery, suspense, and romance; his suggestion led to Rinehart's first serialized full-length novel, *The Man in Lower Ten* (1906). The combination of mystery and romance, characterized by Ogden Nash (among others) as the "Had-I-But-Known" genre proved enduringly popular and Rinehart became the first mystery writer to have a novel make annual best-seller lists. The play she cowrote with Avery Hopwood, *Seven Days*, was a long-running Broadway hit, as were the two other plays she wrote with Hopwood, *Spanish Love* (1920) and *The Bat* (1920).

Rinehart was also a frontline correspondent for the *Saturday Evening Post* in 1915, writing articles about the fighting in France and Belgium. The War Department, impressed with her abilities, asked her to return to France in late 1918. She stayed there until January 1919, writing her impressions and observations about France in wartime and after.

Her mystery stories became increasingly popular during the '20s and '30s, earning unprecedentedly large sums of money—particularly for a woman writer. In 1938, for instance, the *Saturday Evening Post* paid over sixty thousand dollars to serialize her novel *The Wall*. In 1929, Rinehart's sons formed a publishing company, Farrar and Rinehart, and they published their mother's detective fiction until her death, including the novel that many critics think her finest, *The Door* (1930). Rinehart's novels are characterized by multiple subplots (and often, multiple murders), emotional undercurrents, and usually a spinster narrator who solves the mysteries or to whom the mysteries are revealed at the last minute. One of Rinehart's most famous spinsters, Tish Carberry, was the subject of a series of short stories—sometimes solving mysteries, sometimes simply offering observations about her small town and its inhabitants. Rinehart's spinster detectives are detectives in spite of themselves, often pulled into a mystery through circumstance, or out of a desire to facilitate the romance of a young couple.

Although Rinehart's mystery novels are not now held in such high regard as other works of the golden age—the 1920s and 1930s—of mystery writing, her independent heroines mirror Rinehart's own independence, and her ability to defy gender roles. Rinehart was a devoted wife and mother, roles that she discusses in great detail in her autobiography, *My Story* (1931), but Rinehart was also a woman who traveled widely, became independently wealthy through her own productivity, and made the detective novel a respectable—and profitable—genre for the American women writers who followed in her footsteps. She died on December 22, 1958, and is buried with her husband in Arlington National Cemetery.

CRITICAL EXTRACTS

GRANT M. OVERTON

The novel *K.*— or story *K.*, if we accept Mrs. Rinehart's disclaimer as to novel writing—is possibly more representative of her work than any other single book. It illustrates perfectly her ingenuity in contriving and handling a plot; for the book ends on page 410 and the most necessary revelation does not come until page 407. It exemplifies her finished gift for telling a story; there are no wasted words and in half a page she can transport you from laughter to tenderness. Half a page? On page 70 you may see it done in seven lines. The girl Sidney Page has slipped from a rock into the river, alighting on her feet and standing neck deep. Rescued by K. Le Moyne, she remarks:

"'There wasn't any danger, really, unless—unless the river had risen. . . . I dare say I shall have to be washed and ironed.'

"He drew her cautiously to her feet. Her wet skirts clung to her; her shoes were sodden and heavy. She clung to him frantically, her eyes on the river below. With the touch of her hands the man's mirth died. He held her very carefully, very tenderly, as one holds something infinitely precious."

K. shows its author's power to portray character effectively in sweeping outlines filled in, on occasion, with solid or mottled masses of color. K. himself is the kind of a person that Mary S. Watts might have put before us in some 600 closely printed pages. It is a difference of method merely and while not every one would be able to appreciate the thousand little touches with which Mrs. Watts drew her hero, Mrs. Rinehart's more vigorous delineation is effective at all distances, in all lights, with almost all readers. She manages in this tale to present a wide variety of persons and a great range of emotions and she manages it less by atmospheric details and a single setting—the Street—than by an astonishing number of relationships between a man and a woman; or, in the case of Johnny, "the Rosenfeld boy," and Joe Drummond, a youth and a woman or girl. It will be worth the reader's while to note that the story contains no less than ten such relationships. First there are K. and Sidney and Joe and Sidney. Then there are Max Wilson and Sidney, Max Wilson and Carlotta Harrison, Tillie and Mr. Schwitter, Christine Lorenz and Palmer Howe, Grace Irving and Palmer Howe, Grace Irving and Johnny Rosenfeld, K. and Tillie and K. and Christine. This is very complicated and unusual art—if it is not novelizing, then we do not know what novelizing is. Consider the gamut run. K. and Sidney are the ripe lovers. Joe's unrequited love for Sidney is the desperate passion of immaturity. Max Wilson's feeling for Sidney is the infatuation of a nature inherently fickle where women are concerned. Carlotta Harrison's love for Max Wilson is the dark passion. The relation between Tillie and Schwitter goes to the bedrock of human instincts, is a thing Thomas Hardy might have concerned himself with. It is pathetic; he would have made it tragic as well; we are satisfied that in her disposition of it Mrs. Rinehart is sufficiently faithful to the truth of life. Christine Lorenz and Palmer Howe are the disillusioned married; but in this case, as Christine said: "'The only difference between me and other brides is that I know what I'm getting. Most of them do not.'"

Grace Irving and Palmer Howe bring before us the man and the woman in their worst relationship in the story, or in life either. Grace Irving and Johnny Rosenfeld are a picture of thwarted motherhood and a blind feeling for justice. K. and Tillie are proofs of the reach of friendship and the efficacy of understanding. K. and Christine give us the woman saved from herself.

The height—or the depth—to which Mrs. Rinehart attains in this story is a thing to marvel at, and just as marvelous is the surety with which she gets her distance. The tenth chapter of K. will not easily be overmatched in American fiction or that of any other country. Here is Mr. Schwitter, the nurseryman, middle-aged or older, not very articulate, with a wife in an asylum playing with paper dolls; and here is Tillie, punching meal tickets for Mrs. McKee, not becoming younger, lonelier every day, suffering heartaches and disappointment without end. Mr. Schwitter has proposed a certain thing.

"Tillie cowered against the door, her eyes on his. Here before her, embodied in this man, stood all that she had wanted and never had. He meant a home, tenderness, children, perhaps. He turned away from the look in her eyes and stared out of the front window.

"'Them poplars out there ought to be taken away,' he said heavily. 'They're hell on sewers.'"

—Grant M. Overton, *The Women Who Make Our Novels* (New York: Moffat, Yard & Co., 1922), 62–65

A. E. Much

Another woman writer of detective fiction who first became celebrated in the early twentieth century (and is still writing popular novels almost fifty years later), was Mrs. Mary (Roberts) Rinehart, born in Pittsburgh in 1876. She produced many sentimental romances of contemporary American life, with rich 'socialites' owning oil wells or cattle ranches; cowboys performing miracles of horsemanship on the range or at the rodeo; inscrutable, revengeful Indians in their reservations. She has also written many humorous tales, but she is chiefly associated in the public mind with her murder mysteries, cleverly devised to pile suspense on suspense, and remarkable for the technical skill that makes the reader share the emotions of those who investigate the mystery. Her best known works in this field are her earliest, *The Circular Staircase* (1908), later dramatised as *The Bat* and played with immense success during the nineteen twenties in this country and in America, and *The Man in Lower Ten*, serialised in 1907 and published in volume form in 1909.

The plot of *The Circular Staircase*, typical of Mrs. Rinehart's crime mysteries, is in many respects reminiscent of the pattern created by Anna Katharine Green almost thirty years earlier, with two lines of detective enquiry being followed, separately and often at cross purposes, by a police official and the strong-minded, inquisitive, kind-hearted elderly spinster who narrates the story. Miss Rachel Innes, in *The Circular Staircase*, is largely a re-incarnation of Miss Green's Amelia Butterworth in her personal qualities, social position and habits of thought, her relationship with her long-suffering maid, her sympathy with young lovers, as well as in her detective methods and her facility for 'happening' to discover important information by accident. Mrs. Rinehart, however, handles this plot technique with greater literary skill than her predecessor, and her first crime novels are particularly interesting because they owe nothing to French or English influences, and represent the emergence of a new vein of purely American detective fiction, with an authentic background of characteristically American social conditions. Mrs. Rinehart is still actively engaged in literary work, and her novel *The Wandering Knife* (1952) once again introduces an efficient detective, Mary Adams, who appeared in earlier stories, but the mysteries she has written in recent decades, though entertaining, are not outstanding, and Mrs. Rinehart's greatest impact on the American detective novel, her influence upon its development, was made in the early part of the twentieth century.

—A. E. Much, *The Development of the Detective Novel* (New York: Greenwood Press, 1958), 212–13

ARNOLD R. HOFFMAN

Being without effort very much an American, and having been born into and come to live in two strikingly different social classes, Mary Roberts Rinehart could be expected to be class conscious, and also conscious that class differences in America were at the best very shaky. Her early crime fiction, even through *The Wall* of 1938, is often told by a narrator whose position makes requisite the introduction of grand old homes (sometimes seemingly haunted), summer resorts, town cars, and servants of all types. Mrs. Rinehart never explicitly says that the good old days of dignified affluence are gone for America, but again and again her narrators or other major characters are now the genteel poor. Very clearly she caters to America's nostalgia for a time when large fortunes and *grande dames* ruled society. In the Twenties and Thirties there was a sharp awareness that the Gilded Age was only a memory, to be clung to by the few of that generation remaining. Finally, in Mrs. Rinehart's mysteries after 1945, there is no longer a concentration upon the details of managing inheritances, houses, and wild children.

Importantly, the wild children of Mrs. Rinehart's fiction in the first half of her career are not the sex-ridden creatures of today's hard-boiled fiction. Yet Mary Roberts Rinehart's crime fiction really is not of "another time"; it is of several times, through which decorous young ladies who might be kissed on the first anniversary of their "affairs" (*K*, 1915) have metamorphosed into witty females who can balance a cigarette, cocktail, and tennis racket all at once.

In the process of this radical change—and the men are a part of it, too—Mary Roberts Rinehart never plays for sensationalism. In only one of the mysteries is there anything other than a conventional marriage or romance (allowed its obstacles of money, position, and distance). And that is *The States vs. Elinor Norton* of 1934. A major portion of the story is involved first with Blair Leighton's attempts to get Elinor away from her husband and his rather offhand dalliance with a sluttish country girl while he maneuvers, and then with Elinor's agony after her husband has been killed and Blair begins sleeping with her, holding out the promise that he will marry her. There are no bedroom scenes, but at one point Elinor appears before the men in lounging pajamas, and it is clear later that adultery is taking place. However, it is the conclusion to the novel that is most important. The narrator, whom one hesitates to call the "hero," for his physical role in the story is severely limited, finally persuades Elinor to marry him, just before she is to enter an Episcopal convent. For the first time, a Mary Roberts Rinehart hero takes a sullied woman to wife.

In an essay on "The Simple Art of Murder," Raymond Chandler refers to Robert Graves' and Alan Hodge's *The Long Week End*, a study of English life and manners after World War I which gives some attention to detective stories. Their observation is that mysteries do not reflect what is going on in the world, because only writers without vision or ability write mysteries, a kind of unreal fiction. This essay differs with that point of view.

A reading of Mrs. Rinehart's "crime stories" and research into her life and the publication history of her books, indicates that there are two views under which her mysteries may be examined: as craft or art, and as a record of social thought and behavior across some fifty years. As a literary craftsman, Mary Roberts Rinehart worked imaginative variations on "mystery formulas" that are partly stock and partly germane to her own work. She was not the first to use notes behind baseboards or re-papered walls, but she often thought to use an old roll of the original paper for the job. And, although it is hardly to her credit, she is generally recognized as the founder of the "Had-I-But-Known" (or HIBK) school. Under the aspect of an artist, she was, in her own words, "primarily interested in people and their motivations," and at times—very irregularly—she does achieve finely drawn, absorbing characterizations. That of Rachel Innes is one.

—Arnold R. Hoffman, "Social History and the Crime Fiction of Mary Roberts Rinehart," *New Dimensions in Popular Culture*, ed. Russel B. Nye (Bowling Green, OH: Bowling Green University Popular Press, 1972), 165–67

JULIAN SYMONS

The books of Mary Roberts Rinehart (1876–1958) ⟨. . .⟩ were stories written to a pattern. All of them deal with crime, and the crime is almost always murder. There is a detective, but his activities are often less important than those of the staunch middle-aged spinster, plucky young widow or marriageable girl who finds herself hearing strange noises in the night, being shut up in cupboards, overhearing odd and apparently sinister conversations, and eventually stumbling upon some clue that solves the mystery. Much of what happens in these stories occurs by chance, and the mystery is prolonged only by the obstinate refusal of the characters to reveal essential facts. Mrs. Rinehart's books belonged to the "Had I But Known" school, the absurdities of which were wittily summed up by Ogden Nash:

Sometimes it is the Had I But Known what grim secret lurked behind
the smiling exterior, I would never have set foot within the door;
Sometimes the Had I But Known then what I know now, I could
have saved at least three lives by revealing to the Inspector the
conversation I heard through that fortuitous hole in the floor . . .
And when the killer is finally trapped into a confession by some
elaborate device of the Had I But Knowers some hundred pages
later than if they hadn't held their knowledge aloof,
Why, they say, Why, Inspector, I knew all along it was he, but I
couldn't tell you, you would have laughed at me unless I had absolute
proof.

These are the first crime stories which have the air of being written specifically for maiden aunts, and they exploited a market which, with the spread of
library borrowing, proved very profitable. From Rinehart's second book and
first success, *The Circular Staircase* (1908), at the climax of which spinster Rachel
Innes finds herself shut up with the murderer in a small secret room behind the
great old chimneypiece ("I knew he was creeping on me, inch by inch"), the
formula of needless confusion and mock-terror did not change. The settings
became more varied, yet also more enclosed. As one commentator has said, "It
does not really matter much to the world view which emerges whether the
backdrop is New York City or Connecticut, a town or a country house, the
stability and balance most usually associated, sentimentally at least, with an
agrarian order are assumed." People in the books die but this is not important,
because in relation to the real world none of them was ever alive. Nobody is
ever doing any work, although suspects may be labelled solicitor, doctor,
chauffeur.

Sometimes the confinement of the society in which violence takes place
is carried to fantastic lengths. Rinehart went on writing until a year or two
before her death, and *The Album* (1933) is typical of her later novels. It deals
with five families living in Crescent Place, "a collection of fine old semi-
country houses, each set in its own grounds," insulated from the city outside
by an entrance gate marked Private "so that we resemble nothing so much as
five green-embattled fortresses." The action literally never moves outside the
Crescent. Reporters and photographers cause no trouble after an initial visit,
and make no attempt to gain access to the houses although four murders are
committed, the first with an axe and the last involving a headless trunk.
Within this totally closed circle none of the characters works, although one
apparently did, since we are told that "he had given up even the pretence of
business since the depression, and spent a good bit of time tinkering with his
car in the garage." Even such tinkering is unusual, for there are cooks, a gardener, a chauffeur, various helpers. These people really have nothing to do,

apart from being suspected of murder. The murderer, naturally, is one of them. Her actions, when her identity is revealed, are outrageously unlikely.

Rinehart's work was naive, but in some ways her world was that of the detective novel after the First World War.

—Julian Symons, *Bloody Murder: From the Detective Story to the Crime Novel* (New York: The Mysterious Press, 1993), 100–2

JAN COHN

Given Rinehart's previous short stories, her three early mysteries are an astonishing achievement. Each written in a matter of weeks and scarcely revised, they are fully developed and richly plotted fictions, blending not only mystery and romance but humor as well. For the mysterious, Rinehart combined intellectually puzzling clues and events with eerie and chilling occurrences— "the creeps." Her murderers leave their share of footprints and bloodstains but much more fascinating to Rinehart, and her readers, were less conventional clues: a stolen basket of crockery, altered numbers on railway berths, slips of paper with the message "1122." The puzzles provoke interest; the creeps provide thrills, and from the earliest of her mysteries on Rinehart's characters encounter terrors. Her heroes and more especially her heroines wander around in the dark, despite the mounting number of local murders, and more likely than not the least they can anticipate is a clammy hand reaching out of the darkness to grab them.

From the beginning, too, Rinehart knew how to develop a richly complex plot. Often, as in *The Man in Lower 10*, there are two separate, but eventually related plots, two lines of evil-doing. The romantic story adds further complexity and, since at least one of the romantic pair in each early novel is victim or suspect (or both), the elements of mystery and romance support one another in mutual suspension until the denouement.

Despite similarities in the structures of these early works, they are different enough to indicate how far Rinehart yet was from developing any kind of pattern or formula for her mysteries. The three have different settings and social environments, present widely varying motivations for crime, and demonstrate considerable uncertainty about the source of evil except perhaps to suggest that it lies in greed. Theft is a much more important element in early Rinehart than it would become in her mature works. ⟨. . .⟩

Lawrence Blakely, hero and narrator ⟨of *The Man in Lower 10*⟩, travels from Washington to Pittsburgh to take a deposition from steel-magnate West about a forgery case. Returning to Washington on the train, his papers are stolen and, the numbers on the berths in the sleeping car having been altered during the night, his assigned berth is discovered to contain a dead body. A train wreck follows and Blakely finds himself sitting on an embankment, sooty and shaken, with Alison West, the steel man's granddaughter and his own partner's fiancée.

Although the mystery opens with the problem of forgery compounded with the theft of some bonds from Blakely's briefcase, a second criminal conspiracy soon appears. Alison West is the prize in this network of villainy: a particularly wicked woman forces her weak-willed brother Sullivan to woo Alison. Although Alison is already engaged (and Sullivan married!), he manages to press his suit to the point where he compromises her—unfairly of course—and, her reputation apparently ruined, she elopes with him.

Blakely confronts a mass of difficulties. He must recover the bonds, prosecute the forger, release Alison from her false (bigamous) marriage, and persuade her to break her engagement to his partner. These tasks are undertaken in an atmosphere of considerable creepiness: a hand appears mysteriously out of a trap door; a carriage ride to a deserted country mansion brings Blakely into the darkness of an old and unfamiliar house to be terrorized by enemies both human and feline.

Sometimes Rinehart develops comedy in *The Man in Lower 10* by deliberately deflating the horror of the creeps, as she does with the black cat who terrorizes Blakely in that dark mansion. But there is another source of humor as well and it probably had its origin in Rinehart's self-consciousness about writing thrillers. Just as she had burlesqued the mystery genre in her early poem, "The Detective Story," so she parodies the detective himself in the character of Wilson Budd Hotchkiss. Hotchkiss is an altogether disinterested person; he involves himself in the murder in Lower 10 for intellectual reasons alone. As he tells Blakely, "I use the inductive method originated by Poe and followed since with such success by Conan Doyle" (31). Armed with enthusiasm and a small notebook, he collects clues and tails suspects, finally announcing his discovery of the murderer. Unfortunately, he sends the police off to arrest Blakely's own confidential clerk, the most innocuous of men. ⟨. . .⟩

Curious changes have been rung on Rinehart's reputation. Until about 1940 she was thought of as a novelist and short story writer, not a mystery writer primarily. Her enormous public apparently preferred her serious and romantic novels, for they were generally the ones that made the annual bestseller lists between 1910 and 1936. Reviewers, however, began as early as 1920 to see significant flaws in the romances and equally significant successes in her mysteries. That judgment has been echoed since Rinehart's death in 1958 and her name has been altogether associated with the mystery novel, her romances nearly forgotten.

Most recently, in the Dell paperback reprints of her work, Rinehart is being promoted as a writer of Gothics. Dell apparently made a change in marketing strategies for Rinehart novels about 1968. During most of the 1960s, Dell Rinehart covers promoted mystery and crime, with pictures of bodies, weapons, and clues. Subsequently, reissues turned to Gothic images with dark-haired maidens fleeing sinister houses. No doubt the decision to place Rinehart among the Gothics on supermarket shelves was part of an effort to capitalize on a hot market, based on what might seem a reasonable argument that recurrent elements in Rinehart mystery fiction are the elements of Gothic novels: the mansion as setting, the supernatural as a source of mystery, the young woman as narrator and hence *apparently* as central figure.

In fact, these elements are not handled in the Gothic mode. Rinehart mansions are not castles, merely excessive expressions of bourgeois over-reaching. There are, after *The Circular Staircase,* no hidden rooms, secret stairs, or locked chambers. Midnight intruders gain entry not through hidden passageways but by means of unlocked window screens. Similarly, the supernatural is treated in ways that are distinctly anti-Gothic. Seances and spirit-return were part of popular, and sometimes even intellectual, science in the early part of the century, and so they were for Rinehart.

Most important is the role of the female narrator. For one thing, she is central only to the surface romance. Both the surface mystery and the buried story have other characters for their focus. It is also significant that the female narrator is only marginally endangered; she is not the object of murderous violence. Nor is she the object of sexual violence, real or threatened, for this young woman is pursued only by the romantic hero, a man of the purest intentions.

The Gothic label may be hard to detach, however, and not only for reasons of marketing. Rinehart's mysteries do not fit tidily into either of the two schools of detective fiction that dominated mystery writing in her lifetime. She clearly does not belong to the American school of tough guy detectives. And just as surely she is not part of the British school of intellectual puzzles and country-house murders, and for two important reasons. First, her use of the past, while not in itself unique, is so in its complexity and its intensity. Second, despite the comic elements in her mysteries, Rinehart lacks the wit of British mystery fiction, the tone that brings it close, murders notwithstanding, to comedy of manners.

Rinehart started her career ashamed of her mystery thrillers and for a very long time, perhaps for her whole life, she viewed her crime novels as less significant than her serious fiction. Still, as she reviewed her work in the 1948 edition of her autobiography, she paid tribute to the skill that her mysteries demanded, a skill far beyond that her other fiction required: she assured her readers that "ponderous tomes" are relatively easy to write; in fact, "the more easily anything reads, the harder it has been to write," for "almost anyone with sufficient determination can make a roast beef. But it takes a light hand to make pastry."

—Jan Cohn, *10 Women of Mystery*, ed. Earl F. Bargainnier (Bowling Green, OH: Bowling Green State University Popular Press, 1981), 184–85, 216–17

KATHLEEN L. MAIO

It was Ogden Nash who gave Had-I-But-Known its name. In a poem entitled "Don't Guess, Let Me Tell You," he proclaimed: "Personally, I don't care whether a detective-story writer was educated in night school or day school./So long as he doesn't belong to the H.I.B.K. school." Nash's use of a male pronoun to describe the authors of such tales is nothing more than a case of semantic sexism, for HIBK has had, from its very beginnings, a distinctly female character. Needless to say, Nash was not alone in his disdain. Howard Haycraft once called HIBK "a school of mystery writing about which the less said the more chivalrous." Julian Symons dismissed HIBK as "the first crime stories which have the air of being written specifically for maiden aunts."

Now that chivalry is dead, now that one does not have to be apologetic for being a maiden aunt, it seems appropriate that we reexamine the "feminine" detective novel, HIBK, a detective fiction formula that celebrates its roots, Gothic romance.

The ties between Gothic and detective fiction are strong and undeniable. Even male critics will acknowledge that the official "father" of detective fiction, Edgar Allan Poe, was also a master of Gothic horror. Also, as Devendra Varma has pointed out, "the ingenuity of plotting, characterization and background, the perennially fascinating situation of pursuit, coupled with the chief detective ware of 'suspense' are the gift of Gothic romance."

HIBK is quite obviously a Gothic-detective hybrid, and it has inherited characteristics of both parents. Like the Gothic, HIBK is an exercise in terror which is largely domestic terror and which focuses on a woman and her immediate ménage. An HIBK, like the Gothic, is unabashedly a thriller. While the detective story claims to be an intellectual exercise, the HIBK story openly appeals to our emotional sensibilities of sympathy, outrage, horror—and triumph. But HIBK, as a modern formula, employs a modern setting. Removing the Gothic from the crumbling castle and replanting it in a recognizable modern environment makes the HIBK-Gothic a less detached, more ominous, journey into fear. Mabel Seeley reported that if she had a "premise, it was that terror would be more terrible, horror more horrible, when visited on people the reader would feel were real in places he [sic] would recognize as real."

HIBK is also a form of detective story. Like detective fiction, HIBK is, almost always, a "murder mystery" wherein the mystery is finally solved without recourse to the supernatural. A combined force of professional and amateur detectives solves the mystery, and captures or stops the murderer. But HIBK is unlike the "pure puzzle" detective story in many ways. The pure puzzle detective story generally features a single, nicely delineated murder for its primary mastermind sleuth to ponder—and eventually solve through the exercise of sparkling, detached logic. One feels secure that the hero-sleuth has everything firmly under control. The same is not true of HIBK. Here, there is no sense of security—no sense that a heroic male figure has things under control. In an HIBK novel, no one ever says "It's elementary, my dear Watson," because it never is. The situation is always complicated with sub-plots and emotional cross-currents. Events occur in a rapid and confounding chain reaction. Often there are multiple murders. Seldom is there a professional detective, and when there is, he is never a mastermind. Law and male authority figures are clearly not the heroes in HIBK. ⟨. . .⟩

Mary Roberts Rinehart (1876–1958) is the "mother" of HIBK. Although there was a large body of first-person-female narrative mystery fiction before Rinehart (Anna Katharine Green's "Amelia Butterworth" novels are charming examples), it is Rinehart who clearly developed the narrative technique into a formula that went beyond pure detection. Rinehart's first nonserial novel, *The Circular Staircase* (1908), is the cornerstone work of HIBK. The narrator, spinster Rachel Innes, rents a summer country house called Sunnyside and is soon embroiled in a plot of multiple murder (five die) and general mayhem. She is clearly an innocent bystander to the original plot. But soon the reputations of her niece and nephew, and her own safety, are threatened. For a while she waits for the police to resolve things, but she soon finds their inaction "deadly," and the situation increasingly dangerous. In self-defense she becomes a detective, ferreting clues and suppressing those that implicate her household.

The official sleuth, Mr. Jamieson, his band of detectives, and the confused innocents involved all stumble at cross-purposes through a plot that becomes more deadly and dangerous with every moment. Miss Innes makes most of the key discoveries because she is not plagued by the need for "logical" (linear) thinking like the classic male sleuth. She does not expect human behavior to be a rational process. She does not expect physical evidence to tell the whole story. Curiosity and leaps of insight stand her in good stead. She tells us:

> Halsey always says: "Trust a woman to add two and two together and make six." To which I retort that if two and two plus x make six, then to discover the unknown quantity is the simplest thing in the world. That a household of detectives missed it entirely was because they were busy trying to prove that two and two makes four.

Rinehart would later freely admit that *"The Circular Staircase* was intended to be a semi-satire on the usual pompous self-important crime stories."

The Circular Staircase was followed by many more Rinehart mysteries, and almost all are within the HIBK formula. Rinehart was masterful in the use of the older woman as spinster-heroine and narrator. While these women are sharp, fiercely independent, and skeptical about men, they often help foster the obligatory romance by playing fairy-godmother-as-vindicating-sleuth for one or more sets of young lovers. Other mysteries feature younger (but still mature) women as central figures. In *The Wall* (1938) and *The Great Mistake* (1940), young women are actively brave in working to rid their households of danger. They are rewarded with romance and a happy ending. But theirs is a happy ending tempered by the need to look back, to reevaluate, and even to regret the past.

Rinehart, unlike most of her successors, made frequent small concessions to the supernatural demands of the Gothic. An example is her use of omens. In *The Case of Jennie Brice* (1913), the widow-narrator, Mrs. Pitman, finds that a dead kitten has floated into her flooded rooming house—a sure omen of misfortune. In *The Wall*, a servant observes a flock of crows overhead and predicts "bad luck"—which turns out to be the understatement of the year. In the same book, the mysterious ringing of certain bells by a "ghost" is never fully explained.

Rinehart was the innovator, and she was followed by many other HIBK practitioners.

—Kathleen L. Maio, "Had-I-But-Known: The Marriage of Gothic Terror and Detection," *The Female Gothic*, ed. Juliann E. Fleenor (Montreal: Eden Press, 1983), 82–85

NANCY WALKER

Before Dorothy Parker and H. L. Mencken openly attacked sentiment and conventionality as the spirit of *The New Yorker* proclaimed America's urban tenor in the 1920's, such writers as Carolyn Wells, Josephine Daskam, Alice Duer Miller and others wittily questioned old stereotypes of women, and frequently presented images of strong, independent women who demonstrate women's capacity for skepticism. While the styles of humorous writing these women use vary widely—from satire to parody to the most delicate irony—the message is constant: that women are bound by neither piety nor innocence, but are free to question and alter their lives.

Two characters from women's humor of this period exemplify the cleverness and strength that characterize the capacity for humor itself. Susan Clegg, in Anne Warner French's series of stories, and Letitia Carberry, Mary Roberts Rinehart's "Tish" in a similar series, both embody self-determination, even though their personal situations are quite different. French's "Susan Clegg" stories, published in several volumes between 1904 and 1920, recall the settings of American humor—and particularly of women's humor—during most of the nineteenth century: the small, rural town inhabited by unsophisticated people who occupy fixed relations to each other—the kind of town satirized by Sinclair Lewis in the 1920's. Rinehart's Letitia Carberry, on the other hand, though not an urban woman, is distinctly more urbane and mobile than is Susan Clegg: she travels frequently, in both Europe and America; she is an early devotee of the automobile; and she has an attitude toward established authority that borders on iconoclasm. Rinehart, though known as a mystery writer, wrote more than a dozen non-mystery novels and as many volumes of short stories, several of which feature the redoubtable Tish.

Susan Clegg and Letitia Carberry are both spinsters, a fact that enhances their independence. In contrast to the stereotypical unmarried woman of American humorous literature, whose every effort is bent toward snaring a man, these two women, like Louisa in Mary Wilkins Freeman's "A New England Nun," have *chosen* their single state. ⟨. . .⟩

Letitia ("Tish") Carberry differs from Susan Clegg in her far greater physical mobility; in fact, a popular volume of Tish stories is titled *Tish Marches On*. Not tied to a small town and a fixed social milieu, Tish foreshadows the "flapper" of the 1920's—albeit in the form of the eccentric maiden aunt. Yet the dialogues that form the basis of the "Tish" stories, are, like those in the Susan Clegg stories, conversations between and among women. In the stories about Tish Carberry, Rinehart uses a narrator named Lizzie to tell of the adventures of the fearless triumvirate composed of Lizzie, Tish, and Aggie, all of whom have no fear of embarking upon an adventure if it seems to serve a cause. The only time marriage surfaces as an issue among these three women is when some younger person or couple seems to them to be in a sufficiently interesting dilemma to warrant their intervention.

Whereas the humor in French's Susan Clegg stories arises from the difference between Susan's rather cynical attitudes toward her conventional nineteenth-century milieu and the obvious cliches of her life (her tie to the invalid father, her compulsive efficiency as a housekeeper), Rinehart's Tish is a different kind of anomaly. In an early-twentieth-century society that has begun to resemble today's mass culture, Tish stands for old-fashioned decency and individual courage. At the beginning of "Tish Goes to Jail," for example, Lizzie starts her account of the adventure by confirming Tish's position as an individual who follows her own laws rather than those of society ⟨. . . .⟩

Tish Carberry is not only more accepting of the twentieth century, she also tries to bend its institutions to her own sense of values. Tish is a tough, albeit gracious, lady with the proverbial heart of gold, and she is above all stubborn. A typical description of her is Lizzie's in "Tish Goes to Jail": "anyone who knows Tish Carberry and her hatred of wrong and injustice will know that nothing moved her." (135) In the same story, Tish's involvement with the case of a missing girl has put her under suspicion by the sheriff, and when he comes to question her, the following interchange takes place:

> "Now what have we got? [says the sheriff] Clothes in a field, but no body; two sets of teeth, a missing shutter, and a lost girl. For two cents I'd drag that well of yours."
>   "I wish you would," said Tish coldly. "One of Jeremiah's cats has been gone for a week." (154)

It is this mixture of strength and wit (itself a verbal indication of intellectual strength) that endears Tish to the reader, even though she is often a figure of fun in the stories because of her well-intentioned but decidedly eccentric escapades.

Although the image of woman-as-victim lingered as a staple of American humor well into the twentieth century—and still persists, especially in television comedy—Susan Clegg and Letitia Carberry are two examples among many in early-twentieth century literature of an effort to change that image. Both characters are based upon unfortunate stereotypes of women: the gossip and the meddling eccentric. Yet both women, because of their refusal to bow to the expectations society has for them, earn our respect at the same time that they amuse us. Susan Clegg, instead of mourning her single state, finds the flaws in the rosy picture of married life her culture offers her; and Tish Carberry tries to bend the world to her sense of right—a sense that rejects the dehumanizing effect of institutions. In humor as in many other ways, women at the turn of the twentieth century posited their own strength as an argument against the discrimination of society.

—Nancy Walker, "Susan and Tish: Women's Humor at the Turn of the Century," *Turn of the Century Women* 2, no. 2 (Winter 1985): 51–53

JAMES C. DANCE

From about 1908, when *The Circular Staircase* was published in book form, until her death in 1958, Mary Roberts Rinehart reigned as the queen of American mystery writers (a title she professed to despise). Her 1909 book *The Man in Lower Ten* has the distinction of being the first American detective novel to appear on the annual bestseller list.

Critics have credited her, on the positive side, with the injection of humor and informality into the formal detective story, and, on the negative side, with the "Had I But Known" (HIBK) device in which the narrator, usually a heroine, teases the reader with intimations of events further along in the plot which could have been avoided except for her indiscreet behavior.

Both of these accomplishments can be seen, in retrospect, to rise out of her use, in most of her mystery novels and many of her short stories, of a fairly standard stock company of characters, chief among them the unmarried female whose domestic calm is shattered by the intrusion of murder.

An examination of MRR's spinster heroines produces the following discoveries:

1. MRR did not, with one possible exception, cast these women in the roles of major sleuths, thus observing Howard Haycraft's dictum that "women . . . do not make satisfactory principal detectives." They are, at the most, Watsons or assistants to various sheriffs or investigators; at the least, involved observers.

2. MRR's heroines, probably reflecting changes in American society and public taste, evolved from wealthy dowagers into less-well-to-do younger women.

3. MRR's technique of placing her heroines in dangerous situations to which they were not, by upbringing or experience, accustomed, provided more or less subtle learning stimuli in which their powers of intuition and observation were stretched and they tended to become, in the language of this decade, more liberated.

As early as 1907, when *The Circular Staircase* in its original serial form was being written, MRR created the character of an indomitable middle-aged spinster who is on the scene of the crime and assists in the detection. Of her first ten books, five were to feature such a heroine. After 1930, her novel-length mysteries continued to employ unmarried women in the major roles, but these were much younger—in their twenties and thirties—than the fifty-ish spinsters of her earlier works. MRR's autobiography *My Story* (1931, 1948) does not indicate why, just when she herself was reaching the age she had been attributing to her popular heroines, she should suddenly (in 1933's *The Album*) lop some 25 years off her narrator's age, and continue that pattern through the remainder of her full-length mystery fiction. One can surmise that, since most of those novels were first published serially in *The Saturday Evening Post*, she may have had editorial advice as to the kind of heroine to which her readers would most readily relate; but that is strictly conjecture.

It may be significant that MRR's early spinster heroines, self-described as "elderly" and "middle-aged," were actually, on closer reading, in their forties and fifties. The notion that people in this age span were "old," and that it was unusual, or eccentric, or humorous, for them to involve themselves in crimes and other adventures, quickly became a literary convention. But the speed with which the stereotype of "old" was changing is suggested by Agatha Christie's decision, in 1930, to make Miss Marple 74 years old in order to achieve the effect.

In addition to the reverse aging of her heroines, there was a progressive decline in their fortunes. From *The Circular Staircase* through *The Door* (1930), MRR's spinsters were, with one exception, depicted as women of wealth and social position. The modern reader gets an unintended chuckle when Elizabeth Bell, narrator of *The Door*, writes, "I live alone in the usual sense of the word," and then goes on to introduce her secretary, butler, cook, chauffeur, housemaid, laundress, and gardener.

The exception is the narrator of *The Case of Jennie Brice* (1931), who is not only a widow, breaking her out of the otherwise invariable spinster mold, but also an impoverished boarding-house keeper.

The families who inhabit The Crescent, locale of *The Album*, however, begin to show the inroads of the Depression. By the time of *The Wall* (1938), the young heroine is hard-pressed to maintain both the town house and her family's traditional summer home on "the island," as well as give employment to her elderly butler, cook, and maid. By 1940's *The Great Mistake*, she is so bad off as to have to seek work. The family in MRR's 1945 book *The Yellow Room* has to cope not only with a diminished fortune but also with the deprivations of World War II—rationing, no gas, no telephone, no male servants. The heroine of *The Swimming Pool* (1952, MRR's last full-length mystery novel) has given up the town house and is living in the country house, managing by augmenting her brother's income as an attorney with her earnings as a writer. ⟨. . .⟩

In 1933, MRR produced *The Album*, with its gallery of eccentrics—one might say grotesques—unmatched in any other of her novels, and her youngest heroine-narrator to date. Louisa Hall is 28, the "baby" of the inhabitants of The Crescent, an elegant but declining block where five mansions front on a common lawn. One matriarch insists that all doors in her house be locked at all times, with herself the keeper of the keys. An elderly invalid keeps a fortune in a trunk under her bed. One husband and wife have not spoken to each other for years. Louisa's mother has worn deep mourning for her late husband for two decades. The newlywed Wellingtons, having recently moved into the house he inherited, with their wild parties and loud music, represent to the other inhabitants the worst of the Jazz Age. When the wealthy invalid is axed to death in her bed, and other murders follow, The Crescent is shaken to its foundations; but in the ensuing investigation Louisa loses many of her repressions and falls in love with Herbert Dean, a criminologist with sufficient eccentricities of his own.

The Album, besides being a thrilling if gory whodunit, is an excellent portrayal of a young woman suddenly forced to reassess all the values and priorities she has accepted unquestioningly all her life. Louisa blossoms visibly, and, although her behavior (including the cliché of walking alone into a dark, empty house where a trap has been set for the killer) tends to reinforce the

criticisms of the HIBK name-callers, in context it seems logical (she is obey-
ing her mother's command to retrieve her late father's portrait).

1938's *The Wall* was a high point in MRR's output. In the aftermath of the
Depression, Marcia Lloyd must carefully husband her resources to be able to
maintain two houses and keep a handful of elderly family retainers. The very
day that she reopens Sunset House for the summer, her brother's amoral ex-
wife and her maid show up and give every sign of entrenching themselves until
Arthur makes a cash settlement, which will get Juliette out of some unspeci-
fied kind of trouble. Marcia co-operates with the bucolic local sheriff to solve
Juliette's murder, but they are unable to prevent the deaths of her maid and the
local doctor. A large roster of suspects (so large, in fact, that one begins to
question how so many people with concealed connections to the dead woman
should all turn up at the same time at the same place) is gradually whittled
down. At the last, it is the sheriff's tenacity and not Marcia's intuition that
identifies the murderer.

Orchidaceous Juliette dominates *The Wall* even after her death. She is
MRR's best drawn "bitch" and served as a model for unsympathetic females
that the author was to use in most of her subsequent mysteries. Marcia pales
by comparison, and her reaction to the threatening events is chiefly anxiety.
Her romance with the secretive artist Allen Pell seems perfunctory and imma-
ture; her interaction with the middle-aged countrified sheriff is much more
interesting and well done.

—James C. Dance, "Spinsters in Jeopardy," *The Armchair Detective* 22, no. 1 (Winter 1989):
29–30, 33–34

B I B L I O G R A P H Y

A Double Life. 1906.
Seven Days (drama, with Avery Hopwood). 1908.
The Circular Staircase. 1908.
When a Man Marries. 1909.
The Man in Lower 10. 1909.
The Window at the White Cat. 1910.
The Amazing Adventures of Letitia Carberry. 1911.
Cheer Up. 1912.
Where There's a Will. 1912.
The Case of Jennie Brice. 1913.
The Secret Seven. 1914.
The After-House. 1914.
"K". 1915.

Tish. 1916.
Bab: A Sub-Deb. 1917.
Long Live the King. 1917.
The Amazing Interlude. 1918.
Twenty Three and a Half Hours Leave. 1918.
Dangerous Days. 1919.
Love Stories. 1919.
Affinities and Other Stories. 1920.
The Bat (drama, with Avery Hopwood). 1920.
Spanish Love (drama, with Avery Hopwood). 1920.
A Poor White Man. 1920.
The Breaking Point. 1921.
The Red Lamp. 1925.
Nomand's Land. 1926.
Tish Plays the Game. 1926.
Lost Ecstasy. 1927.
The Romantics. 1929.
The Strange Adventure. 1929.
Mary Roberts Rinehart's Mystery Book. 1930.
The Door. 1930.
My Story.1931; revised and updated in 1948.
Miss Pinkerton. 1932.
The Crime Book. 1933.
The State vs. Elinor Norton. 1933.
The Album. 1933.
The Doctor. 1936.
Tish Marches On. 1936.
Married People. 1937.
The Wall. 1938.
Writing is Work. 1939.
The Great Mistake. 1940.
Familiar Faces. 1941.
Haunted Lady. 1942.
Alibi for Isabel and Other Stories. 1944.
The Yellow Room. 1945.
Episode of the Wandering Knife. 1950.
The Swimming Pool. 1952.
The Frightened Wife and Other Murder Stories. 1953.
The Mary Roberts Rinehart Crime Book. 1957.

MARI SANDOZ
1896-1966

MARI SANDOZ was born on May 11, 1896, in northwestern Nebraska, the setting for most of her novels and nonfiction. The daughter of Swiss homesteaders who expected her to be a farm wife, Sandoz's literary career was alien to her family, particularly to her father, whose life she chronicled in *Old Jules* (1935).

Because her childhood home was near two Lakota reservations, and because her father was an early supporter of Indian rights, much of Sandoz's work is dedicated to revising aspects of Indian history. Her nonfiction is supplemented by her ability to draw on accounts of historical events told to her by Indians, giving Sandoz's work a veracity not often found in mid-twentieth-century accounts of conflicts between Indians and whites. In *Cheyenne Autumn* (1953), for example, she draws on the memories of an old Cheyenne woman, who was one of the last survivors of the violent encounters that Sandoz writes about in the book. *Cheyenne Autumn* attempts to explain the discrepancies between the U.S. Army's version of a Cheyenne rebellion and stories of the rebellion told by the Indians, white eyewitnesses, and records in pictograph books.

Much of Sandoz's work is politically oriented, either implicitly or explicitly. In New York she was involved with various leftist organizations, and she often spoke out against what she perceived to be the rapacious and destructive exploitation of the Western frontier. Her Great Plains series documents changing attitudes toward the land, and in the struggles between man and nature, her sympathies seem usually to be with nature. The first book in the series, *Old Jules*, tells the story of how the immigrants "settled" the west, using her family as an example. Unlike other representations of immigrant settlement, however, Sandoz's book portrays the brutality and ugliness of life on the farm, particularly in the ways that women were treated by their husbands, brothers, and fathers. In the same series, Sandoz also included two biographies of Indians: *Crazy Horse* (1942), and *Cheyenne Autumn*.

In what many consider to be her finest novel, *Slogum House* (1937), Sandoz continues the process of desentimentalizing the West. Gulla Slogum is an unscrupulous woman who deceived her husband into marrying her, and she drives her daughters to prostitution and her sons to everything but murder. Gulla's greed comes close to destroying the entire family; it is only through the efforts of her one good daughter, Libby, that the family name is salvaged. Family life in *Slogum*

House and in *Old Jules* is rough and inhospitable, reflecting, perhaps, the landscape of the Nebraska sandhills that provides the background of much of Sandoz's work.

Sandoz's mixture of historical fact, anecdotes, and interpretation has made it difficult for critics to know exactly how to draw the line between fiction and nonfiction when considering her work. Furthermore, her fiction is often didactic and polemical, which led to negative and even hostile reviews, as was the case with her novel *Capital City* (1939), which is actually an allegory of sorts, using the city of Lincoln, Nebraska, as the subject for Sandoz's antiwar sentiments and her support for the proletariat. Recently, however, much of the research she did has been verified by other historians, and sociologists, ethnologists, and anthropologists all praise her meticulous details. Mari Sandoz died on March 10, 1966.

CRITICAL EXTRACTS

HELEN WINTER STAUFFER

Mari's own literary influences came primarily through her reading and studies. She had read Conrad as a child but was introduced to other major authors later. Hardy, whom she read shortly after she first came to the university, made a profound impression on her; the structure of *Slogum House* was based on that of his novels. Of later discoveries, the Russians strongly affected her, as did Shakespeare and, finally, the Greeks, with whom she saw so many parallels in her Indian heroes. "I've always felt that the underlying theme of Crazy Horse, the destiny fore-ordained for him and the people he led, no matter how great his personal virtue, is Greek in its tragic implications," she wrote to her friend Mamie Meredith in 1957. "I've always felt, ever since my introduction to Greek literature, that the Plains Indians had a close affinity for the Greeks in their sense of honor and honor lost." At some point she read Whitman and was strongly impressed by both his philosophy and his style, as were so many other western writers. His American romanticism influenced her indirectly as well, through such writers as Carl Sandburg and Willa Cather. Her reading of Adolph Hitler's *Mein Kampf* was an experience she never forgot. Eliot's *The Waste Land* was a major discovery, as was Céline's *Journey to the End of the Night*. Kafka's *The Castle* she found especially illuminating of her own occasional sudden sense of being lost in the world, "a complete unfamiliarity with even the commonest things." For her, Kafka's book was terrifying and yet one she returned to every year or so. That she came to so many of the classics late, when she was a mature woman but while still formulating her own writing style and ideas, made them especially vivid to her, in the same way that her delayed learning to read affected her when she was nine: "I learned reading late . . . learned *cat*—a tremendous revelation—could always recognize it . . . [as] the greatest gift in the world, and I was old enough to appreciate it," she told an audience.

By conventional literary standards, Mari Sandoz's nonfiction measures up well. Strongly affected by her sense of history, of time and of place, she wrote powerful and effective histories when working with protagonists whom she could identify with her own region. She mastered the art of recreating a man and his culture, emphasizing the moral issues involved when one culture destroys another, and illustrating her own romantic view that man has dignity and worth. She adhered closely to carefully researched information, and the strength of her artistic imagination lay in creating a verisimilitude of actual events, rather than in creating imaginary scenes. In her biographies particularly she succeeds in re-creating the living past. She accepted the artist's purpose: "The crude matter of life assumes significance from the shaping hand of the artist."

The re-creation of early settler life abounds in Plains literature, but Mari Sandoz's *Old Jules* is so unusual it has few imitations. Her ability to fuse Jules's importanace to the region with scenes from his domestic life, while involving herself, is rare. (The only biography I know that manages similar emotional material so unemotionally, achieving aesthetic distance, is Edmund Gosse's *Father and Son*, about life in the 1800s in England.) In 1935, *Old Jules* shocked people, not only because of the domestic scenes but because it showed the public a stark, unromantic view of the frontier. The strong language, the sometimes brutal realism, the frankness were all criticized vigorously, but they made the book powerful. The swearing no longer shocks contemporary readers, who are frequently confronted with pungent, and often pointless, profanity, but the realism and frankness are just as gripping now as they were then. The children cowering under the bed, Henriette's fright when a shot breaks the lamp in her hand, Uncle Emile shot down in front of his family by a hired gunman—these scenes as well as the descriptions of the prairie's beauty are still as effective as ever. The conflicts described best in *Old Jules*, *Crazy Horse*, and *Cheyenne Autumn* still hold significance, although the specific incidents are well in the past. The West is now tamed, and the Indians are, legally at least, freer to move about as they please, but the emotions engendered by those conflicts are universal. Mari's people experience love, hate, ambition, jealousy, sorrow, fear, satisfaction and joy. Some are caught by forces too large for them to control—by a government gigantic and relentless and sometimes apparently mindless. Some learn their fate is controlled by men too small for their responsibilities, too ignorant or too greedy to value human life. And some fight back. These things have been going on since long before the Greeks wrote of them, and we see them today. The theme of man and his fate is timeless. Mari Sandoz hoped to match her subject matter with her art. In these three books she succeeded.

—Helen Winter Stauffer, *Mari Sandoz: Story Catcher of the Plains* (University of Nebraska Press: 1982), 6–8

MELODY GRAULICH

Sandoz conceived her biography of her father, a notorious "locator" in frontier Nebraska, as "the biography of a community, the upper Niobrara country in western Nebraska," and she focuses on her family as representative pioneers (p. vii). Exploring the unequal conflict between men and women in the West, Sandoz shows through repeated example that women are often the victims of the West's celebrated freedom. She presents her father as the archetypal frontiersman, whose desire for absolute free will and freedom makes him in some ways romantic and heroic—America's much-discussed and well-respected rugged individualist who is usually presented in only the barest and most stylized relations with women. Sandoz focuses on her father's marriages, and most readers finish the book shocked at his violent treatment of his four wives. When his first wife disobeys an order, "Jules closed her mouth with the flat of his long muscular hand"; when his second wife asks why he does nothing, "his hand shot out, and the woman slumped against the bench. . . . [Later] he pretended not to notice [her] swollen lip, the dark bruises on her temple, and the tear-wearied eyes"; when Sandoz's mother Mary asks Jules to help do the farm work: "'You want me, an educated man, to work like a hired tramp!' he roared, and threw her against the wall" (pp. 5, 102, 199).

But Jules is no more brutal than most other men in the book and is, in fact, most representative when he is beating his wives. Sandoz shows through his conversations with his friends that they believe women are to be used and controlled, their individuality of little consequence. The men mock and belittle women, making crude sexual comments. Sandoz makes it clear that Jules defines women as his society does: a woman is something to exploit. A man needs a wife to work, obey, and bear children, and the laws and culture support his attitudes. Although the "community" knows which wives are victims of battering, it never interferes. The legal system, such as it is, sides with the male. ⟨. . .⟩

As the violence teaches girls what to expect from men, it also influences boys' attitudes about and behavior toward women. One of the grisliest scenes in *Old Jules* concerns Mrs. Blaska, whose husband uses her love for her sons to "coax" her back after she dares to leave him. After she is found dead, "stripped naked, in the open chicken yard," her husband admits he whipped her. "She started to run away again and, handicapped by his crutch, he sent her sons to bring her back. They held her while he pounded her" (p. 412).

The Blaska boys, like many of the sons in these works, suffer from what Talcott Parsons has called "compulsive masculinity," characterized by aggression toward women who "are to blame." By the end of *Yonnondio*, Mazie's brother Will becomes "sullen" and "defiant," having learned "a lust to hit back, a lust not to care" (p. 71). The books demonstrate that violence is circular: society's devaluation of women and implicit support of male domination cause violence, while men learn to further devalue women through watching them being beaten. Recent feminist theorists who argue that gender identity is based on a child's relationship to the mother show how traits that these writers link to violence are formed in childhood. Carol Gilligan has suggested that because boys must separate from their mothers to develop a masculine gender identity, while femininity is defined through attachment, "male gender identity is threatened by intimacy while female gender identity is threatened by separation." The boys learn to reject women, but the books reveal a good deal more about how the girls attempt to deal with identifying, with being "attached," to a victimized woman.

Sandoz, Smedley, Le Sueur, and Olsen focus on how the daughters resist, reject, and come to understand themselves through their mothers' lives. Some suffer from what Adrienne Rich ⟨in *Of Woman Born* (New York: Bantam, 1976), 237–38⟩ calls "matrophobia": the fear "of becoming one's mother . . . the splitting of the self, in the desire to become purged once and for all of our mothers' bondage." Rich argues that daughters often see their mothers as standing "for the victim in ourselves," "as having taught compromise and self-hatred," as "the one through whom the restrictions and degradations of a female existence" are passed on (pp. 238, 237). While the authors do not find wholly adequate solutions to the blurring and overlapping of personality that Rich analyzes, they do not resemble the daughters she describes who find it "easier by far to hate and reject a mother outright than to see beyond her to the forces acting upon her" (p. 237). Partially through identifying these forces, they resolve their feelings about their mothers in various ways. In a sense, each book bears testimony to the daughter's inability to separate herself from her mother, to her belief that her mother's life had value.

—Melody Graulich, "Violence Against Women in Literature of the Western Family," *Frontiers* 7, no. 3 (1984): 14–15, 17

HELEN WINTER STAUFFER

The second book in ⟨Sandoz's Great Plains⟩ series, *Crazy Horse*, was not part of her early plan. A novel based on the Indian chief's life was originally to have been written by Sandoz's friend Eleanor Hinman. The two traveled over three thousand miles the summer of 1930 in a Model T Ford Coupe, visiting the Rosebud and Pine Ridge reservations in South Dakota, the Little Bighorn and Rosebud battlegrounds in Montana and Wyoming, and other sites important in the Indian wars of the 1800s. They interviewed a number of ancient Indian veterans still living on the reservations, some Sandoz had known in her childhood. Sandoz returned alone to the reservations the following two summers for further information. ⟨. . .⟩

Once again Sandoz uses the chronicle form for a biography, but there are a number of differences between this and *Old Jules*. Everything in *Crazy Horse* points to the death of the hero at the end. Moreover, in Crazy Horse she had a man who manifested characteristics of the classic Virgilian hero. Because of the vast area, the large number of people involved, and the importance of the events to the Indians and the whites, the book is close to the classical epics in subject matter. Sandoz's serious treatment of her materials, her veneration for her hero and his civilization, her sorrow at the destruction of that civilization, all suggest her awareness of ancient Greek literature and history.

In addition, Sandoz applied a rather unusual technique for that time in using Indian terms and idiom to tell the story from their point of view. The method reinforces her objective of relating events primarily from the Indian view, using symbols compatible with their culture. The reader usually knows only what the Indians knew. Seeing events from that perspective, one understands their actions in their conflicts with the whites.

While those steeped in Plains Indian lore found the book excellent, many others had difficulty with the strange terms and the sometimes elliptical comments of the author. Footnotes are scanty and the bibliography lists only her most unusual sources, so researchers wishing to follow up on the book are frustrated.

In spite of these legitimate criticisms, *Crazy Horse* is one of the most important books of its genre in Western American literature, introducing readers to details of Indian belief and life on the Plains, and bringing out information never before known to the whites about the Indian wars.

Action begins in 1854 with the incident Sandoz considered the fuse that ignited the long struggle, the Grattan affair at Fort Laramie. Lt. Grattan, an arrogant, inexperienced young West Point officer, led his detail of men into a large Indian village near the fort and mortally wounded a major chief there. The infuriated Indians swarmed over the soldiers and killed them all. Among those witnessing the struggle and its aftermath was the twelve-year-old Crazy

Horse. In addition to identifying the first incident in the wars, she also describes in this chapter the causes of the conflict and many of the major characters who will dominate the book: Red Cloud, here almost a villain; Spotted Tail, Crazy Horse's maternal uncle, who eventually betrays him; Pretty One, later called Woman's Dress, already jealous and always anxious to belittle or hurt him; He Dog, Crazy Horse's best friend, loyal to him all his life (and one of Sandoz's most important sources in 1930).

One of the strengths of the book lies in the authenticity of detail. As always, Sandoz pays close attention to the importance of the environment in the hunting, the fruit and vegetable gathering, the homes, and the travel: the details of a life attuned to the Plains. She shows, too, the heat of summer, the cold and snow of winter that contributed to the defeat of the Indians.

Sandoz also used great effort to trace the intricate relationships of the Oglala and Brulé Sioux, as she did later for the Cheyennes. Since much Sioux loyalty is based on family ties, this was of major importance in determining the motives of the participants. Her book also revealed for the first time the love affair between Crazy Horse and Black Buffalo Woman and its consequences in later events.

The empathy between Sandoz and her hero is important. Her close sympathy with him gives power to the story and helps her to succeed in recreating a man and his time as it must have been, one of the primary purposes of a good biographer.

    —Helen Winter Stauffer, *Mari Sandoz* (Boise, ID: Boise State University Western Writers Series, 1984), 20–23

CLAIRE MATTERN

The Sandhills of Nebraska are long and tall and vast. They were desert once, but now support a tough, nourishing grass cover that makes the coats of horses and cattle sleek. Fifty acres of it will support one cow for a year, and to gain this nourishment, the cow must watch her step and walk carefully along the slopes of the hills, making frequent switchbacks to wend her way up and down. To walk straight down would make her choke and suffocate, and to walk straight up would tax her unduly, and perhaps invite a fall. In the valleys, cattle ranchers harvest hay in summer to sustain her when the snow is deep, and they keep their windmills in good order to provide her water where there are no streams to quench her thirst. The thoughtful rancher will feed her cattle cake to supplement her rations from time to time, especially during calving season. Through the past 100 years some trees planted by ranchers and farmers have survived, especially on the homesteads which, however, are located far back from paved roads, and are miles and miles from each other. The people who settled the sandhills and survived had to be tough. They learned to be loners, if need be, to be wary of strangers yet hospitable, and to depend upon themselves.

One hundred years ago, a young man ". . . left his home on the blue waters of Lake Neuchatel alone, crossed the sea, and came as far west as his money permitted . . ." (Mari Sandoz, *Old Jules*, Little, Brown, and Company, Boston, 1935). That man was Jules Ami Sandoz, father of Mari Sandoz. The eldest of six children, she would experience corporal abuse, endless duties and hard work, the care of younger siblings, the loss of the sight of one eye from snow-blindness hunting cattle after a blizzard, the wrath of her father over her desire to be educated and to write, and the displeasure of her parents and family for ending a marriage of almost five years to go to the city of Lincoln in Nebraska to pursue education and a writing career. When Jules Sandoz believed he was dying of snakebite he spoke what he thought were his last words to her: "'Your mama's a good woman . . . You'll get like her. Marry a farmer and help build up the country.'" (ibid, p. 332) He would survive for many more years, but his sentiments did not change. When he was in his last illness, Jules and Fritz and James, and the other two girls, Caroline and Flora, lived near. "Only Marie was gone, like a seed washed far by a flood, and that was not good." (ibid, p. 415) Only a short time before he died, Jules ". . . looked through the papers and found a small item announcing a prize for a short story awarded to Marie. He tore the paper across, ordered pencil and paper brought, wrote her one line in the old, firm, up-and-down strokes: 'You know I consider artists and writers the maggots of society.'" (ibid, p. 419). ⟨. . .⟩

Sandoz believed and said frequently that there could not be a story without a conflict, and in book after book written by her, conflicts raged and were somehow resolved, for better or worse. The protagonist in *The Tom Walker* returns from the Civil War minus one leg, to find his family wealthy as a result of war profiteering. He leaves Ohio and goes west to pioneer and tame the land. The generations that spring from him also sustain injuries in subsequent wars. Thus, three generations of a family swim against the current to struggle for social change, especially in the aftermath of war. ⟨. . .⟩

Sandoz treated her rebels tenderly and with great sympathy, although the exception may be General George Armstrong Custer, whose ambition to be President overrode his good judgment when he elected to go against overwhelming odds in order to make a name as a great Indian fighter on the road to high office. Crazy Horse and the Sioux were the victors that thwarted Custer's great plans on that fateful day at the Little Big Horn.

The tales of Young Elk in *The Horsecatcher* and Young Lance in *The Story Catcher* reveal the struggles of young men who met opposition within their tribes when they elected to pursue professions other than that of warrior. Both must go through difficult trials in order to gain respect despite their choices.

Morissa Kirk, in *Miss Morissa*, is a frontier physician in the days of the Gold Rush to California. She, too, just by the nature of her profession, is a rebel and an outsider, and her life is an embattled one. Her marriage, also, is stormy, and in dissolving it, she again is running against the social expectations of her time.

Sandoz kept her own marriage and divorce a secret when she left the sandhills and established a new life ⟨. . .⟩ in Lincoln, dropping the name Macumber and four years off her age. ⟨. . .⟩ She understood rebels, aliens, and outsiders thoroughly, having been one. She took up the cause of Native Americans, lobbying in Congress against the selling of reservation lands to oil, mining, and lumber interests. She wrote letters and campaigned tirelessly in behalf of settlement between the United States government and the Sioux tribes in the matter of compensation for Black Hills land. She knew that life was a struggle, for she was born to it in her sandhills.

—Claire Mattern, "Rebels, Aliens, Outsiders, and the Nonconformist in the Writing of Mari Sandoz," *College English Association* 49, no. 2–4 (Winter 1986–87): 102–3, 110–12

THOMAS MATCHIE

"American Literature is essentially subversive," says Anthony Burgess in a recent review of the newly published *Columbia Literary History of the United States*. He mentions Thoreau, Whitman, and Henry Adams as examples. "It does not boost America," concludes Burgess, "except satirically" (91). This may be true, but it may also be true that this subversion is done, not in the name of destruction, but of growth. Especially important in 19th century literature, a time when our societal mores were being severely tested, is the *bildungsroman*, the novel of education or growth. Here widely differing kinds of rebels reject our so-called free society, but I contend they do it as a call to change. Three of these rebels are Mark Twain's pre-Civil War vagabond Huckleberry Finn escaping down river with "nigger Jim," Edna Pontellier, Kate Chopin's late-Victorian lady living among Louisiana Creoles, and the Sioux warrior Crazy Horse, whose life leading up to the Battle of Little Big Horn was recreated in 1942 by Mari Sandoz. ⟨. . .⟩

Crazy Horse is another novel about the 19th century in which possession of property is a major factor in the main character's rebellion. And if Twain used his skill with language to put us in the shoes of young Huck, Sandoz experimented with a new idiom to help readers experience the mentality and viewpoint of the Plains Indians at a time when white settlers, hunters, and miners were coming west to replace the Indians' "savage" (42) culture with their own "civilized" one. Young Crazy Horse is, like Huck and Edna, coming to a new consciousness about his place in the universe, and his vision at the end of Part I shows he will play a key role in his people's fate as they fight to ward off a culture whose view of ownership is foreign to the Sioux. Part II depicts the major battles of the 1860s over possession of the Yellowstone River Basin west of the Black Hills, a fertile area for the buffalo upon which the Indians rely for their whole livelihood. The buffalo is "the brother of the Indian" (57) and an integral part of his religion.

By contrast, the whites want hides for the market, and by the 1860s were shipping them back East by the ton on the newly constructed "iron road." But more importantly, the Bozeman trail (144) is becoming the gateway to Montana gold, which together with the Sand Creek massacre, makes "a firing in his (Crazy Horse's) breast" (151). He knows the whites' interest in land, buffalo, gold; indeed his success as a warrior in battles like Fetterman and Wagon Box grows out of his opposition to their greed. But the Sioux also know they don't have the guns, the ammunition, or (with the continued loss of buffalo) the food to hold out against the growing number of whites (213, 217). For reasons like these Red Cloud agrees in 1868 to stop the violence in exchange for exclusive rights to the Black Hills. Crazy Horse, a mystic idealist, refuses to accept the Laramie Treaty because he doesn't trust the whites, prone to greed and hungry for land. Later, he is proved right when gold is discovered in the Black Hills, whites swarm in by the thousands in violation of the treaty, and the area is lost forever to the Indians. But Crazy Horse remains a leader of the hostile Sioux, a rebel whom the U.S. Government now sends Generals Crook and Custer to subdue.

It is interesting that Crazy Horse, like Huck and Edna, reacts to possessiveness by going to someone he loves. His maturation as a warrior parallels his growing affection for Black Buffalo Woman, who unexpectedly marries his rival No Water. Still, her "eyes" (143, 156, 178) remain on Crazy Horse who visits her regularly. It is not until things become most hopeless for the Sioux, however, that he moves instinctively to make her his woman. When Red Cloud signs the Treaty of Laramie, Crazy Horse takes her from her camp to his own. Though this is a legitimate Indian practice (240), it ends in tragedy, for No Water shoots Crazy Horse to get her back. She leaves, but upon recovery and even "after gifts had been accepted" (248), Crazy Horse chases No Water from the area. As a result, he loses his title as shirt wearer and the chiefs' society he helped form in the 1860s to unify the Indians against the whites is disbanded. Crazy Horse is discouraged, but he sees in the whole affair a sign that his own pleasure is less important than the people, who need his leadership against new white encroachment. If the failure of Edna's amorous relationships gives her new insight into her oppressive society, so does Crazy Horse's failure in love serve to redirect his energies against oppression.

In Part III, in spite of huge odds, he emerges as a successful strategist against Crook on the Rosebud and Custer at the Little Big Horn. Now he marries Black Shawl, a good woman who serves him well at home as she provides him fresh horses on the battlefield. Later, after he comes into the white agency, Crazy Horse is given a white wife, who is also loyal, keeping him in contact with the larger white political world. But, faithful as these women are, they don't fulfill in Crazy Horse the special affection he has for the woman he lost. For some critics, this love story is more imaginative than the epic history in the novel (Gannet), but through it Sandoz demonstrates, like Twain and Chopin, the causal connection between possessiveness in the white culture and the deep human need for personal love and acceptance. The effects of his affair resemble Edna's, for they are deep and lasting; they also generate new insight into the meaning of life in a gold-driven white culture.

Near the end of the novel Crazy Horse, like Huck and Edna, has to make a key decision regarding the white society. Unlike Sitting Bull, he does not flee to Canada, but remains chief of the northern Oglalas—as though the midwestern plains belonged to his people. Then, when old Black Elk comes to ask him to surrender, Crazy Horse says:

> Uncle . . . you notice the way I act, but do not worry. There are caves and holes for me to live in, and perhaps out here the powers will help me. The time is short, and I must plan for the good of my people (359).

To keep his people from starving, Crazy Horse elects to come into the white agencies. Here he finds that even his former friends, Red Cloud and Spotted Tail, are seeking power and control over land like the whites. Their jealousy keeps him from having an agency, as each of them does, or having the freedom to go out and hunt. He is purposely misinterpreted, and rumors fly that he will again stir up the hostiles, causing soldiers and Indian police to bring him to Fort Robinson, where he is stabbed by a white guard when he refuses to be jailed. Unlike Huck and Edna, he elects to join the white society at the end, but he does this as a chief for his people, though he knows they have already lost their freedom. Like Huck and Edna, however, he rejects the white's final enslavement—for him, the jail. He, too, chooses against confinement, and his death, like theirs, becomes symbolic of a lack of freedom, not its presence in America. So his act is also subversive, undercutting the original reason for which whites went west. ⟨. . .⟩

Crazy Horse also gives his life, for he cannot live in the restricted white world symbolized by the agency. He actually dies twice. The first is a symbolic death—his decision to come into the agency to save his people. He is unlike Huck and Edna in this way—riding in and joining the society. But he does it as a leader; left to himself he would live in the "caves and holes" of

nature. His second and real death results from his refusal to go to jail, the ultimate symbol of possession by whites. Now his end, like Huck's going to the
territory, and Edna's to the sea, seems to call the white society on some basic
denial of freedom. That is why they are subversive actions. But they are acts
of bravery nonetheless, calling for new internal growth in this so-called "land
of the free."

   —Thomas Matchie, "The Land of the Free, or the Home of the Brave?" *Journal of American
   Culture* 11, no. 4 (Winter 1988): 7, 9–10, 12

Barbara Rippey

Though it is true Sandoz did not follow historical or literary guidelines without making exceptions that would further her own historical perspective, she
rooted that perspective in basic characteristics of the West, characteristics that
continue to influence our own time. These elements include economic conflict
based on ownership of land, problems of racial and cultural pluralism, ambivalence toward federal aid, the profound effects of economic cycles, and the
complexity that is revealed when those with naive dreams meet hard reality.
According to Patricia Nelson Limerick in her recent book, *The Legacy of
Conquest: The Unbroken Past of the American West*, these are issues that are still viable
concerns today and provide a new paradigm for understanding the history of
the West. I believe that Sandoz' work can provide scholars with valuable material that links yesterday's concerns with those of today. ⟨. . .⟩

   Sandoz, by her didactic emphasis and judgment, exposes the dichotomy
between expectations and a more complex reality. In her narratives she
demonstrates the expectations of people and then ironically exposes those
individuals' vulnerability because of those expectations. In effect, she is always
saying—"There is more to this than story." Consequently, Sandoz' stories, in
fiction and nonfiction, preserve culture, sometimes within the popular mythic
patterns of the West, while her judgment shows the reality of that West. For
example, in *Old Jules* (1935), the story of her western Nebraska frontier father,
Sandoz shows that Jules' first reaction on witnessing frontier justice fits with
his expectations and confirms the myth with which he is familiar. But then
Sandoz conveys Jules' consternation as he realizes the threatening and complex human reality. When a young man near Jules in a frontier bar is shot and
killed because he questions the rightness and power of vigilante justice, Jules
thinks at first the shot is gunplay, ". . . the Wild West of which he had read,
with a great smell of powder and brag." Then he realizes, bewildered, angry,
and "a little sick," that this is Western justice and the murderer will not be
apprehended. Sandoz continues throughout the book to question law, order,
and justice even when Jules is the man behind the gun, including questions
about equality of justice and control of the justice system. Sandoz keeps

expanding the expected view to encompass questions of value that are relevant today. ⟨. . .⟩

In her next book, *Slogum House* (1937), Sandoz' character, Libby, loves nature as her father Ruedy does. Ruedy digs ditches along the bluffs by his home and gardens so that he may use rain water for irrigating, and he builds terraced pools, "bordering them with arrowhead lilies, water grasses, and brown-eyed Susans," while Libby uses wisely what the land has to give, collecting buffalo berries by pounding "the thorny branches with sticks, raining the close-clustering little orange berries into an umbrella, clean-lined with sugar sacking" or crawling up on a flock of mallards on a river sandbar to first admire and then take a few for dinner. Sandoz' concern for the environment parallels Limerick's concern about our thoughtless destruction of our environment today. Since Sandoz' death in 1966 the concern for environment and the wise use of our natural resources has accelerated, becoming global. We see appreciating and protecting the environment as crucial to our survival. Sandoz wrote complete books about the exploitation of the beaver and the buffalo and planned one to attack irresponsible oil drilling in the plains.

The second focus of Sandoz' historical perspective is the underdogs of society, or "victims and villains," as Limerick calls them. Sandoz' depiction of women victimized by men reveals a picture of the victim as sometimes involved in the cause of her predicament; and, furthermore, the ability of some of these women victims, in the best of instances, to rise above the victimization. Sandoz wanted victims to recognize their predicament and try to escape. Limerick suggests that the people of the West tended to not recognize or admit how they were implicated in their own victimized situation, and that this is an ongoing attitude for the country as a whole.

—Barbara Rippey, "Mari Sandoz' Historical Perspective: Linking Past and Present," *Platte Valley Review* 17, no. 1 (Winter 1989): 62, 64–66

BETH BOHLING

In her Foreword to *Love Song to the Plains*, Mari Sandoz explains that in her earliest writing she found that ordinary words were "poor saddlebags" to transport her sense of either the gaiety or the hardships and violence of homestead life. "I began to maneuver," she writes, "for special relationships, special rhythm patterns, the string of words perhaps as abrupt as a cut bank or vagrant as a dryland whirlwind; as gentle as a June morning, or harsh as blizzard snow driven in endless, twisting drifts."

Even in this description of her writing style, composed many years after she began maneuvering with words, she turns for her figures of speech to the land of her origin, disdaining other comparisons which would be less appropriate for *Love Song*. By examining her use of metaphors and similes in this book and two others—*Old Jules* and *Cheyenne Autumn*—one can see that this fitting of the phrase to the subject is purposeful—a part of that very maneuvering.

At least ninety percent of the figures of speech in *Old Jules* are drawn from the animals and other natural phenomena of the sandhills and adjacent flatlands of northwestern Nebraska, or from articles used by the early settlers. Jules and his neighbors razed the Freese place, "tearing it as buzzards would a rabbit" (140); cattlemen were "running fraudulent proofs like wild steers through a chute" (106); the crowd was "still as a lull in a dry-land thunderstorm" (113); the people flowed toward the building, "breaking about its walls like the waters of a cloudburst about a settler's shack" (141); to Mary, "Jules's masculine boasting was as the wind on the dry buffalo grass" (183); she sifted "the chaff from Jules's accounts of himself and his country" (185); time moved heavily, "like a plodding old woman with her shoes full of sand" (390).

Sandoz takes as much care with her non-frontier metaphors when they are appropriate. To describe the pioneer Jules's eyes she reaches back to his native Switzerland—"eyes as strange and changing as the Jura that towered over his homeland" (4).

In *Cheyenne Autumn* Sandoz says in the preface that she tried to keep "something of the rhythm, the idiom, and the figures of Cheyenne life" (vii). For instance, she expresses time in the Indian manner. Referring to the distant past, she writes, "long before the first white man's tracks shadowed the buffalo grass" (19); a short span of time is said to be "barely longer than an arrow's flight" (138).

An examination of other figures of speech indicates they were also tuned to Indian life. More than one-half of the Sandoz similes in *Cheyenne Autumn* have birds, animals, and insects for their point of reference. The Cheyennes of the old days were "bold as the gray wolf who stalks the ridges with his tail straight up in the air" (36); or "like the fox sneaking up a gully" (36). Soldiers gathered in "clouds as thick as fall blackbirds in a strip of corn" (53); whites strung talking wires "like spider ropes all through the morning grass" (53); the snowdrifted log buildings of Fort Robinson were "scattered like a half-buried prairie-dog town along the bluff slope" (209).

Approximately another one-third of the figures of speech are concerned with plants, land features, and natural disasters: the noise of gunfire "like a rolling hailstorm" (89); eyes "cold as the blizzard wind" (50); women and children "scattering like leaves in a whirlwind" (116).

The rest of the figures refer to items used by the Indians: "The mocassin was a whisper where the hoofs of a horse would have been loud as a war whoop" (55)—or relate to the white men who had encroached on the area: the gray clouds described as being "like herds of dirty *veho* sheep" (172).

Love Song to the Plains, which draws upon the area's history from pre-historic times to the 1960's, provides a wider latitude in figurative language Sandoz speaks of the "tiny eohippus who, tiptoeing like a ballet girl through geologic ages, lost all his five toes but the center one" (2). ⟨. . .⟩

While Sandoz sprinkles fresh figures of speech throughout her works, she has some favorite similes and metaphors which reappear frequently, either in a single work or in two or more books. For someone who takes such pains with her use of language, such repetition is certainly intended, and the heightened impact of the repeated figures is purposeful, not accidental.

—Beth Bohling, "Mari Sandoz' Saddlebags," *Platte Valley Review* 17, no. 1 (Winter 1989): 84–85, 88–89

KATHERINE A. MASON

All her life Sandoz paid homage to the pioneer ethic which enabled the survivors to succeed; at the same time she decried the actions of opportunists who fed on the weak and became rich on the miscalculations of losers. She learned early on that greed and corruption feed on failure and misfortune and she returned to this theme in her writings. Three novels which illustrate her quarrel with greed are *Slogum House* (1937), *Capital City* (1939), and *The Tom-Walker* (1947).

In *Slogum House* Sandoz traces the events evolving from the Slogum family's obsessive desire for private wealth and power. The family's underhanded acquisitions are engineered by the principal antagonist, Gulla Slogum, an aberration, a caricature of motherhood.

> Gulla—as she was called—watched her daughter on the hogback, the mother's little eyes half buried in the flesh of her broad face. . . . And in the meantime she rocked her body so like a keg in its dressing sacque over a drawstring petticoat, or tipped herself forward to find her lean mouth in a small handglass while she plucked at the dark fringe of hair on her upper lip. (*SH* 11)

Gulla is the personification of avarice, a woman who, in an attempt to become acceptable, tricked a gentle young man into marrying her, first by seducing him, then by telling him he had gotten her pregnant. Shunned by his family, she is obsessed with the desire to get even with her husband's people for not accepting her when she married Ruedy. Sandoz exaggerates Gulla's physical and spiritual ugliness in order to create a character who personifies evil. The few good qualities she possesses are subverted to the characteristics which enable her to become powerful. She will stop at nothing, including murder, to get what she wants. Only once does she react with horror at what has been done by her sons, Hab and Cash, and that is when she learns that they have castrated a man who thwarted their plans.

Gulla exerts her will on other members of her family as well. She condones and encourages her twin daughters' prostitution in order to form political alliances throughout the county; for example, Annette is obligated to maintain a relationship with the sheriff of Dumur County to make sure that Hab and Cash will not be indicted for any crimes they have perpetrated. Cellie, her twin, is encouraged to cultivate relationships in concert with those of her sister.

The activities of the Slogum family validate the theory that a little igenuity makes it possible to acquire whatever one needs; whether it be lumber for a house (a result of nighttime foraging expeditions) or immunity to the law as a result of one's associates.

> The trend to lawlessness was a gradual one, beginning with River Habor's [the grandfather] occasional night sack of chickens when the grub pile was extra slim, and Ruedy couldn't very well complain with a cleanpicked drumstick in his fist. Now there was a complete cattle rustlers' layout on Hab's claim in Lost Valley, deep in the chop hills, with Libby to stand guard on a high point against the sky. (*SH* 47)

Gulla buried any tenderness early in her life. She had trapped Ruedy because she was obsessed by the notion that he could provide her with respectability. Ruedy was unable to do so, and Gulla rejected him, only using him sexually to create more pawns to be used in her machinations. As she continues to turn her ambitious schemes into reality she has increasingly little contact with Ruedy until it is no longer necessary to keep him with her. When he builds his own soddy, a house constructed of cut blocks of sod, across the creek, Gulla is merely annoyed that he would not live in her house. Most of the time Gulla ignores Ruedy, only raging at him when he protests one of her schemes.

Gulla's power rests in her ability to coerce and intimidate others into doing her dirty work; and she is never actually responsible for the harm she creates, although everyone around her knows she masterminds the events. ⟨. . .⟩

People like Gulla succeed because they see only the weakness in others. Compassion, commitment to others' needs, a sense of self have no place in Gulla's worldview, and her greed feeds only on ignorance, fear, and disloyalty. Libby and Ruedy transcend greediness because they are not committed to their own selfish desires.

The protagonists in *Slogum House* are also Slogums, so the family is divided in its attempt to extend its influence. Ruedy, Gulla's estranged husband, and Libby, her eldest daughter, are allied in their purpose: to block Gulla's "will to power." In doing so, they become the voices of Sandoz' social concerns.

Libby successfully rebuffs any of Gulla's attempts to include her in the twins' activities. The only household functions in which she will participate are housekeeping and cooking; she withdraws from other activities of the family. Not completely isolated from those she cares about, Libby spends time with her father on his allotment. Her duties in the house are necessary, and she takes pride in her ability to keep house; furthermore, housekeeping provides her with a means to acquire information about the rest of the members of the household without becoming involved in any of its nefarious activities. ⟨. . .⟩

Through Libby the reader is given a glimpse of frontier life as Sandoz experienced it. The reader recognizes the environment which shaped many pioneer women: an ongoing battle with dirt and insects; the necessity for harvesting and preserving whatever wild food was at hand; and the task of making clothing, linens, and curtains from material sent from distant cites. The reader also witnesses the self-made entertainments in the settlements: barn dances, horseback trips, and sewing bees, and the vignettes serve to illustrate a woman's life on the plains. Libby serves as the embodiment of plains women just as Mari's father gives us a portrait of a Nebraska settler. Her conviction that an individual does influence his world is a thread woven into her writing.

—Katherine A. Mason, "Greed and the Erosion of the Pioneer Ethic: Selected Novels of Mari Sandoz," *Platte Valley Review* 17, no. 1 (Winter 1989): 92–95

MICHAEL R. HILL

Capital City was Sandoz' third major project, following *Old Jules* and *Slogum House*. She began work on *Capital City* (initially conceived as a satiric stage play and tentatively titled *State Capital*) when her ethnographic research with the Cheyennes was interrupted in the fall of 1938 by her mother's illness and subsequent death. She wrote to her publisher:

> Because Mother's uncertain health and my unfinished research
> prevented my departure for Montana until too late for camping
> out for my Cheyenne interviews, I'm left with the winter rather
> unoccupied. I might play, except that a growing uneasiness about
> some of the social trends in the middlewest, particularly in the capital
> towns, won't let me. So I decided upon a play, a satire, if I could
> manage it, to be called "State Capital" and started to go through my
> files of notes. Two weeks of this and the accumulation of material and
> the growing importance of the theme convinced me that I should put

this into a novel,—covering a short space of time, say two or three
months, and immediately contemporary. This would not be any
special state capital and yet might be any one or all those that have
little commerce, produce nothing much—just live off the capitol and
the adjacent university. In other words, parasites, as Washington is
the arch parasite, of all the world, so far as I know just now.

Capital City was a new form for Sandoz—"an interesting experiment in writing"
as Stauffer (1983: 130) put it—in which the city itself was cast as a principal
dramatic actor. ⟨. . .⟩

In 1939, Sandoz saw her too complacent neighbors drifting toward fascism, and she wrote critically to arouse her fellow citizens to the possibility of
this outcome so that it might be averted by timely and intelligent social
action. She wrote, "You people in the East are probably not aware of the real
danger of a growing fascist set-up in the middlewest." She did not undertake
her project lightly, and early in the writing of *Capital City* she discovered in
herself "a few isolated cases of mild jitters at what I may be doing." For Sandoz,
Capital City was an urgent project: "I suspect that for my time this is the most
important thing I have done or could do." About red-baiting by a critical
Omahan, she wrote, "my kind of person is much more dangerous . . . than a
whole nest of communists." She noted, "The Sandoz family has been fighting
for the underdog for over 700 years," and concluded, "Surely I would be less
than true to my heritage if I held my pen now." Pen to paper, Sandoz did not
duck the sociological obligation to become an empirically-grounded and
logically-disciplined critic.

After publication of *Capital City*, Sandoz saw growing evidence that her
basic thesis was correct. In 1940, she wrote,

> Almost every day the papers reveal more truth in the basic premises
> of *Capital City*, with rifle ranges for Silver shirts in Oklahoma, the
> National Association of Manufacturers setting up spy rings to check
> up on the freedom of speech of teachers, newspaper men and
> preachers.

She wrote to alert society, but by 1940 the global community of nation-states
was already plunging into the darkness of World War II. In July 1940, Sandoz
mused, "About *Capital City*, all I can say [is] that it came four, five years too late
to save the world, even if I had made its message powerful enough." American
society changed during the 1940's, and the foundations of the 1950's "cold
war" were set in place. The modern relevance of Sandoz' social critique must
be weighed in light of subsequent developments in technology, the global
nuclear threat, the multi-national corporate economy, and the institutional-
ization of surveillance bureaucracies such as the U.S. Central Intelligence

Agency. Issues fundamental to the preservation of democracy have changed dramatically since 1939, and so have the techniques and charactersitics of fascist oppression, as Bertram Gross (1980) demonstrates in his analysis of modern life, *Friendly Fascism: The New Face of Power in America.*

The specifics of Sandoz' social world are significantly altered now, but her criticism looked toward the future we share today. She wrote in 1938, choosing words reminiscent of her father, Old Jules, that young people are

> the Nebraska of the future, and in their keeping lies the heritage of a vision followed by their fathers the wide world across, a vision of a land free of intolerance and oppression and want. Let them guard this heritage well.

The need to remain alert, to advance social criticism based on thoughtful and reflexive research, is the continuing sociological message of *Capital City.* This is a Nebraska heritage to honor and celebrate. ⟨. . .⟩

Mari Sandoz' (1939) novel *Capital City* is a recognized allegorical experiment. Beyond this achievement, however, I conclude that *Capital City* is also a first-rate effort at ideal-type analysis and sociological ethnography. Further, Sandoz exhibited the essential elements of sociological imagination throughout the work. As a discipline, sociology has too often shrunk from the obligation to provide meaningful social criticism (Hill 1984). Thus, *Capital City* is especially important today as an exemplar of one scholar's willingness to take an unflinching and critical look at American life.

—Michael R. Hill, "Mari Sandoz' Sociological Imagination: *Capital City* as an Ideal Type," *Platte Valley Review* 17, no. 1 (Winter 1989): 102–3, 112–13

HELEN STAUFFER

The 1878–79 trek of the Cheyennes is treated as a relatively minor event in American history, dealt with either in general terms or as an isolated event, and embellished with great detail but not tied into its causes and effects. Sandoz's primary achievement, other than the literary style (which is outside the purview of this essay) is her carefully detailed presentation of the effects of past actions on the present, as seen from the Indian's point of view. Sandoz's intent in *Cheyenne Autumn* was to show the progress of events from the first contacts of the Cheyennes with the whites, up through negotiations, the Plains tensions, and the actual encounters that affected them. Her stress of detail would be on the final results, including the outbreak at Fort Robinson in 1879, and its causes. ⟨. . .⟩

The episode began in the spring of 1875, when a group of Southern Cheyennes, desperate and frightened by events at their reservation in Indian

Territory, left the reservation to join their relatives in the north. At that time, such travel off the reservations was forbidden, and Lt. Austin Henely was sent with two companies of cavalry and infantry from Fort Lyons, Colorado, and Fort Wallace, Kansas, to intercept the Indians, separate them from their horses, and attack them if they did not surrender. En route to the area where the Indians were camped he was joined by several civilians, one of whom was the Fort Wallace trader Homer Wheeler, who had originally called on the army for help in removing the Indians after they had stopped some of his men from bringing in a herd of horses. Wheeler himself led Henely and his troops to the Sappa camp and, although a civilian, participated in the battle, which he describes in terms of a game: "I thought it best to go on foot, lest my horse whinny if taken away from the others, which would have alarmed the Indians, and our game would have decamped" (Wheeler 145). "We moved up and ordered the Indians to surrender, making signs which they well understood . . . . Then they fired on us, and the fun commenced" (148). "It was near noon when we finished destroying the camp" (140). Wheeler frankly admits he tried to keep some of the horses belonging to the government, but was stopped by a sergeant who recognized them. Nevertheless, for his part in the action Wheeler was commissioned into the army as a second lieutenant.

Lt. Henely's official report is brief. It mentions only three buffalo hunters joining the troops and lists nineteen dead warriors. It states that "eight squaws and children were unavoidably killed by shots intended for the warriors" (quoted in Wheeler 156). Sandoz's investigations resulted in a considerably different version than either Henely's or Wheeler's.

The accounts Sandoz saw were full of discrepancies, murky, offering her the kind of challenge she enjoyed most. She had been locating information for a number of years, at home in the sand hills, in Lincoln, and later, when living in Denver. From 1940 to 1943 she had used the Colorado State Historical Society extensively, for the Cheyennes had used the Colorado area as part of their hunting territory before being pushed onto their southern reservation, and the infamous Sand Creek massacre led by Col. Chivington took place in 1864 in southeastern Colorado. She had another excellent source as well, Albert Roenigk's *Pioneer History of Kansas*, which included accounts of local participants and witnesses of the 1875 fray. ⟨. . .⟩

Sandoz's interpretation of events of the 1875 episode has been challenged by other historians, and in some detail by C. Derek West in his "Battle of Sappa Creek" in *Kansas Historical Quarterly* (150–78). West based his conclusions primarily on evidence of four white participants in the battle—Henely, Wheeler, a Sergeant Platten's account found in *Sergeant Fred Platten's Ten Years on the Trail of the Redskins* (10–12), and Marcus M. Robbins's story in Beyer and Keydel's *Deeds of Valor* (vol. 2. 198-99). West also was familiar with the published accounts of Roenigk, Street, and Lockard. His sources are extensive, but his article is as strong an apology for the military and white participants as Sandoz's is for the Cheyennes. He lacked the Indian information Sandoz had, and nothing in his article suggests that he himself visited the site or talked with local residents. Sandoz, in addition to the invaluable Indian interviews and notes, did indeed see the battle site, in 1949 and again in 1950. Walking over the terrain, visiting with neighborhood historians, she felt justified in envisioning events as she wrote them. Even much later, after her book was published, she returned to the area, again accompanied by interested history buffs.

She had a clear mental picture of the site, even before seeing it. An enthusiastic amateur cartographer, she had obtained official government maps of every battle site involving the army, as well as local topographical maps of the entire route of the 1878 trek. In addition, she had her own homemade maps that she took out on the trails with her, and in her apartment one wall was covered by a six-by-nine-foot map on which she marked the 1878 route of the fleeing Cheyennes in red mystic tape, their camps in green, the camps of the pursuing army in blue; she also inked in the topography. On another, smaller, portable map, she marked the routes of previous flights. This map is included in *Cheyenne Autumn*. This thorough physical investigation of the territory was essential to her understanding of events taking place there. It allowed her a sense of the ambience of the land and clarified the importance of what happened to its inhabitants.

—Helen Stauffer, "Two Massacres on the Sappa River: Cause and Effect in Mari Sandoz's *Cheyenne Autumn*," *Platte Valley Review* 19, no. 1 (Winter 1991): 32–34, 39–40

BIBLIOGRAPHY

Old Jules. 1935.
Slogum House. 1937.
Capital City. 1939.
Crazy Horse. 1942.
The Tom-Walker. 1947.
Cheyenne Autumn. 1953.
Buffalo Hunters. 1954.
Winter Thunder. 1954.
Miss Morissa. 1955.
The Horsecatcher. 1957.

The Cattlemen. 1958.
Hostiles and Friendlies. 1959.
Son of a Gambling Man: The Youth of an Artist. 1960.
Love Song to the Plains. 1961.
These Were the Sioux. 1961.
The Story Catcher. 1963.
The Beaver Men. 1964.
Christmas of the Phonograph Records. 1966.
The Battle of Little Big Horn. 1966.
Sandhill Sundays and Other Recollections. 1970.
The Story Catcher. 1973.

JEAN STAFFORD
1915-1979

JEAN STAFFORD was born on July 1, 1915, the youngest of four children of a California walnut rancher. When she was five, her father moved the family to San Diego, and when his business dealings there failed to pan out, he moved the family again, this time to Boulder, Colorado. Stafford earned her bachelor's degree from the University of Colorado, Boulder, and received a fellowship for a year of study at the University of Heidelberg.

After returning from Germany, Stafford supported herself as a teacher. In the late 1930s Stafford met the young aspiring poet Robert Lowell, and after a stormy courtship—including a near-fatal car accident caused by Lowell's drunk driving that put Stafford in the hospital for several months—they were married in 1940. The accident, which necessitated extensive reconstructive surgery on Stafford's face, became the basis for her often-anthologized short story, "The Interior Castle," in which Pansy Vanneman becomes the mouthpiece for Stafford's rage at Lowell's negligence and destructiveness.

Stafford's marriage to Lowell ended in divorce; they were both heavy drinkers and both prone to bouts of depression. Despite being hospitalized for depression in 1946, Stafford managed to complete work on *The Mountain Lion* (1947), a bildungsroman that draws on her unhappy childhood and adolescence in Boulder. In the late 1940s and early '50s, Stafford's short stories began to appear regularly in *The New Yorker* and other magazines. Her *Collected Stories* (1970) won her a Pulitzer Prize. Her short fiction has been favorably compared with other American masters of the form, such as Hemingway, Wharton, Cather, James, and Twain. She herself praised the writing of Cather, Evelyn Scott (with whom she had a long epistolary friendship), and other women writers. Although she did not define herself as a feminist writer, Stafford's fiction is often quite critical of the roles available to women in contemporary society, particularly women who have artistic ambitions.

Her third novel, *The Catherine Wheel* (1952) was written while she lived in Connecticut with her second husband, a writer for *Life* magazine. That marriage also ended in divorce and in 1959, Stafford married for a third time. In the late 1950s, Stafford began to write nonfiction more and more regularly and almost entirely ceased to publish fiction. Some biographers suggest that nonfiction was more profitable than fiction writing; others suggest that she suffered writer's block that would not let her make progress on *The Parliament of Women* (an unfinished novel). She regularly published essays, reviews, and interviews, including a book based on her interviews with Lee Harvey Oswald's mother, titled *A Mother in History* (1966). Aside from her Pulitzer Prize, Stafford was also awarded two Guggenheim fellowships. She died on March 26, 1976.

CRITICAL EXTRACTS

LOUIS AUCHINCLOSS

Second to Henry James, Proust was probably the strongest influence on young American novelists of the 1940's and early 1950's. It became the fashion to see his guiding hand in every reference to time and childhood. But when *Boston Adventure* appeared in 1944, it was apparent, to many of us at least, that here was a first novel that caught the very essence of the master's flavor: the continual contrast of a dreamlike childhood, nostalgically recaptured, with a highly vivid, specific study of the more contemporary "great world." Sonia Marburg, one by one, gradually identifies the objects in the fanciful red room, the refuge that her imagination has seemingly created out of a void, with items in her past that she has not, until they spring to mind, consciously remembered, while Miss Pride, a Bostonian Guermantes, is engaged in distinguishing carefully the exact social positions of an Emerson and a Revere.

While the themes are everywhere interrelated, Jean Stafford nonetheless, in dividing her novel into two parts, assigns one to each part. The first deals with Sonia Marburg's childhood at a seaside town near Boston where she works as a chambermaid in a hotel for summer residents; the second, with Boston society in which, through Miss Pride, she at last gains a brief and precarious foothold. The atmosphere of the first chapters admirably conveys the cloudy coldness of a winter beach. The descriptions of the sea and the deserted hotel have the eeriness of Dickens and fit perfectly with the unreality of Sonia's background: her lunatic Russian mother, her German cobbler father, the memories of a Europe that has nothing to do with New England or the gold dome of the distant State House in Boston. Sonia has no life but that of her dreams. She rejects the vulgar world of the Brunsons who employ her to wait on table and chooses for her fantasies the Boston of Miss Pride, the grim old aristocrat whose room at the summer hotel she cleans. Like Marcel in Proust's novels, she has only one ambition, though hers is simpler. He yearns to be a part of the magic world of the Guermantes, and she wants to go to Boston, merely to live in Miss Pride's house. That is all. Love, marriage, children, a career, none of these things matter. If she can attain a room in that house, she will have attained nirvana.

And in the second part of the book she attains precisely that. She learns what she has deep down always known: that there is nothing particularly admirable or even particularly interesting about Miss Pride's circle of blue bloods. Like the Guermantes family they pretend incessantly not to care about the only things they *do* care about: their own birth and position. Hopestill Mather, Miss Pride's beautiful and reckless niece, marries the young doctor who has engaged Sonia's own rather vague affections, but she marries him only because she is pregnant by another man and needs a father for her child. And Miss Pride herself turns out to be a selfish and heartless old woman who pays to put Sonia's mother in a private asylum only to bind Sonia to her as the companion of her long, fretful old age. Yet Sonia has not been entirely the loser in taking this gift borne by the Greeks. In facing Boston she has fought her way out of her own fantasies, and she knows now that she will not lose her sanity as her mother has.

It is difficult to convey a sense of the unique aesthetic appeal of *Boston Adventure*. It is perhaps in the contrast between its dreaminess and its sudden specificity: characters like the Brunsons, large, ugly, wonderfully droll, suddenly emerge, as if out of a fog, to startle and delight. Nathan Kadish, the young Jewish radical, with the purple birthmark on his cheek and the chip on his shoulder, is as vivid as Marcel's friend, Bloch, when he hisses "Slave!" at a Boston butler. And there is hilarity, too, when Sonia, drunk, staggers home and wants to suggest to Miss Pride, awful in the doorway, that she have a nightcap with her. Miss Stafford has a poet's eye for the slang, the slogan, the comically vulgar detail that will suddenly superimpose twentieth-century commercial civilization on the dignity of the ancient past.

Ellen Glasgow found this novel an "endless exercise" and protested that to "anyone who has known Boston and Back Bay, the setting of that adventure is more ludicrous than amusing." Many who profess to have known the old Faubourg Saint-Germain have said as much of Proust. But it must be remembered that we see society in *Boston Adventure* through Sonia's eyes. People forget how constantly they label themselves in their acts and talk, particularly to the Sonias of this world who are looking for labels. Society people invariably maintain that they are interested in everything in the world *but* society; indeed, it is their constant pose that society, in *their* sense of the world, no longer exists. But Proust and Miss Stafford chose not to be contained by this.

—Louis Auchincloss, *Pioneers and Caretakers: A Study of 9 American Women Writers* (St. Paul: University of Minnesota Press, 1965), 152–54

BLANCHE H. GELFANT

That women are judged by appearance, whether beautiful or ugly, Stafford sees as their misfortune. In her Jamesian story "The End of a Career," Stafford's heroine discovers that being blessed with rare and exquisite beauty is a form of curse. All her life she has cared for her beauty as though it were a sacred jewel whose brilliance must not be allowed to dim; that has been her career and the waste of her life. For at the end she learns what we should have known all along, that appearance is superficial, though it may be all in a woman that society values. The young woman in another story, "The Echo and the Nemesis," finds beauty and intellectual brilliance burdens too heavy for her to carry. So she splits her personality in two, bestowing beauty on one self and brains on the other: a solution of insanity, painful and full of diabolical self-punishment. She eats herself into obesity—a fate worse than death for the American woman. In *The Mountain Lion*, Molly's brains cannot save her from the blight of her looks; and her character is demoralized by her acceptance of society's judgment that her looks are ugly. The ugly looks she gives to others—making gross faces at them—reflect what she has seen mirrored to her as an identity and a judgment. Molly collaborates in her own destruction when she accepts this image as her own. She is Stafford's brilliant study in introjection. Finally hating herself for the same reasons others hate her, because she assaults their sense of female beauty, wants to erase herself from view, to disappear, to die. Though she is precocious, ambitious, critical, and discerning, her talents go to waste; her epitaph is "trash." Conventional beauty and simpering ways would save her, she thinks: "If only she had yellow hair, she thought, she would be an entirely different kind of person". But the image in the mirror does not reflect Shirley Temple. She comes to hate the image so much that shortly before she dies she adds her own name to her "list of unforgivables". Then she breaks down and cries, "and all the time she cried she watched herself in the mirror, getting uglier and uglier until she looked like an Airedale". In death she resembles "a monkey." Her limp body evokes the judgment with which the book ends: "The pore little old piece of white trash".

Although *The Mountain Lion* is Ralph's story, it tests us by our judgment of Molly. We sympathize with Ralph's desire for autonomy, and we see he has been betrayed by the male tribe that he thinks will grant it. In time the stereotyped "gosh darn" weekend-whooping cowhands at the ranch deprive him of his dream of the West. In time Uncle Claude, his only possible model for manhood, reveals "a ponderous stupidity, a sort of virile opacity" that masks indifference to suffering, and malice to those who suffer or allow themselves, like Molly, to be "unhealthy"—that is, introspective, thoughtful, "bookish," critical, and smart (like Jean Stafford). But though he is alone, Ralph can enter and be entertained in the world closed to Molly—because he is male, and hand-some, and willing to accommodate to the "fat merchants" against whom he and Molly were once allied. But Molly remains intransigent; perhaps that is what we mean when we call her neurotic. And even if she would accommo-date to the world as shown in the novel, she would not be accepted because her looks are hopeless. She tries. Even at the last, grown tall, her latest mis-fortune as a girl, she is still trying to cope, by stooping and sidling through the school hall like a crab. But such maneuvers make her more of a freak: more eccentric, more isolated, more unhappy, and finally, hopeless.

Can we imagine for Molly a life that does not end in futility, madness, or death? In 1947, reviewers of *The Mountain Lion* did not trouble themselves over this question, though they admitted being shocked by the "unexpected hor-ror" with which the book ended. They were troubled, however, by the possi-bility that readers might miss the "terrible" "underlying truth" concealed almost entirely, they feared, beneath a brilliant surface—that of Stafford's witty, subtle, and highly sophisticated style. In his *New York Times* review, Howard Mumford Jones expressed the worry that "naive readers may miss the deeper psychological developments of the tale." This was a shared apprehen-sion. As another reviewer wrote: "'The Mountain Lion' is likely to beguile many a reader into thinking that he has hold of merely a shrewdly perspective and amusing novel of children, when what he really has in his hand is a charge of psychological dynamite." Such doubts about the common reader's ability to understand *The Mountain Lion* show the critics responding to an uncertain ten-sion within the novel between form and theme, or between expectation and fulfillment. This is the tension I ascribe to *The Mountain Lion's* revolutionary turnings, its radical movements away from the expectations that its traditional forms arouse. That this tension produces in the reader both pleasure and pain—pleasure at the expectation of the familiar, and shock at "unexpected horror"—still another reviewer clearly discerned: "though you read it [*The Mountain Lion*] with amusement, you will feel it aching in you like a tooth for days." All these responses suggest that *The Mountain Lion* creates confusion in the reader: she thinks she is reading one kind of book, a traditionally amusing one, but she feels and reacts to another. No doubt Jean Stafford imagined her-self writing one kind of book, a humorous satire well within the tradition of the American Western; but she could not imagine within that tradition a life for an odd young adolescent girl since, traditionally, none existed.

—Blanche H. Gelfant, *Women Writing in America: Voices in Collage* (Hanover, NH: University Press of New England, 1984), 55–57

MARY V. DAVIDSON

The Scott-Stafford correspondence deepened from strictly professional interest to personal intimacy as the months passed. An undated letter written when Stafford's courage had begun to flag shows how important the young writer's success was to her mentor. Scott insisted "In short I shall be bitter and hate it i[f] you don't come through (as you will), though I shall love you for being a poor kid in hard luck anyhow. This is both a gentle kick in the pants and a maternal hand on the fevered brow." Indeed, Stafford later credited Scott with maintaining her very will to write when she began to doubt her own talent and creative strength. Scott gratefully acknowledged Stafford's trust:

> Naturally your first paragraph makes me happy, though it cannot
> be really I who have kept alive your desire to write. What I would
> like to think that meant . . . is that my conviction in respect to you
> saved you from some moment when the water might have seemed
> to close over your head. But even if it had closed over you, you
> would have come up just as surely, and the third time—it is a fatality
> of temperament.

In addition to keeping up her correspondence with Scott, Stafford developed another epistolary relationship during the fall of 1937. At the Colorado writers' conference many other students traveled to participate in the event. For Jean Stafford, only one of them would make a lasting impression. His name was Robert Traill Spence Lowell. We do not know whether Stafford met Evelyn Scott or Robert Lowell first; it does not matter, since the influence each was to cast on her life's work was equally significant. When Lowell returned to Kenyon College for the fall term following the conference, he carried with him the image of a strangely attractive and elusive young woman whose demeanor and talent had caught his attention. The interest, Scott would discover from Stafford's letters, was entirely mutual. Stafford was intrigued by the lanky young Yankee poet, and his connection with east-coast high society magnetized her. Still, in Colorado their relationship scarcely had time to flourish, and Stafford's characteristic voluminous correspondence would serve to augment what was begun in Boulder.

Scott, herself once a partner in a traumatic, passionate love affair described intensively in her autobiography *Escapade*, changed from literary mentor to personal confidante as she shared her own experiences in matters of the heart with Stafford. By the fall of 1938, one year after the initial meeting, Stafford began to reveal the depth of her feeling for Lowell in her letters to her friend. She feared the complications inherent in romantic involvement with him, sensing the danger she courted by loving a man whose mercurial artist's temperament often resulted in erratic, unpredictable behavior. There is no question but that Stafford felt drawn to Lowell. She found his Yankee decorum (he continued to call her "Miss Stafford" for the entire first year of their acquaintance) and his literary ancestry, as well as his imposing physique, appealing, and Stafford's lifelong desire to escape the bonds of financial dependence was tantalized by Lowell's almost invulnerable social status. But more significantly, Stafford was captivated by Lowell's intense commitment to his poetic gift. Their common devotion to the manipulation of language signaled a spiritual affinity which, at least in the early stages of their relationship, seemed to reinforce their initial attraction.

Scott was apparently the only woman to whom Stafford could confide her conflicting feelings openly at this time. Her fears about pursuing Lowell—for it had come to that—were mirrored in Scott's response:

> One can make mistakes by accidents of blindness and survive their effects; but to make mistakes, as it were, "on purpose" really is suicidal. And the comparative ambition—isn't that the most dangerous? If two artists marry they avoid the risks of such a combination only if each has the urge with an equal fanaticism. Otherwise, surely, the superior talent is half wasted by the need to pour into the possessor of inferior talents the conviction that comes with nature's gifts. Even that might be done and some happiness result if it *could* be done; but it seems to me inferiorities cannot be mended by anyone's conscious effort—the flatteries they demand as cure only aggravate the disease. It seems to me the love of something has to be as proud and positive as the hatred or it is likely the hater will be discovered to hate himself, his contempt for the world turning out, in the end, only the translation into false terms of a corrosion in his own guts.

Thus Scott confirmed the danger Stafford herself recognized in assenting to a romantic involvement with Lowell. Still, if Stafford were determined to follow through with the relationship, Scott urged her to be fully aware of the consequences of any truly serious partnership: "Oh, don't marry your man if it is as you describe, for heaven's sake. . . . . You do have to begin by presuming equality, even if you are proved wrong later." Stafford was evidently ready to accept the risks involved, and her actions during the following three months proved the extent to which she compromised her own life to accommodate Cal Lowell.

—Mary V. Davidson, "'Defying the Stars and Challenging the Moon': The Early Correspondence of Evelyn Scott and Jean Stafford," *Southern Quarterly Review* 28, no. 4 (Summer 1990): 30–32

CHARLOTTE M. GOODMAN

In contrast to *The Mountain Lion*, in this novel ⟨*The Catherine Wheel*⟩ Stafford chose a male rather than a female character to embody her younger self. While in doing so she might merely have been trying to create a character who at least superficially was different from Molly Fawcett, her use of a male protagonist to portray her earlier self might have psychological significance as well. As a young girl, the bookish Stafford preferred males like her father and her brother to females like her mother and her older sisters, and thus in thinking about herself at the age of twelve, it was as easy for her to represent herself in the guise of Andrew Shipley as it had been to see herself as Molly Fawcett. Always sympathetic to the plight of neglected children, Stafford identified with the "lost boy" Andrew Shipley just as she had identified with Molly Fawcett. "My theory about morality is my theory about children," she said in an interview soon after *The Catherine Wheel* was published. "The most important thing in writing is irony, and we find irony most clearly in children. The very innocence of a child is irony . . ."

One crucial difference between Andrew Shipley and Molly Fawcett is that Molly Fawcett is killed at the end of *The Mountain Lion* whereas Andrew Shipley, another incarnation of Stafford's younger self, survives. It is to Andrew that the dying Katharine Congreve entrusts the sacred task of burning her diary with all its revelations of her secret life and hidden desires. In a letter to Lowell that Stafford had written when she was a patient at Payne Whitney, she had described how she had burned her old letters in the fireplace on their last night in Maine. Recalling, perhaps, that terrible final night in her house in Damariscotta, she concluded the novel with Andrew feeding the pages of the dead Katharine Congreve's diary into the coal stove, "Leaf by leaf, without reading a word of them, . . . his big tears hissing and skittering away in minute bubbles on the iron lids."

While Andrew Shipley exhibits many of the characteristics and attitudes of the young Jean Stafford, Katharine Congreve appears to be a fictional representation of Stafford as an adult. ⟨. . .⟩

Given to "lapidary speech," as was Stafford herself, Katharine Congreve enjoys many of the same pastimes that Stafford did: she loves flowers and once took up the study of botany, as Stafford had done; she enjoys old-fashioned pastimes such as playing Patience, doing needlepoint, and making potpourris with sun-dried petals; she is a voracious reader of esoteric texts such as the writings of Sir Thomas Browne; and she records her thoughts and feelings in a diary. Though she is rather aloof, she is also generous to her relatives and friends. Such details help make Katharine Congreve an attractive if somewhat eccentric character. However, Stafford also anatomizes unsparingly the less savory characteristics of her protagonist, something she failed to do when she described Sonie Marburg in *Boston Adventure*. Fiercely competitive with other women, as was Sonie in *Boston Adventure*, Katharine comes to despise her cousin Maeve, who first became a rival for her father's affections and then stole her lover, John Shipley. Even before John Shipley fell in love with Maeve, Katharine was jealous of her and actually prayed that a skin disorder with which Maeve was afflicted would prove to be incurable. And now in middle age, as she contemplates being the cause of the breakup of Maeve's marriage to John Shipley, Katharine admits to herself: "The fact was that she had never really forgiven poor Maeve for anything though she had struggled to. Bending every effort of her will and intelligence, she had tried to love Maeve and failing, had come at last to this ultimate betrayal." Into her description of Katharine's antagonism to Maeve, Stafford projected her own recollections of her competitive relationships with other women: with her sisters, with Lucy McKee, with Bunny Cole, and with Gertrude Buckman. The connection between the events in the novel and Gertrude Buckman's visit to Damariscotta that fateful summer of 1946 is evident, for example, in a passage in which Stafford describes Katharine Congreve painfully observing Maeve and John Shipley falling in love:

> As if it had been yesterday, she remembered her demeaning anguish
> when on idle afternoons, they begged her to read aloud to them *The
> Georgics.* . . . They sat the while demurely far apart, stealing glances
> and mouthing pet names. In the intoxication of their romance,
> furthered—even created—by this house, these grounds, this lake, this
> river that Katharine's father and grandfather and great-grandfather
> provided them with, in this lavish, extravagant Roman holiday, they
> had had energy and lunacy to spare and had showered her with it.

In some of the most remarkable passages in *The Catherine Wheel*, Stafford describes her protagonist's mental disintegration. Just as women writers such as Sylvia Plath, Janet Frame, Doris Lessing, and Antonia White have recorded their own mental breakdowns in the pages of their fiction, so did Stafford draw on her recollections of the mental and physical torment she too had experienced in Damariscotta and later in New York. Insomniac and prey to momentary hallucinations, Katharine Congreve writes in her diary: "Poor, lonely, obsessed Katharine. For I am snatched by moments of hallucination when reality disgorges me like a cannon firing off a cannon ball and I am sent off into an upper air where there is no sound and my senses are destroyed by the awful, white, paining light. . . . At the same time that I rise, ejected from the planet into the empyrean, I plummet through the core of the world."

One of the several books on psychology that Stafford owned was psychiatrist Karen Horney's *Self-Analysis*. In this book Horney, a revisionist Freudian psychiatrist especially interested in the psychology of women, presented a case history of a patient named Clare. Focusing on the subtle pattern of female devaluation in a patriarchal society, Horney used the fictitious Clare's experience to explore the conflicts she herself had experienced in her lifetime. In *The Catherine Wheel*, Stafford, too, used a fictitious character to explore her own conflicts, as she had done earlier in both *Boston Adventure* and *The Mountain Lion*. It is worth noting, however, that although Katharine Congreve has many intellectual pastimes, as did Stafford, she is not a writer. Rather, we are informed that, like her father, "she would read astutely and never write, observe wholeheartedly and never paint, not teach, not marry god." During a trip to Germany in her youth, Katharine had begun to write a novel, but she was told by a German youth she liked, "You should take up the harp. Or paint ring-around-a-rosy on saucers." Just as Charles Tansley in Virginia Woolf's *To the Lighthouse* maintains that women should not paint or write, so this young German maintains "women should never try to write," and his teasing remarks about her novel make Katharine Congreve suffer "small fractures of the heart." The only writing Katharine Congreve does as an adult is contained within the pages of her diary, and the diary, as she had wished, is destroyed by Andrew after she dies. Although Stafford never actually wrote a *Künstlerroman*, she incorporated into *The Catherine Wheel* many of the conflicts she had experienced as a woman and a writer.

—Charlotte M. Goodman, *Jean Stafford: The Savage Heart* (Austin: University of Texas Press, 1990), 220–23

ANN HULBERT

Boston Adventure, as its original title, *The Outskirts*, suggests, was a story of exile—of social, but also of spiritual, exile. It was a version of the story that Stafford had tried to tell in *Autumn Festival*, and her protagonist this time, named Sonie Marburg, was a relative of Gretchen, like her an outcast from her family, searching for salvation in an alien society.

But in Sonie, Gretchen's temperament was tamed by a more mature imagination—her own and her creator's. Where Stafford's earlier heroine had been consumed by adolescent self-loathing and disgust with the world around her, Sonie was more patient and ironic in her explorations of her alienation; if Gretchen was a damned soul, Sonie was a spirit in purgatory. It marked the kind of tempering of sensibility that, interestingly, was not much in evidence in Lowell's *Land of Unlikeness*, which consisted largely of poems that emerged under the Tates' roof at the same time that *Boston Adventure* was taking revised shape. As R. P. Blackmur wrote of Lowell's poems, "There is not a loving metre in the book," echoing the Atlantic Monthly Press's reactions to Stafford's earlier novel. "What is thought of as Boston in him fights with what is thought of as Catholic; and the fight produces not a tension but a gritting. It is not the violence, the rage, the denial of this world that grits, but the failure of these to find *in verse* the tension of necessity; necessity has, when recognised, the quality of conflict accepted, not hated." Stafford had discovered the tension of necessity in Sonie's narrative. In mesmerizing prose, she created a character who confronted the divisions in herself with an eerily calm, fatalistic curiosity.

Stafford's novel was not religious in the same sense that Lowell's contemporaneous poems were. She was not working with explicitly Christian symbolism, aiming to articulate an apocalyptic religious myth, as he was. (He said later that he had been "much more interested in being a Catholic than in being a writer.") But her basic inclination, like that of her teachers Tate and Ransom (and, behind them, T. S. Eliot), was to see, as Taylor observed in his letter, mankind as fallen and art as a kind of redemptive witness to that plight. And like Lowell, Stafford was fascinated by the opposition between Catholicism and Boston. Dividing her novel into two parts, she juxtaposed an Old World vision of spiritual damnation with a New World vision of social salvation. Sonie hoped to escape her lowly, blighted past and redeem herself amid high Boston society. But Stafford didn't grant her such a simple pilgrimage. Boston was hardly the salvation Sonie expected, and Stafford offered another alternative, the life of art—only to deny her that as well. Stafford was not proposing Sonie's tale as a portrait of the artist as a young woman. The only prospect of transcendence she held out for Sonie was a contemplative, not a creative, retreat from the corrupt world—a retreat that threatened to mean losing her mind rather than finding her soul. ⟨. . .⟩

If James was one lurking literary model whose international theme Stafford in a sense transposed, Proust was the presiding influence. Here too Stafford inventively adapted. "With its first page, tuned to the glazed and dying night-music of Proust's Overture," Alfred Kazin wrote in his review, "'Boston Adventure' brings us into the mind of a young girl so high in her style and so low in society that one's first impression is that Gorky's tramp characters have stolen into the cork-lined room." The strange tension at the center of Stafford's novel was the disjunction between Sonie's sensibility and her circumstances. She sounded, as Stafford herself said early on, like C. K. Scott Moncrieff's translation of Proust—elevated and archaic—yet her origins and her destiny were a world away from Marcel's. Although *Boston Adventure*, narrated in the first person, was proof of Sonie's prodigious imagination, Stafford emphatically denied her character the fruitful circuit that Proust granted Marcel. Sonie was Miss Pride's disillusioned secretary—an amanuensis charged with a hopeless project, the old lady's memoirs—not a real writer. She never enjoyed Marcel's miraculous triumph of simultaneously renouncing the corrupt world and possessing it in the creation of a work of art.

That is what made Sonie such a peculiar, and powerful, heroine. Stafford's Proustian and Jamesian ingredients resulted in an idiosyncratic mix. Sonie was neither an artist nor really an heiress. What stood in the way of art was that she aspired to be an heiress—that she wanted to be, and then was, adopted by Miss Pride—more than she wanted to pursue a literary life. What undermined her role as heiress was that she had the ironic spirit of an artist, the imagination to see the distance between pretension, aspiration, and reality. She made not only the opposite of James's journey, but also the opposite of Proust's journey—that is, she chose society over art, even though society was an imprisonment. Yet Stafford shared with both writers a focus on disillusionment, on spiritual alienation and social subjugation. In fact, her vision was completely dark. She allowed no bridging of American and European values, no synthesis of art and life.

—Ann Hulbert, *The Interior Castle: The Art and Life of Jean Stafford* (New York: Knopf, 1992), 144–45, 147–48

MAUREEN RYAN

Let me disclaim: there is no question but that Jean Stafford was—by talent and by vocation—an artist, **not** (as she said) a journalist. Her novels and short stories are valued for their poignant, exquisitely crafted presentation of the horrors of modern life for the memorable misfits and outcasts who populate her world. But to dismiss her nonfiction as hackwork written, begrudgingly, for money is to underestimate a body of work that illuminates Jean Stafford's fiction as well as mid-twentieth century American society. ⟨. . .⟩

Now, in the 1990s, we know that those mid-century reports of the death of the novel were premature, but these experiments with and challenges to traditional, realistic fiction constituted a significant literary movement in the sixties and seventies. Informed, as her own nonfiction writing showed her to be, about contemporary culture, Jean Stafford would surely have been aware of the New Journalism. Though older and more culturally conservative than Wolfe, Mailer, and the others, her withdrawal from fiction and immersion in nonfiction in the sixties and seventies may well have been precipitated by the same forces that propelled Capote to write *In Cold Blood* or Didion to pen *Slouching Toward Bethlehem.* ⟨. . .⟩

Her best essays are her most autobiographical: reminiscences about her past, like "Souvenirs of Survival: The Thirties Revisited," in which she describes her youth in Colorado and her college years during the Depression; or poignant attempts to make peace with a troubling world, such as "The Art of Accepting Oneself" and "It's Good to Be Back," in which Stafford writes about her inability to feel completely secure abroad. In a foreign country, she writes, "confronted at every turn by strangeness, I become a stranger to myself; my identity is suspended . . . . It's not until I am at home again . . . that I can reflect and winnow, reduce, deduce, arrange" (26). Only at home, she maintains, is she confident of her ability to understand her experiences, and the experiences she prizes are the "unimportant and undramatic" ones: a tan cow grazing in the Adirondacks, the sight of the Rocky Mountains from a morning train. Significantly, home for Stafford is not Colorado or Boston or White Plains, but America. "I hold equally dear the violent and outraged Colorado River and the peaceable, shapely Hudson," she writes, in this essay that articulates some of her greatest strengths as a writer: her diverse geographical settings; her eye for the familiar, even humble, detail; her quietly confident narrative voice (113).

Among Stafford's most interesting personal journalism is her only non-fiction book, *A Mother in History*, and this, her most sustained essay, perhaps most clearly demonstrates her appropriation of the conventions of the New Journalism. Published in 1966, the book was an expansion of a commissioned 1965 *McCall's* article based on a three-day interview with Marguerite Oswald. Using Wolfe's scene-by-scene construction, Stafford structures the book in three sections to correspond with her sessions with the assassin's mother (which Stafford, who in the book considers and rejects various conspiracy theories, presumes her to be). She captures Mrs. Oswald and her garrulous, illogical attempts to vindicate her son in the driven woman's own words, accurately recording (literally, beginning with Day Two, when Stafford arrives with a tape recorder) the "soliloquy," or "recitative," in which Marguerite Oswald offers her bizarre theories of her son's involvement in the Kennedy assassination and her earnest exoneration of herself as "a mother in history."

While most of the 120-page book consists of Mrs. Oswald's own words, Stafford, using the New Journalist's adaptation of the novelistic technique, deftly inserts those "everyday gestures, habits, manners, customs, styles of furniture, clothing, decoration . . . and other symbolic details . . . of people's *status life*, using that term in the broad sense of the entire pattern of behavior and possessions through which people express their position in the world or what they think it is or what they hope it to be" (Wolfe 32). She describes Mrs. Oswald's "round," "lineless," small-boned and "affable face" and her "plump and faultless bun," which top a short, "tubular, well-corseted construction" (13). Lee Harvey's mother, neither educated nor sophisticated, is nonetheless a woman with a certain style:

> I had the feeling that, except when she was in bed, she was never *en deshabille*, but was always dressed ready to receive anyone who wished to have the scales removed from his eyes. . . . She was one of those

women who can go directly to the one appropriate thing on a rack of cheap clothes. . . . She would never make the mistake of going in for conspicuous novelty; if she wore costume jewelry, it would not be gauche. If she were to travel with those bands of women that you see in the summer in Europe, her drip-drys would do what they were advertised to do and not dissolve or come out irremediably wadded up. (92–93)

Whether graciously holding court in her modest, neat bungalow with its poly-ethylene furniture and its artificial flowers, or deftly maneuvering her "dapper" new car through a Texas storm on her Mother's Day visit to her son's grave, the mother in history remains focused on her obsessive subject.

Jean Stafford, however, who eschews the New Journalists' third person point of view in favor of her own voice, punctuates her subject's ramblings with her characteristic asides on a range of subjects; her short, parenthetical discourses on coffee drinking in Texas and on Southern women, and her reactions to the news of JFK's death, provide a necessary respite from the relentless ramblings of Mrs. Oswald.

—Maureen Ryan, "Green Visors and Ivory Towers: Jean Stafford and the New Journalism," *The Kenyon Review* 16, no. 4 (Fall 1994): 106, 108–9, 112–13

ELSA NETTELS

Jean Stafford, in her essay "Truth in Fiction" (1966), suggests that her reading of Edith Wharton's novels had a profound influence on her own writing during a critical period in her life, the winter of 1948–49. At that time, Stafford had published two well-received novels, *Boston Adventure* and *The Mountain Lion*, and was living alone in New York struggling in vain to write a third novel, to be titled 'In the Snowfall.' To escape the noise in her apartment building, she recalls, she went to the New York Public Library to write. "In the quiet there I would come to terms with my book. But I tended to come to terms with the books Edith Wharton had written rather than with the one I had not" (4562). Shortly afterwards she put aside her own novel, which she never finished.

Stafford does not say which novels of Wharton she read, or what moved her to read them, or what effects, if any, her reading had on her decision to abandon her own work. But one may surmise that she turned to Edith Wharton's fiction because she felt affinities with her predecessor. Indeed, reviewers of Stafford's novels identified her with both James and Wharton. For instance, Richard Hayes found in *The Catherine Wheel* (1952) "the oppressive concern with elegance and *decor* which afflicts even the best of Edith Wharton's fiction" but concluded that "like Mrs. Wharton, Miss Stafford has written a novel to compel the imagination and nourish the mind" (404–405).

Another reviewer of *The Catherine Wheel*, John McAleer, declared Jean Stafford "properly linked" with Jane Austen, George Eliot, Henry James, and Edith Wharton (113).

Henry James was always Stafford's idol, but of the four writers, Edith Wharton is the one with whom Stafford has the most in common. The resemblances between them are especially notable in their short fiction. Characters rendered powerless by the roles they feel they must play, women seeking escape from marriages that threaten to destroy them, the vacuity and cruelty of fashionable society made significant only by the value of what it destroys— these themes so prominent in Wharton's fiction are developed as powerfully by Jean Stafford as by any other of Wharton's successors. Wharton's narrative techniques were congenial to Stafford as well: the transformation of objects and settings into symbolic representations of mental states; the critical exposure of a pleasure-loving society by dialogue which engulfs and isolates its victims; the ironic turns of plot culminating in revelations of truth long unsuspected or unacknowledged but implicit in the opening paragraphs. ⟨. . .⟩

Jean Stafford herself identified Edith Wharton with an earlier generation, but she did so in a startling way. In a sharply ironic story "The Captain's Gift" (1946), Stafford portrays the disillusionment of an elderly widow, Mrs. Ramsey, who lives in a once fashionable square in New York, wears black taffeta dresses of her mother's era, and preserves the rituals of a vanished world, making her house an "ivory tower," "impregnable to the ill-smelling, rude-sounding, and squalid-looking world which . . . now surrounds her" (439). Her grandsons are in the army fighting the Axis powers in Europe, but she has no comprehension of the war. "She speaks of Germany and Japan as if they were still nothing more than two foreign countries of which she has affectionate memories . . . If someone speaks of the mistakes of Versailles, she quite genuinely believes he refers to the way the flower beds are laid out in the palace gardens" (441). She has "refused to acknowledge the death of the past" (439), but she "remains altogether charming," gracious mistress of a wit "bright and Edwardian" (440). In short, she is an "innocent child of seventy-five" (440); to the younger generation, "she is their link with the courtly past, she is Mrs. Wharton at first hand" (442).

The reader is astonished that Stafford could identify "an innocent child of seventy-five" with Edith Wharton the novelist, who in her seventies was writing *The Buccaneers* and completed several of her greatest stories, including "Roman Fever," "Pomegranate Seed," and "All Souls'." Far from being oblivious of European politics in the 1930s, she was, in R. W. B. Lewis's words, "more alert than ever to the changing world around her, and the major dramas of the day" (504). She listened to Hitler's speeches on the wireless, appalled by the spread of fascist tyranny in what she called "this angry sombre world" (Lewis,

505). She created the ironies in "Roman Fever," in which the two mothers know nothing of the government served by "those young Italian aviators" entertaining their daughters and think that, unlike the city of their own youth, Mussolini's Rome poses "no more dangers than the middle of Main Street" (II, 834, 837).

Intentionally or not, in. "The Captain's Gift" Stafford created a caricature of a pervasive idea of Edith Wharton as the *grande dame* encased in privilege, frozen in the past, cut off from the lives of her contemporaries outside the walls of her protected world. Wharton herself acknowledged her pained awareness of the popular view in letters to younger writers who sent her their books. To Sinclair Lewis, who dedicated *Babbitt* to her, she confessed herself "long since resigned . . . to the idea that I was regarded by you all as the—say the Mrs. Humphry Ward of the Western Hemisphere, though at times I wondered why" (Lewis, 433). Thanking F. Scott Fitzgerald for *The Great Gatsby*, she wrote, "I am touched at your sending me a copy, for I feel that to your generation, which has taken such a flying leap into the future, I must represent the literary equivalent of tufted furniture and gas chandeliers" (*Letters*, 481).

Stafford wrote "The Captain's Gift" before her reading of Wharton in the New York Public Library. Perhaps those months there gave her a different impression of the novelist. But she was acquainted with Wharton's grimmest work of fiction before then. Sonia Marburg, the protagonist of Stafford's first novel, *Boston Adventure* (1944), spends a morning "dream[ing] over *Ethan Frome*" (138).

Possibly Stafford is satirizing the satiric narrator of "The Captain's Gift," but the shocking conclusion of the story belies such a reading. (At the end, Mrs. Ramsey unwraps a package from her favorite grandson in Europe to find a braid of blond hair, "cut off cleanly at the nape of the neck" and "shining like a living snake" (445).)

One is left to ask whether Stafford, consciously or not, needed to reduce her formidable predecessor to a figure she could satirize. If so, she acknowledged the power of Wharton's legacy in the very act of denying it.

—Elsa Nettels, "Thwarted Escapes: *Ethan Frome* and Jean Stafford's "A Country Love Story," *Edith Wharton Review* 11, no. 2 (Fall 1994): 6, 8, 15

ANN FOLWELL STANFORD

In Jean Stafford's well-known short story, "The Interior Castle," the figural patterns embedded in the language frequently slide between physical and mental pain, destabilizing neat divisions between body and mind. More interesting, however, is the language Stafford employs to describe her main character, Pansy Vanneman's, brain and the restorative facial surgery she undergoes. In this language, images of female sexuality, violation, and rage flicker beneath the surface of a sometimes ironic, and always distantly removed, narrative voice. This distancing is an attempt to objectify pain, to keep it in the mouth and body of the fictionalized other. But for Stafford, while on the one hand objectifying the pain allows her to represent it, the attempt at distance fails as the narrative of pain gives way to voices of ambivalence, rage, and resistance at the gendered body's violation. ⟨. . .⟩

For Jean Stafford, a writer deeply committed to keeping the woman and the writer separate (Ann Hulburt notes that she resisted "any conflation of her life and her art, or just as important, of her identities as a woman and a writer" xii), and who was involved in a troubling and ultimately destructive relationship with a prominent writer in the 1940s, the terms of literary articulation were, indeed, limited. In "The Interior Castle," like Cocteau's body in pain, the wound and wounding of the main character, Pansy Vanneman, become the mouth for Stafford's own ambivalence and rage. ⟨. . .⟩

"The Interior Castle" first appeared in the *Partisan Review* in 1946, and, eight years later, in Stafford's short story collection by the same name. Based on a harrowing incident out of Stafford's life, "The Interior Castle" does what relatively few stories do; it takes physical pain as its subject. The story was highly unusual for Stafford, since it was based on a personal event. (Stafford claimed that "The Interior Castle" was one of those rare occasions when "I wrote directly out of my life" [Roberts 161].) The narrative, whose title refers to St. Teresa of Avila's meditation on the soul's journey toward love, is a vivid representation of the visceral quality of pain. In Stafford's story, Pansy Vanneman has had a protracted stay in the hospital after having been seriously injured in an automobile accident. The centerpiece of the story is the description of a painful "sub-mucus resection or removal of fragments of gristle and bone from her nose" (Roberts 161), while she is only partly anesthetized. Her struggle with pain and with the doctor who inflicts it, interlaced with seemingly disconnected memories, makes up the bulk of the narrative.

The story as it stands is quite remarkable; Stafford is one of the few writers who manages to capture so vividly (and excruciatingly) the experience of the body in pain, a task made possible by objectifying the pain, by giving it a voice by way of an other. The story is, however, puzzling. Pansy's ruminations consist of awkward memories connected only loosely by the color pink—her mother reading *Lalla Rookh*, an "inappropriate" pink hat Pansy had worn to a party, a pink sky, "three dogs' voices . . . like bells from several churches," trees on the horizon that "looked like some eccentric vascular system" (200). The color extends to Pansy's image of her brain as a "pink pearl" as she fights obsessively to protect it from the onslaughts of pain and her doctor's ministrations. ⟨. . .⟩

In "The Interior Castle," the body, violated by pain itself, is doubly violated by the surgeon who comes to make it right. Charlotte Goodman compares "The Interior Castle" to William Carlos Williams's "The Use of Force," where a pediatrician, facing a resisting child, forces "a heavy silver spoon back of [a child's] teeth and down her throat till she gagged" (60). Goodman argues that both Williams and Stafford depict "the examination a doctor performs on his female patient as a kind of violation, almost a rape" (95). What is particularly interesting, however, is not just the suggestion of the doctor as rapist, but how Pansy's images of her brain, like an optical illusion, shift into representations of female genitalia. Here, the pain inflicted both by the surgeon and by the body itself is figured in terms of sexual violation. Pansy's body, then, becomes the site of conflict between violation and resistance, a site that mirrors Stafford's rage at and ambivalence about her own violation at the hands of Lowell.

—Ann Folwell Stanford, "Through the Mouth of Her Wound: Pain, Sexuality, and Resistance in Jean Stafford's 'The Interior Castle'," *Women's Studies: An Interdisciplinary Journal, Special Issue: Women and Medicine* (Amsterdam: Overseas Publishers Association, 1995), 586, 589–91

MARY ANN WILSON

"The End of a Career" is the story of Angelica Early, whose unearthly beauty makes her an international celebrity and a frequent guest at glamorous dinner parties, where she graces the table like a glittering ornament. Married to an obtuse, rather insensitive big-game hunter whose frequent absences give her considerable freedom to pursue her beautifying rituals, Angelica feels an obligation not only to herself but to her admirers to maintain the beauty that so animates their lives. In an artfully compressed introductory paragraph, Stafford describes Angelica in the words of her adoring public as a "nymph in her cradle" and a "goddess" in her "silvery coffin," thus framing this woman's pathetic life in a few sentences and foreshadowing the story's inevitable conclusion (*CS*, 447).

When her hands begin to show her age, Angelica hides from the world, spreads the rumor that she is dying of cancer, and takes to her bed. Angelica's aunt visits at the end of the story, bringing the languishing invalid a beautiful pair of embroidered gloves. After her initial hysteria Angelica slips the gloves on as she lies in bed. As the story ends, the maid who comes in later in the day finds her dead of a heart attack.

From the beginning of the story, Stafford depicts Angelica as a beautiful object, a passive, shallow woman not rich enough to be interesting to the truly rich, not chic enough to set fashion trends, not intelligent enough to utter any profound observations, not even flirtatious enough to incur the wrath of other women. Childless, without any center to her life except the religious devotion to her face and body, Angelica recalls Edith Wharton's Lily Bart from *The House of Mirth*, a beautiful adornment in her rigidly hierarchical, ultimately fickler world, and like Angelica, a victim of her own innocence. Angelica has no friends, but an "entourage" like a "public personage," though her smitten male admirers quickly discover that very little substance lies under the beautiful facade (CS, 450). With nunlike dedication Angelica has withdrawn from life and—like far too many American women, Stafford implies—devoted herself to the religion of the body: "[S]he was consecrated to her vocation and she had been obliged to pass up much of the miscellany of life that irritates but also brings about the evolution of personality; the unmolested oyster creates no pearl" (CS, 450–51).

Little do Angelica's admirers suspect the tortuous rituals she undergoes, from applying her makeup in front of mirrors that cast "an image of ruthless veracity" (CS, 451) to making yearly trips to a plastic surgeon in France who painfully scrapes her skin to maintain the illusion of youth. These annual trips incite her friends to speculate that the renewed passion they see in Angelica comes from a secret lover who has given her life new purpose. Angelica's "passion" is, of course, herself and the endless attention her now aging face and body require. Significantly, she assumes an alias when she visits the sanitarium, thereby divesting herself of any personal identity and intensifying Stafford's implication that, for women like Angelica, the image *is* the self. Faced with the prospect of aging beyond the control of her masterful plastic surgeon (who advises her to get a lover), Angelica fears the emptiness ahead and regrets not "lay[ing] up a store of good things against the famine of old age" (CS, 457).

The adoring public that contributed to Angelica's narcissism also victimizes her. When she overhears a cruel comment about her hands spoken by two young men, Angelica begins her painful downward spiral, withdraws from the world, and finally loses the will to live.

The story's numerous pointed references to art and the artist, beginning with the title, make the analogy clear and add another dimension to this parable of an ill-fated beautiful woman. Like Angelica, the artist labors to construct an illusion—a fiction—requiring constant labor and devotion that are largely invisible to her audience: "The world kindly imagined that Mrs. Early's beauty was deathless and that it lived its charmed life without support" (CS, 451). Both beauty and artistic talent imply obligation and incur expectations: a fickle public is quick to see the chinks in the edifice, the flaws in the marble. As Jean Stafford found the writing of fiction increasingly difficult in the last 20 years of her life, as literary fashions inevitably shifted, she might well have voiced the request Angelica poses near the end of the story: "I was faithful to your conception of me for all those years. Now take pity on me—reward me for my singleness of purpose" (CS, 460).

Jean Stafford placed "The End of a Career" last in her 1969 Collected Stories, thus punctuating her life's work with a story whose obvious subject is woman but whose deeper subtext is writer. Mediating between these two often conflicting identities was never easy for Stafford, though in stories like "The End of a Career" she articulates the tensions and demands of both roles more lucidly than she ever would in life. Studiously avoiding artist figures in her work, Stafford nevertheless wrote, in various guises, a composite portrait of the woman artist—from the childhood adventures of Emily Vanderpool to the wistful meditations of the aging Angelica Early.

—Mary Ann Wilson, Jean Stafford: A Study of the Short Fiction (New York: Twayne, 1996), 74–75

Susan J. Rosowski

If gender makes a difference in reading the West, it makes an even greater difference in writing it. In The Mountain Lion (1947), Jean Stafford uses her pen as a divining rod to reveal sources of the psychosexual violence so thinly veiled in formula western fiction. The setting of a cattle ranch, the plot of male bonding, the action of the hunt: these familiar ingredients of the formula western are laid bare in Stafford's novel. The cattle ranch is a breeding business, at the heart of male bonding is sexual anxiety, and the hunt represents undisguised aggression against women. Exposed, too, is the experience of women, given voice in the character of a girl who, finding herself in a world structured by the western formula, is inevitably the victim of its action. But The Mountain Lion extends as well as exposes the literary West, for it is also Stafford's künstlerroman and, as such, the novel in which she treats directly the theme running as an undercurrent throughout her oeuvre: the story of a girl destined to be a writer who is born into a literary tradition that, as Jane Tompkins has argued, sprang from hostility toward precisely that destiny. As such it is one of the most radical explorations of gender, creativity, and the significance of the West in American literature and it offers a paradigm for feminist criticism. 〈. . .〉

Forbidden the language of love, Stafford's western men give voice to inchoate longings when they talk of hunting, the one subject they can speak of freely. Describing the prey they are tracking, Claude displaces onto the yellow mountain lion the image of the golden girl of cultural myth: Ingrid Bergman and Carole Lombard—today we would add Marilyn Monroe and Madonna. "He thought about her so much that he had given her a name,"

Claude tells Ralph, "he called her Goldilocks because, running the way she had in the sunlight, she had been as blonde as a movie star." By deciding to let Ralph hunt her too, Claude formalizes their bond: by resolving "that it would be *he*, not the man, who got the lion," Ralph defines the bond as competitive. The hunt as displaced sexuality, driven by fear of its articulation, emerges in the violence of its language as well as in the violence of its action. The men name their prey "Goldilocks" because she reminds them of a movie star. They determine to "have her," swear to "blast the yellow bitch," identify the house-keeper's daughter with a cat, and tell stories with double entendres about hunting beavers.

Given such a code, it is inevitable, perhaps, that Molly is sacrificed, for as Blanche Gelfant has written, the male initiation story demands the exclusion of the female. It *is*, after all, a female mountain lion that the men hunt, its femaleness intensified by Ralph's fantasy of finding her in her den with her cubs and killing them all. Ralph comes to resent Molly's intrusion into the "pure masculinity" of his friendship with their uncle. But such an explanation acknowledges only half of Stafford's story, that concerning male initiation. By means of her double protagonist, Stafford presents a second story of initiation: Molly's. As a girl/woman Molly simply represented the "other" in the male script, but she is the *subject* of her own female script, a transference that demands a rereading—this time from Molly's point of view.

On one level, Molly tells the female version of the male initiation story of the hunt. Like Ralph, Molly is coming of age sexually, and her dawning awareness is as complex—as enticing and foreboding—as is his. Beneath Molly's social awkwardness is her secret femininity revealed in her fantasy of herself as beautiful. In a "bag which she kept locked and hidden away on the topmost shelf of her closet," Molly has assembled products designed to transport and transfigure her: bathsalts that give off "a sweet scent" and with which she can "imagine that she was in a garden," soap "in the form of a yellow rose, Armand's talcum powder, a bottle of Hind's Honey and Almond, a jar of Daggett and Ramsdell vanishing cream, a bottle of Glostora shampoo, a jar of Dr. Scholl's foot balm, a jar of freckle remover." Were these salts, soaps, powders, and creams to work as their advertising promises, they would transform Molly into a golden girl. And here, chillingly, Molly's fantasy joins with that of the male hunt, from the perspective of the hunted rather than that of the hunter. The fundamental lesson of growing up female, Stafford suggests, is that to be beautiful is to be desired, and to be desired is to be pursued. When Molly finally sees the mountain lion and identifies with it, wishing to be golden, small, and beautiful, she articulates her role in the masculine myth. When she dies because she is mistaken for the lion, she fulfills that role.

Yet while her fantasy may be one of being beautiful, Molly is actually becoming a writer. Whereas Ralph's initiation into manhood proceeds inevitably from a gendered culture, Molly's initiation into writing proceeds inevitably from her character. The central fact about Molly (and about *The Mountain Lion*) is that she is truly defined not by her appearance but by her sensitivity to language. Though she plans "to be a salesman for the *Book of Knowledge*, a grocer, a government walnut inspector, a trolley conductor in Tia Juana; . . . her real vocation was writing and these were to be only sidelines."

By giving to Molly the vocation of writing, Stafford announces a second initiation story for which she appropriates the symbolic forms of the literary West. Claiming the metaphor of the hunt, Stafford describes the vocation of the writer as a "hunt for the proper words." The quotation is from a talk Stafford gave the year that *The Mountain Lion* appeared; she could be describing Molly's story.

—Susan J. Rosowski, "Molly's Truthtelling, or Jean Stafford Rewrites the Western," *Reading the West: New Essays on the Literature of the American West* (Cambridge: Cambridge University Press, 1996), 158, 164–66.

BIBLIOGRAPHY

Boston Adventure. 1944.
The Mountain Lion. 1947.
The Catherine Wheel. 1952.
The Interior Castle. 1953.
Children Are Bored on Sunday. 1953.
Elphi: The Cat with the High I.Q. 1962.
Bad Characters. 1966.
A Mother in History. 1966.
Collected Stories of Jean Stafford. 1969.

GERTRUDE STEIN
1874-1946

GERTRUDE STEIN was born on February 3, 1874, in Allegheny, Pennsylvania, the youngest of five surviving children of Daniel and Amelia Stein. She spent her childhood in Vienna, Paris, and Oakland, California, and later attended Radcliffe, where she studied under philosopher and psychologist William James.

Stein was especially interested in psychology and her first published work, "Normal Motor Automatism," cowritten with Leon Solomons, was published in the *Psychological Review* in 1896. She studied medicine at Johns Hopkins University from 1897 to 1901 but left without receiving a degree. In 1903 she moved to Paris with her brother Leo and lived there for the rest of her life. She returned to America only once.

In 1904, Stein and her brother began collecting paintings, including early works of Cézanne, Matisse, Picasso, and Braque, and started what became their famous Saturday evening gatherings frequented by members of the expatriate and French avant-garde. In 1907 Stein met Alice B. Toklas, who became her lifelong lover and assistant; they lived together until Stein's death.

Influenced by the aesthetic philosophies and styles of the artists she collected and by Flaubert's *Trois contes*, Stein wrote *Three Lives* (1909). Likewise, the cubism of Picasso—for whom Stein sat for a portrait—informs her astonishing prose-poem, *Tender Buttons* (1914). Over the next 40 years she wrote almost constantly, producing nearly 500 works, including portraits, plays, poems, and scores of books, only a few of which were published in her lifetime. While some critics hailed her stream-of-consciousness techniques as liberating and illuminating, others thought her work self-indulgent, deliberately obscure, and intellectually dishonest.

Among her best-known works are *Tender Buttons*, *The Making of Americans* (1925), and the popular *The Autobiography of Alice B. Toklas* (1932); the opera *Four Saints in Three Acts* (cowritten with composer Virgil Thomson) premiered in the United States in 1934. By the time Stein recorded her experiences in France during World War II in *Wars I Have Seen* (1945), her reputation in America was firmly established. She died on July 27, 1946.

Stein was undoubtedly one of the most influential writers of her time and was central to a significant segment of the European artistic community; Sherwood Anderson and Ernest Hemingway are among those most directly in her debt. Her experimental writing has influenced generations of poets concerned with the sound of words and the portrayal of consciousness.

A "famous lesbian," Stein also aroused keen interest in her sexuality; she has been the subject of a number of biographies. She herself addressed lesbianism in several works: her early novel, Q. E. D. (1903), for example (published posthumously as *Things As They Are*), examines the rivalries and desires among three young women, and her *Autobiography of Alice B. Toklas* explores her lifelong relationship with Toklas. One of Stein's most intriguing works on the subject is "Lifting Belly," an extensive "encoded" poem of lesbian eroticism.

CRITICAL EXTRACTS

VIRGIL THOMSON

Gertrude not only liked people, she needed them. They were grist for her poetry, a relief from the solitudes of a mind essentially introspective.

Alice Toklas neither took life easy nor fraternized casually. She got up at six and cleaned the drawing room herself, because she did not wish things broken. (Porcelain and other fragile objects were her delight, just as pictures were Gertrude's; and she could imagine using violence toward a servant who might break one.) She liked being occupied, anyway, and did not need repose, ever content to serve Gertrude or be near her. She ran the house, ordered the meals, cooked on occasion, and typed out everything that got written into the blue copybooks that Gertrude had adopted from French school children. From 1927 or '28 she also worked petit point, matching in silk the colors and shades of designs made especially for her by Picasso. These tapestries were eventually applied to a pair of Louse XV small armchairs (chauffeuses) that Gertrude had bought for her. She was likely, any night, to go to bed by eleven, while Miss Stein would sit up late if there were someone to talk with.

Way back before World War I, in 1910 or so, in Granada Gertrude had experienced the delights of writing directly in the landscape. This does not mean just working out of doors; it means being surrounded by the thing one is writing about at the time one is writing about it. Later, in 1924, staying at Saint-Rémy in Provence, and sitting in fields beside the irrigation ditches, she found the same sound of running water as in Granada to soothe her while she wrote or while she simply sat, imbuing herself with the landscape's sight and sound. In the country around Belley, where she began to summer only a few years later, she wrote *Lucy Church Amiably* wholly to the sound of streams and waterfalls.

Bravig Imbs, an American poet and novelist who knew her in the late twenties, once came upon her doing this. The scene took place in a field, its enactors being Gertrude, Alice, and a cow. Alice, by means of a stick, would drive the cow around the field. Then, at a sign from Gertrude, the cow would be stopped; and Gertrude would write in her copybook. After a bit, she would pick up her folding stool and progress to another spot, whereupon Alice would again start the cow moving around the field till Gertrude signaled she was ready to write again. Though Alice now says that Gertrude drove the cow, she waiting in the car, the incident, whatever its choreography, reveals not only Gertrude's working intimacy with landscape but also the concentration of two friends on an act of composition by one of them that typifies and reveals their daily life for forty years. Alice had decided long before that "Gertrude was always right," that she was to have whatever she wanted when she wanted it, and that the way to keep herself always wanted was to keep Gertrude's writing always and forever unhindered, unopposed.

Gertrude's preoccupation with painting and painters was not shared by Alice except in so far as certain of Gertrude's painter friends touched her heart, and Picasso was almost the only one of these. Juan Gris was another, and Christian Bérard a very little bit. But Matisse I know she had not cared for, nor Braque. If it had not been for Gertrude, I doubt that Alice would ever have had much to do with the world of painting. She loved objects and furniture, practiced cooking and gardening, understood music. Of music, indeed, she had a long experience, having once, as a young girl, played a piano concerto in public. But painting was less absorbing to her than to Gertrude. ⟨. . .⟩

Gertrude lived by the heart, indeed; and domesticity was her theme. Not for her the matings and rematings that went on among the amazons. An early story from 1903, published after her death, *Things as They Are*, told of one such intrigue in post-Radcliffe days. But after 1907 her love life was serene, and it was Alice Toklas who made it so. Indeed, it was this tranquil life that offered to Gertrude a fertile soil of sentiment-security in which other friendships great and small could come to flower, wither away, be watered, cut off or preserved in a book. Her life was like that of a child, to whom danger can come only from the outside, never from home, and whose sole urgency is growth. It was also that of an adult who demanded all the rights of a man along with the privileges of a woman.

—Virgil Thomson, "A Portrait of Gertrude Stein," *Virgil Thomson* (1966), excerpted in *The Chelsea House Library of Literary Criticism: Twentieth-Century American Literature*, vol. 6, ed. Harold Bloom (New York: Chelsea House Publishers, 1987), 3766–67

RANDA K. DUBNICK

Tender Buttons represents a radical change from the early prose style of *The Making of Americans* and of other works to that which ⟨Stein⟩ called poetry. From prose, with its emphasis on syntax and its suppression of vocabulary, she moved to a concern for poetry with its emphasis on vocabulary and its suppression of syntax. This change manifests itself in a shift of linguistic emphasis from the operation of combination (horizontal axis) to the operation of selection (vertical axis).

Tender Buttons attained "a certain notoriety" in the press and attracted polemical criticism, perhaps because it seemed to "veer off into meaninglessness," at least in conventional terms. But the work is more than a literary curiosity. Its marked stylistic change appears to have been a breakthrough that influenced the direction of much of Stein's future work. "*Tender Buttons* represented her full scale break out of the prison of conventional form into the colorful realm of the sensitized imagination." ⟨. . .⟩

As the concerns of Stein's writing gradually shift from an interest in orderly analysis of the world to an interest in the immediate perception of the world by the consciousness, her writing appears to deal more and more with the word itself; with the mental images called up by and associated with the word (signifieds), and with the qualities of words as things in themselves (signifiers). "Her imagination was stimulated then not by the object's particular qualities alone, but also by the associations it aroused . . . and by the words themselves as they took shape upon the page."

Perhaps coincidentally, a similar shift in emphasis was occurring in the painting of the Cubists around the time *Tender Buttons* was composed. ⟨. . .⟩

This new interest in the word itself, and especially in the noun and the associative powers of the word, was what Stein considered the essence of poetry. In *Tender Buttons* and other works that she held as poetry, the chief linguistic operation is association (given various labels by structuralists such as substitution, selection, system) and choice of words. The association of words and concepts by similarity or opposition, and the selection of a word from a group of synonyms, are operations that function along the vertical axis of language. Interestingly enough, the *Tender Buttons* style also suppresses syntax (the horizontal axis) while it is expanding vocabulary. Construction of syntax becomes increasingly fragmentary until syntax disappears altogether in some of the more extreme passages. ⟨. . .⟩

It is ironic that, in spite of Stein's intention in writing *Tender Buttons* to capture immediate experience while consciousness grapples with it, there have been so many problems in the reading of this book. One problem inherent in the work itself is the disjunction of the two axes of language making it almost impossible to read the work for conventional discursive content. Moreover, this problem leads to another: the effort of trying to "figure it out," to reconstruct the content, not only exhausts the reader, but overdistances him from the work itself. Such an effort is futile anyway, for *Tender Buttons* demands to be dealt with in its own terms. The reader is given none of the literary allusions that the reader of Pound, Eliot, or Joyce can hold on to. ⟨. . .⟩

As Sutherland suggests, perhaps what the reader of Stein is required to do is to look *at* the work, rather than *through* it. One cannot look *through* it because it is an opaque, rather than transparent, style. If one does look *at* the work, what does one see in *Tender Buttons*? He sees the word presented as an entity in its own right. By forcing the reader to attend to the word, Stein makes the word seem new, again. In this effort, she does not ignore the meanings of words, as so ma⟨n⟩y critics have claimed. However by presenting each word in an unusual context, she directs attention not only towards its sound but towards its sense as the reader is forced to grapple with each word, one at a time. One is forced to attend to the word, and to language, with a sense of bewilderment and perhaps with a sense of wonder and discovery.

—Randa K. Dubnick, "Two Types of Obscurity in the Writings of Gertrude Stein," *The Emporia State Research Studies* 24, no. 3 (Winter 1976), excerpted in *American Women Poets*, ed. Harold Bloom (New York: Chelsea House Publishers, 1986), 84–85, 87–88, 90, 94–95

CLIVE BUSH

The Making of Americans shows us the authorial voice breaking with "society" by creating a magnificent epitaph for it. For Gertrude Stein it meant a long apprenticeship, reaching a threshold of release from the tyranny of the sentence with all its implications of reality. The completeness of the break is described in her essay "The Gradual Making of *The Making of Americans*" and realized halfway through *A Long Gay Book*, written after *The Making of Americans*.

We have, of course, described the process too clearly. Gay, *déracinée*, living among bohemians *and* artists, herself exempted from "necessity," Gertrude Stein also had to escape from the pseudo-alternative of American bourgeois life: bohemianism. The *life-style* (a term as dogmatically aesthetic and significant of *behavior* as "way of life") included an interest in psychoanalysis, managing art, collecting, or, as Gertrude Stein herself said in a particularly vicious mood in "The Notebooks," teaching ballet to little girls. We should, therefore, expect from the novel a variety of tones, and indeed contradictory attitudes toward the fate of American history turning into social behavior. The movement goes between inner and outer perception, between nostalgia and hatred, ironic approval and obsessive criticism, chilly analysis and praise of courage face to face with invisible neurosis, between pride and despair. Indeed the tone of the authorial voice matches these varieties as it changes the terms of its address from "gentle reader" of Swiftian memory to "stranger" of twentieth-century nihilistic angst.

Various disciplines merge in the novel. From her training at Harvard and Johns Hopkins she brought the experimental legacy of a classificatory habit of mind, a distrust of teleologies, and a disposition toward evolutionary psychology as a model for human behavior. In Europe she immersed herself in literature and painting. The curious thing to emerge from her prodigious excursions into literature is a double leaning toward eighteenth-century novels, many written by women, and toward histories of military leaders. There is a sexual differentiation of direction toward the private and public realms. It seems as if she needed to ascertain the poles of traditional "feminine" and "male" behavior: the one expressing its conflicts in the early bourgeois novel whose class, economic, and social conflicts mythicized themselves in the Gothic romance; the other betraying her fascination with violent male power games which lasted throughout her life. Thus we may at least speculate that in the paralleling of the search for a husband with the search for glory she was looking for the historical origins of psychological types, a favorite nineteenth-century activity.

In satire she found comedy and public tragedy by characterizing human activity as behavior, and by mocking the linear continuities of idealism and destiny.

—Clive Bush, "Toward the Outside: The Quest for Discontinuity in Gertrude Stein's *The Making of Americans*," *Twentieth Century Literature* (Spring 1978), reprinted in *American Fiction 1914 to 1945*, ed. Harold Bloom (New York: Chelsea House Publishers, 1987), 82–83

LYNN Z. BLOOM

⟨By⟩ letting the reader in on the joke of the real authorship of the *Autobiography* right from the start, instead of publishing it anonymously or pseudonymously, Stein's strategy is to take the reader into league with her. Once she has him on her side as a participant in her joke, it's hard to turn against the perpetrator of it. Thus the reader is more inclined to accept Stein's image of herself (as seen by Toklas and by herself) as true than he might if he had the judgment of a bona fide intermediary biographer to question. Again Stein, through Toklas, controls the reader as well as her material.

If the subject's personality or psyche were suppressed, flattened, distorted, or falsified, some of the advantages of autobiography-by-identification would be lost. But none of these occur in *The Autobiography of Alice B. Toklas*, in which both Gertrude Stein and Alice B. Toklas are very much alive and very well. All in all, the advantages of this innovative form are manifold, and as practiced by Stein it has no conspicuous disadvantages—except unrepeatability.

Another innovative aspect of *The Autobiography of Alice B. Toklas* is that, despite its intense focus on Gertrude Stein, a biographical portrait of the alleged autobiographical subject does emerge quite clearly. The work is a double portrait, of Stein and of Toklas. The *Autobiography* is further unusual in that Stein deliberately wrote it to emulate the oral speech mannerisms of another person—in choice of words, level of language, syntax, speech rhythms—rather than precisely her own, though the two are not incompatible. Indeed, she succeeded very well, judging from Toklas' own style in *What Is Remembered*, ⟨. . .⟩ even allowing for the possibility that in the latter volume Toklas could have imitated Stein's imitation of herself. Stein always treats Toklas-as-narrator the way she evidently treated Toklas-as-intimate-lifelong-friend, with the respect that maintains Toklas' integrity and never makes her feeble or foolish, never jokes at Toklas' expense (unlike Boswell's sometimes silly sycophancy, with which Toklas is occasionally wrongly compared). Thus Alice, like her biographical creator, is a vivid, witty, personable tartly gracious presence in her own pseudo-autobiography, an enduring tribute to a friend and to a friendship, among other things.

—Lynn Z. Bloom, "Gertrude Is Alice Is Everybody: Innovation and Point of View in Gertrude Stein's Autobiographies," *Twentieth Century Literature* (Spring 1978), excerpted in *The Chelsea House Library of Literary Criticism: Twentieth-Century American Literature*, vol. 6, ed. Harold Bloom (New York: Chelsea House Publishers, 1987), 3778

Mary Allen

Gertrude Stein's story "Many, Many Women" is riddled with the word *one*, which appears three thousand six hundred and sixty-three times. The phrases "she is one" and "she was one" occur hundreds of times. Frequently seeking a larger whole, Stein actually perceives oneness in the smallest unit—object, word, or person. Her belief that only matter broken into its most basic components exists in its integrity has everything to do with the fragmented effect of her writings. She shatters things that are commonly stuck together—related objects, words in familiar patterns, people bound to each other—so that the individual unit may flourish. Her new arrangements emphasize formerly unexpected characteristics of the individual parts rather than the creation of new entities. While Stein's critics observe that her work falls into pieces, what is not conceded is that a sense of wholeness comes after the shattering. Like other moderns she sees that things fall apart. But for her there is virtue in this condition. Stein tenderly breaks the world into pieces, and although she sometimes tries, she never puts it back again.

Well in the American tradition of individualism, Stein does not hold to the convention that alienation and loneliness inevitably accompany that theme.

The strong may earn a tough-minded pleasure in accepting the uniqueness and the aloneness that everyone inherits. The connections most desire, she sees, are too often based on destructive illusions. In combination, something is lost. Above everything, Stein values liberty, and her idea of freedom calls for the fresh view of a child who has not yet learned to put things together. His world is new, and it is pleasingly small. Excitement comes from seeing nearby things in original ways rather than in looking far for the exotic. ⟨. . .⟩

The marvelously playful *Tender Buttons* is a logic-defying work that has received a due amount of ridicule. But where it refuses analysis, it does not refuse pleasure, yielding the fun a child gets from poking at a world he would not expect to understand. A curious enjoyment can be derived from not "understanding" *Tender Buttons*, with its conscious attempt to dislodge logic. Critics continue, however, in their efforts to establish connections in this book of non sequiturs. In *Gertrude Stein in Pieces*, Richard Bridgman observes that objects share common qualities: a tiger skin and a coin are the same color. But when a common characteristic is located, with the suggestion of a true association, the essential differentness and impossibility of connection become even more noticeable. A coin and a tiger skin are so very *unlike*. *Tender Buttons* makes sly fun of the predilection of the highly trained, logical mind in its attempt to create meaningful wholes. The fresher child's approach is to accept the individual object and to probe it for new significance. He plays with it. The art of play is the method of *Tender Buttons*, although the book is touched by a maternal tenderness for the strangely arranged "Objects," "Food," and "Rooms." Nothing in this small world, however, is grown up or dead. Things smash, but they are not destroyed. In fact, Stein had a particular weakness for breakable objects.

—Mary Allen, "Gertrude Stein's Sense of Oneness," *Southwest Review* (Winter 1981), excerpted in *The Chelsea House Library of Literary Criticism: Twentieth-Century American Literature*, vol. 6, ed. Harold Bloom (New York: Chelsea House Publishers, 1987), 3781–82

ELIZABETH FIFER

Although Stein's writing often assumes a bantering tone, it speaks movingly of the anguish of being misunderstood, of needing a reader who will participate vigorously in the act of creating meaning. Caught in a web of words and struggling to be understood, Stein must use the very obfuscating language that created her previous difficulties. In a passage from *A Sweet Tail*, she admits her need for a reader to "rescue" her meaning: "Suppose a tremble, a ham, a little mouth told to wheeze more and a religion a reign . . . that makes a load registrar and passes best . . . gracious oh my cold under fur, under no rescued reading" ⟨*Geography and Plays*, 1968, p. 67⟩. This monologue is in the conditional—"What if I were like that and no one understood?" Of course, Stein is like that. Her sexual and creative "tremble" is both emphasized and belittled by her use of the word "ham." The "little mouth," a reference to the vagina, is simultaneously the writer's mouth, "hamming it up"; and her text, told to "wheeze," is made purposefully difficult. Her lesbian love, "religion a reign," is identifiable both by its serious and its "royal" nature. The whole "load" of her sexuality must be interpreted by the reader, who either understands her garbled message by correcting it and passing it on, or who misunderstands and lets its truth "pass" unrecognized. This educational metaphor is explicit throughout Stein's difficult texts. Stein fears being unmasked, but she also fears going unrecognized. If she is not read clearly, she will become "cold," and her texts will betray their purpose. ⟨. . .⟩

Why does Stein use this difficult language? She herself gives us a partial answer in *A List*. "Change songs for safety . . . if they were . . . differently decided . . . delighted . . . accidentally relieved and repeatedly received and reservedly deceived." Stein must "change songs for safety." If she were "differently decided," if she were not a lesbian, perhaps she would write differently. Yet, in her trope of contradiction, her positive note is also clear. She claims to be "delighted" and "relieved" by both her writing and her life, indulging herself "repeatedly." She emphasizes two ideas: accident and deception (as opposed to intention) as keys to both her reception and her reserve. ⟨. . .⟩

Stein's coding strategy is a willed and intentional process, a carefully worn mask through which she artfully expresses her thoughts and feelings. But her intrusion "errors," uncensored areas of her discourse which intrude on prosaic statements and make them ambiguous, are far more frequent and far more puzzling. These intrusions seem to enter haphazardly into her texts, creating a randomized surface. It is as if parts of the message have actually appeared against her will or that Stein has no control over its development and logical direction. ⟨. . .⟩

Stein's intrusions usually occur when she is trying to rationalize the problem of sexuality. Just as she is telling us that she will not reveal herself or that it is probably better not to be associated with the idea of sexuality at all, Stein provocatively emphasizes the sexual content of her associations. In the following selection, for instance, the intrusions occur as physical descriptions of the earth, drawn from the vocabulary of mining: "It is as well to be without in their reverberation in the meantime ways which are in opening to their site do unexpectedly deliver it as in a tunnel and they attend the opening and the exit." If, in the beginning, Stein seems to be begging the question of sexuality (using "reverberation" to refer to the movement of orgasm), the very mention of this word causes the appearance of associated kinds of sexualized geological images such as the earthquake or the explosion that mining requires, in turn producing other metaphorically related words: "opening," "site," "deliver," "tunnel," "exit." These words intrude upon her originally framed denial to become a kind of contradictory approval of her original premise.

—Elizabeth Fifer, "Rescued Readings: Characteristic Deformations in the Language of Gertrude Stein's Plays," *Texas Studies in Literature and Language* (Winter 1982), excerpted in *The Chelsea House Library of Literary Criticism: Twentieth-Century American Literature*, vol. 6, ed. Harold Bloom (New York: Chelsea House Publishers, 1987), 3784–85

Marianne DeKoven

As in much impressionist and modernist fiction, narrative tone and temporal structure are at odds in *Three Lives* with the thematic content deducible from close reading and a reconstruction of linear causality. The tone and emphasis are noncommittal, cheerful, naive, at most mildly mocking; the thematic content is bitter, angry, implying a sophisticated social-political awareness and judgment. Temporal structure is preponderantly either a "continuous present" or static, yet each novella plots a classic trajectory of rise and fall. Nothing better epitomizes the contradictions of *Three Lives* than its epigraph, a quotation from Jules Laforgue: "Donc je suis un malheureux et ce/n'est ni ma faute ni celle de la vie." These lines certainly belie the narrator's cheerful innocence, but they equally belie the conclusions we can draw with excellent justification from all three novellas that a cruel "life," at least, is very much to blame for the mistreatment and death of these women.

We need no longer speculate about the psychological reasons for Stein's diverting attention, both her own and the reader's, from her anger and sadness. Richard Bridgman and Catharine Stimpson have shown with great clarity that Stein simultaneously concealed and encoded in her literary work troublesome feelings about herself as a woman, about women's helplessness, and particularly about lesbianism, still very much considered by society a "pollutant," as Stimpson puts it, during most of Stein's life ⟨Catharine Stimpson, "The Mind, the Body and Gertrude Stein," *Critical Inquiry* 3, 1977, p. 493⟩. But Stein did not merely stifle or deny her anger, her sense that she did not fit and that the deficiency was not hers but rather that of the structure which excluded her. In effect, Stein's rebellion was channelled from content to linguistic structure itself. A rebellion in language is much easier to ignore or misconstrue, but its attack, particularly in literature, penetrates far deeper, to the very structures which determine, within a particular culture, what can be thought.

Stein's anti-patriarchal rebellion was not conscious or intentional, as her denial of her own bitterness and anger in *Three Lives* suggests. But for her, as perhaps for Virginia Woolf, there is an extra dimension to the view of experimental writing as anti-patriarchal, because both writers defined themselves in opposition to the notions of women which patriarchy provides.

Stein's attitude toward her gender offers further material for speculation. ⟨. . . W⟩hen this material becomes particularly relevant to Stein's writing, her female self-hatred was such that she was psychologically compelled to identify herself as a man in order to be a happy, sexually active person and a functioning writer. While she lived with her brother Leo, she was a frequently depressed, subservient sister; when Leo left and Alice Toklas moved in, she became a generally happy, very productive husband. This male identification did not shift until the late twenties, when there is evidence that Stein began to feel better about her female identity. Throughout her radically experimental period, therefore, she essentially thought of herself as a man (there is direct evidence of this identification in the notebooks, where Stein says "Pablo & Matisse have a maleness that belongs to genius. Moi aussi, perhaps"). We might posit a speculative connection between this male identification, and the concomitant suppression of her female identity, with the shift of the rebellious impulse from thematic content to linguistic structure, where the subversive implications of the writing are at once more powerful and abstruse.

—Marianne DeKoven, "Three Lives," A Different Language: Gertrude Stein's Experimental Writing (1983), excerpted in The Chelsea House Library of Literary Criticism: Twentieth-Century American Literature, vol. 6, ed. Harold Bloom (New York: Chelsea House Publishers, 1987), 3790

JAYNE L. WALKER

In Tender Buttons Stein channeled the flood of concrete particulars she first tapped in G.M.P. to create an artfully structured composition. Its three sections, "Objects," "Food," and "Rooms," form a provocative sequence. From the external objects we see and touch, the text moves inward to the substances we ingest and, in the final section, outward again to the spaces that surround us. Tender Buttons describes a female world (circa 1912) of domestic objects and rituals—a world of dresses and hats, tables and curtains, mealtimes and bedtimes, cleanliness and dirt. Although a few exotic items, including an elephant and a "white hunter," make momentary appearances, the iconography of domestic life dominates the text. Concrete nouns and adjectives name a wealth of homely particulars. But in its artful rearrangement of these details, the text models a world in which objects, foods, and rooms are liberated from their normal subordination to human routines and purposes. ⟨. . .⟩

While its concrete objects are animated with human qualities, Tender Buttons presents human beings simply as physical objects, equal to all the others named and arranged in these "still lifes": "and so between curves and outlines and real seasons and more out glasses and a perfectly unprecedented arrangement between old ladies and mild colds there is no satin wood shining" (473). Here, as in "A Feather" and many other pieces, spatial contiguity is the ordering principle of this "perfectly unprecedented arrangement," but "mild colds" and "real seasons" mingle with the "curves and outlines" of purely spatial configurations. Sometimes the human body is reduced to a set of synecdoches, as in "Colored Hats": "Colored hats are necessary to show that curls are worn by an addition of blank spaces, this makes the difference between single lines and broad stomachs" (473). Occasionally the discourse creates shocking juxtapositions of human bodies and inanimate objects, as in "Little sales ladies little sales ladies little saddles of mutton" (475). This equation of "little sales ladies" with pieces of meat strikingly illustrates how radically the order of *Tender Buttons* refuses to privilege human meanings and purposes. In her earlier works, Stein portrayed human beings in terms of essential character, abstracted from their concrete daily life in the physical world. The radical reversal in *Tender Buttons* suggests not so much a dehumanization as a new affirmation that human existence is intimately involved with the physicality of matter and of flesh. The physical world portrayed in *Tender Buttons* includes the most intimate realities of the female body. "A Petticoat" shows "a disgrace, an ink spot, a rosy charm" (471). And a "shallow hole rose on red, a shallow hole in and in this makes ale less," an obvious transmutation of Alice (474). ⟨. . .⟩

⟨. . .⟩ Stein's pursuit of "reality" forced her to confront the irreconcilable difference between the order of language and the chaotic plenitude of immediate experience. ⟨. . .⟩ *Tender Buttons* claims that each of its "collections" of words "shows the disorder, . . . it shows more likeness than anything else." By the time she wrote this text, Stein's acute awareness of language as a "necessary betrayal," coupled with her continuing dedication to the "realism of the composition," had led her to conclude that, within language, "real is only, only excreate, only excreate a no since." Uniting the words creation and excretion, the verb "excreate" boldly asserts the inseparable connection between mind and matter. External to more conventional creativity, nonsense is the only viable model of the "real" that language can create. ⟨. . .⟩

In *Tender Buttons*, Stein joyfully embraced what she later identified as the "reality of the twentieth century . . . a time when everything cracks, where everything is destroyed, everything isolates itself." Later in her career she asserted that the "creator of the new composition in the arts is an outlaw until he is a classic," until the time when the "modern composition having become past is classified and the description of it is classical." From our vantage point, we can readily situate *Tender Buttons* within the historical poetics of modernism. In Yeats's "Second Coming," "[t]hings fall apart; the center cannot hold." In *The Waste Land*, a "heap of broken images" is presented as the sum of human knowledge. Fragmentation and the loss of a center have become part of our "classical description" of the themes and structural principles of literary modernism. But Stein remained an "outlaw" long after writers like Yeats and Eliot were enshrined as "classics." The playful, domesticated disorder of *Tender Buttons* is strikingly different from the apocalyptic "rough beast" presaged by Yeats's vision of chaos or the spiritual aridity of Eliot's "waste land." In *Tender Buttons* the absence of a center is presented not as a loss but as a liberation that allows limitless invention of new, purely poetic orders.

—Jayne L. Walker, *"Tender Buttons: 'The Music of the Present Tense,'"* *The Making of a Modernist: Gertrude Stein from "Three Lives" to "Tender Buttons"* (1984), excerpted in *The Chelsea House Library of Literary Criticism: Twentieth-Century American Literature*, vol. 6, ed. Harold Bloom (New York: Chelsea House Publishers, 1987), 3791, 3794

MALCOLM COWLEY

⟨The⟩ great mystery about Gertrude Stein is how this woman with a real influence on American prose, so that her first book marks an era in our literature; this woman famous for her conversation, able to change the ideas of other writers, able to hold and dominate big audiences when she lectures, should at the same time have written books so monumental in their dullness, so many pyramids and Parthenons consecrated to the reader's apathy.

I am not speaking of her exoteric works like *The Autobiography of Alice B. Toklas* and the present volume, but rather of her experimental essay-poem-novels like *Tender Buttons* and *The Making of Americans* and *Lucy Church Amiably*. And the trouble isn't at all that these books have no meaning. If we felt they were pure nonsense, we could find some pleasure in the word patterns, the puns, the rhymes, the mere sound of it all; everything would be dada, would be good fun. The trouble is that they do have a meaning, somewhere in the author's mind: a definite subject that eludes and irritates us and sets us off on a vain search as if through a pile of dusty newspapers for an item which we are sure must be there, but which we are equally sure we can never find. ⟨. . .⟩

Wars I Have Seen starts out to give us more in the same self-centered vein: more about the early life of the very great author, more about her becoming a legend, more about how it felt to be the spoiled youngest child in a family of five boys and girls. ⟨. . .⟩ But her attention keeps being distracted by present events, much as a rheumatic twinge or the ticking of an alarm clock will intrude into a pleasant dream about the past. Soon the sleeper wakens to feel that there are intruders in the house.

The intruders, of course, are the Germans; and here in an occupied village the effects of their presence are felt in a thousand indirect ways. ⟨. . .⟩

At the beginning of *Wars I Have Seen* you are bothered by Miss Stein's American but excessively personal style, with its flatness of statement, its repetitions, its deliberate errors in grammar, and its absence of commas, except where the sense calls for a period or a semicolon. Later you become reconciled to your reading; or perhaps the style itself becomes a little simplified and

humanized through the author's preoccupation with her subject. For the first time she forgets herself in her subject, and her readers forget themselves too, and forget Miss Stein, as they follow the life of a French village from day to day.
—Malcolm Cowley, *The Flower and the Leaf: A Contemporary Record of American Writing Since 1941*, ed. Donald W. Faulkner (New York: Viking Penguin, 1985), 72–75

ESTELLE C. JELINEK

Catharine Stimpson defines the problem of women at the turn of the century who were liberated intellectually but not sexually as the "feminization of the mind/body problem." ⟨. . .⟩

For women like Stein, "the feminization of the mind/body problem" created confusion over "what women might do with their bodies and what they might say about it, especially in public." For Stein, in her time and with her personality, camouflage was the only way she could write about her life. There was no way for her to coexist or synthesize her dual roles as private lesbian and public writer. Thus, fragmented anecdotes and a discontinuous chronology were necessary to conceal her true self in a genre predicated on self-revelation. And they do not contribute to a rounder or more insightful portrait ⟨. . . .⟩ Instead, they represent Stein's lack of trust and faith in a world that does not accept or allow her to write about her sexual preference. ⟨. . .⟩

It is because of this need to hide her private life with Alice Toklas that the autobiography becomes a pretense at self-portraiture, for she must exclude the only meaningful intimate relationship of her life. She hopes to distract her readers from the absence of this personal element by concentrating on amusing portraits of famous people. Nonetheless, Stein does not entirely exclude her personal life from *The Autobiography of Alice B. Toklas*. ⟨. . .⟩

If Stein had written in her own voice about Toklas's wifelike functions, her readers would probably have been shocked or disturbed. But if Toklas chooses to perform these duties, in her own voice, while the genius worked, then the audience may not even notice. Toklas's presence as the narrator legitimized Stein in a world that expected some information stereotypically associated with women in an autobiography by a woman, just as the geniuses Stein gathered around her legitimized her as a professional, if yet unrecognized, writer.

Writing her life story in the voice of her intimate companion serves yet another function. By placing Toklas in the ostensible center of the autobiography and by making her the narrator, Stein pays homage to their—her and Toklas's—personal success story. Stein makes famous the most important person in her life; she makes famous the "wife" of the genius who will one day be famous for her work. ⟨. . .⟩

Stein's need to disguise her relationship with Toklas is not surprising. During a time when most women had little choice between celibacy and domesticity, it was socially acceptable for women to share homes with one another. Jane Addams lived with another woman. So did M. Carey Thomas, Frances Willard, and Susan B. Anthony. Nevertheless, marriage was still the socially preferred relationship. Unpublished diaries and letters from the nineteenth century are filled with passionate and intense descriptions written by women to one another, sometimes explicit about physical contact but most of the time not. Physical relationships were not common until the beginning of the twentieth century because women were so ignorant of their bodies that they did not often connect sexuality with anything save procreation.

Stimpson describes Stein's motive for disguising and "encoding" her lesbian relationship in her earlier novels *Q.E.D.* and *Fernhurst*, both written between 1903 and 1905, as "the need to write out hidden impulses; the wish to speak to friends without having others overhear; the desire to evade and to confound strangers, aliens, and enemies." By 1932 the disguise was reduced to the "openness" of giving Toklas the role of narrator of Stein's autobiography. Stein did not live to benefit from the struggles of the women "who first exemplified the feminization of the mind/body problem," but she "left for contemporary women the consolation that it could be endured, even transcended."

—Estelle C. Jelinek, "Exotic Autobiography Intellectualized," *The Tradition of Women's Autobiography: From Antiquity to the Present* (Boston: G. K. Hall & Company, 1986), 136–37, 143–45

DINNAH PLADOTT

How does one live and create while in exile? The life and work of Gertrude Stein, exiled several times as an expatriate American woman, a Jew, and a lesbian, make the question especially pressing. Her decision to experiment with unprecedented forms of writing gives resonance to the notion of exile formulated by Julia Kristeva, also a double exile. In "A New Type of Intellectual: The Dissident," Kristeva comments that physical banishment implies a dissenting metaphysics: "Exile is already a form of *dissidence*, since it involves uprooting oneself from a family, a country or a language." According to Kristeva, this initial form of exile is compounded in women, who are excluded from participation "in the consensual law of politics and society." A woman, argues Kristeva, is by definition "trapped within the frontiers of her body and even of her species, and consequently always feels *exiled* both by general clichés that make up a common consensus and by the very powers of generalization intrinsic to language." The same terms apply by inference to the Jew and the lesbian, living permanently outside the consensus. The effect of this multiple exile on Stein's contribution to American drama is considerable.

Regrettably, Kristeva never mentions Stein among the writers she valorizes—Joyce, Kafka, Beckett—who "pluralize meaning and cross all national and linguistic barriers." Yet her discussion of avant-garde writing and its ability to use exile as a vantage point from which it displaces established literary forms by "the eruption of the languages of modernity" situates Stein perfectly. Moreover, Kristeva insists that the displacement accomplished by such dissidence is not confined to the purely literary or aesthetic realm but always has political implications. Under the pressure of avant-garde writing, "the master discourses begin to drift and the simple rational coherence of cultural and institutional codes breaks down."

Kristeva provides a belated description of the defiant creative project Stein has already carried out, demonstrating that exile from the mainstream opens for women and avant-garde artists a similar enterprise—undertaking to interrogate and destabilize the most sanctified and most entrenched assumptions about what constitutes reality, knowledge, beauty, and truth. As Stein explains in "Composition As Explanation," the experimental writer composes differently than her contemporaries, and in so doing shatters the habitual modes of seeing and showing, as well as the received emphases and perspectives. In a typical humorous deflation, Stein comments on the refusal of the majority to accept the minority's (re)vision until the artistic innovation has become abstracted from its spatiotemporal context, thus rendering the upstart artist an "outlaw" or exile from the communal framework:

> "Those who are creating the modern composition authentically are naturally only of importance when they are dead because by that time the modern composition having become past is classified and the description of it is classical. That is the reason why the creator of the new composition in the arts is an outlaw until he is a classic . . ."

Faced with the choice of being "an outlaw" or "a classic," Stein unhesitatingly chose the former. I suggest that her creative project of realizing "the new composition" is most central and radical in her operas and plays, which have received much less critical attention than her fiction. It is most radical because Stein takes on the tendency of the theatrical medium to mask more effectively than any other art the fact that it is a structured and codified process of signification. The convergence of the spectator with the physical presence of iconic signs (in Peirce's terms), namely, the actors and the performance's sights and sounds, fosters the illusion that the staged play is an unmediated reality rather than a rule-governed semiotic exchange. Stein repeatedly foregrounds and unmasks this illusion. By refusing to abide by the traditional rules of dramatic writing, she also calls into question many assumptions about the means whereby meaning is produced and about the relationship of signification to the object signified. Furthermore, as we shall see, she confirms Kristeva's prediction that the dissidence from one system of "consensual laws" bears inevitably on a number of theoretical projects. In Stein's case, dissident innovation is pertinent to feminism on the one hand and to theories of art and criticism on the other, because she raises questions about the presumed authority of any text (most notably, "the master discourse") to represent reality.

Stein's dramatic scripts anticipate the deconstructive terminology and methods of Jacques Derrida and Michel Foucault, because she set out intentionally to disrupt all structures or systems that presuppose the existence of a stable, inherent, and infallible meaning (patriarchal structures particularly), including her own writing. The operas and plays exemplify writing that is conscious of its own provisional authority; that is, aware of its own contingency, of its being *sous rature* (under erasure), in Derrida's words. Stein and her practice in her operas and plays, therefore, come into the discussion as both illustrating (although antedating) Kristeva's points and moving the discussion toward a consideration of the relation of the woman-writer-exile to feminism, the avant-garde, deconstruction, and signification. I propose that the capacity to interrogate the signifying practices of theater and other types of discourse establishes an analogy between feminism and the avant-garde in art as well as in science. Moreover, this capacity collapses categories central to the historiography of American drama and theater, such as "the play of social relevance."

—Dinnah Pladott, "Gertrude Stein: Exile, Feminism, Avant-Garde in the American Theater," *Modern American Drama: The Female Canon*, ed. Jane Schlueter (Cranbury, NJ: Associated University Presses, 1990), 111–13

Martha Dana Rust

On one level, then, *The World is Round* portrays Rose's struggle with circularity in the world around her; on another level, it dramatizes her struggle to define herself within the treacherously slippery medium of language itself.

While Rose attempts to master the turning worlds within and around her, a parallel tussle occurs between linear and circular elements in the story's style. On the one hand, Stein's play with syntax creates a prose that swallows up individual sentence "identities"; on the other hand, the multiple lists of nouns that are so characteristic of Stein's poetics, coupled with the linear discourse of narrative itself, seem to form a wedge against the story's almost overwhelmingly circular syntax. Tellingly, though, *The World is Round* concludes with the words "and the world just kept on being round," and circularity does have the "last" word in this story. Rose's quest for stability in her round world leads only to the discovery of new horizons of roundness; the lists of nouns that seemed to interrupt the story's spinning syntax only give rise to dizzying spirals of repetition and rhyme; even the supposedly stable identities produced by the linear narrative mode are eventually proven subject to flux. Stein thus gives her playful tale a subversive message: because our world does keep going around and around, we may never know exactly "who" we are. ⟨. . .⟩

The syntax of *The World is Round* echoes Rose's distressing entanglement in language. Just as Rose's identity is obscured by a circular play with the meaning-making limitations of language, the identities of individual sentences and clauses in *The World is Round* are obscured by a circular play of syntax, one that makes it impossible to tell where one sentence ends and another begins. One variety of this circular word order consists of a pattern in which a sentence constituent may serve as either the beginning or end of a sentence. For instance, consider the constituent "her chair" in the following sentence: "So Rose left early so no one saw her and her chair she held before her" (54). The constituent "her chair" may conclude the clause "no one saw her and her chair," or it may begin the clause "her chair she held before her." Because "her chair" functions simultaneously in two sentence positions and thus seems to belong to both sentences at once, its position blurs the individual identities of both.

A second example of this sort of identity-blurring syntax may be found in the following sentence:

> But she could not keep on remembering and forgetting of course
> not but she could sing of course she could sing and she could cry
> of course she could cry. (22)

Here the ambiguous constituent is "of course." While the first "of course" in this sentence is clearly associated with its first independent clause, "she could not keep on remembering and forgetting of course not," the next "of course" is positioned in such a way that it may serve either as the end of the clause "she could sing of course" or the beginning of the clause "of course she could sing." Because this second "of course" functions as both the end of one independent clause and the beginning of the next, the boundary between the two clauses dissolves and the distinct identity of each is lost. ⟨. . .⟩

Although oral discourse markers do provide *The World is Round* with a narrative thread, these markers in several ways are also thoroughly wound up in roundness. First, in addition to guiding the listener through the story's enigmatic episodes, they comprise one of its most strident reminders of circularity. Indeed, the statement "the world is round" is repeated sixteen times in this short story. Second, oral discourse markers also frequently give way to repetitive sound patterns and thus shirk their guiding function in the interest of repetitive play. Thus, in the following sentence, the oral discourse marker "well anyway" yields its directive force to a larger pattern of sound: "Well anyway just then the hay went away, hay has that way and the water went away and the car did stay and neither Rose nor Willie were drowned that day" (15). Where a practical narrator might have followed "well anyway" with a perfunctory "everything turned out alright," in *The World is Round* the narrator drops the authority of "well anyway" to join in a dance of "ay" sounds. But, third, the narrator's ultimate act of collusion with roundness occurs at the end of the story. Throughout the book, the little boy named Willie has been identified as Rose's cousin, but in the end, "Willie and Rose turned out not to be cousins, just how nobody knows" (94). Since they are no longer cousins, Rose and Willie marry and have children, and they "live[d] happily ever after" (94). Because Stein passes lightly over the mystery of this sudden change in Willie's identity, her narrative sleight of hand flies in the face of the conservative standard of "truth" we expect from narrative even as it seems to provide the tidy closure we expect from a story for children.

The abrupt alteration in Willie's identity also calls into question the possibility of arriving at a fixed and settled sense of self. For if one of the purposes of the narrative mode is to provide an individual with a stable, unique identity, a narrative in which an individual's identity changes so capriciously not only fails to fulfill its function, but also threatens to undermine our sense that it is ever possible to know our "true" selves. If even our narrator thus colludes with roundness, a listener may well ask, as Laura Hoffeld does, "[i]f the world goes on being round, how could [Rose and Willie] live happily ever after?" (53). Indeed, how can any of us live happily ever after on such a slippery planet? The answer to this question, I would argue, lies in the juxtaposition of roundness and linearity found in the last sentence of *The World is Round*: "they lived happily ever after and the world just kept on being round" (94). Blending traditional closure with an affirmation of Stein's "continuous present," this sentence marks a dynamic truce between linearity and circularity. Even though the world is round, even though identities are unstable, and even though stories may never tell the "truth," Rose and Willie do live happily ever after. Their stories blend into the pleasurable, unknowable "continuous present" in which fictions, as Frank Kermode has observed, provide ways "for finding thing out" and "change as the needs of sense-making change" (39). Linear processes— like the stories we tell about ourselves—may be swept into larger circles of return; nevertheless, they are a pleasurable aspect of a round world. Indeed, as *The World is Round* concludes, its linearity is itself swept into a circular narrative discourse. Since it is a picture book for children, we will inevitably begin it again and again.

    —Martha Dana Rust, "Stop the World, I Want to Get Off!: Identity and Circularity in Gertrude Stein's *The World is Round*," Style 30, no. 1 (Spring 1996): 130

BIBLIOGRAPHY

Three Lives. 1909.
Portrait of Mabel Dodge at the Villa Curonia. 1912.
Tender Buttons. 1914.
Have They Attacked Mary. He Giggled. 1917.
Geography and Plays. 1922.
The Making of Americans. 1925.
Descriptions of Literature. 1926.
Composition as Explanation. 1926.
A Book Concluding with As a Wife Has a Cow: A Love Story. 1926.
An Elucidation. 1927.
A Village. 1928.
Useful Knowledge. 1928.
An Acquaintance with Description. 1929.
Lucy Church Amiably. 1930.
Dix Portraits (with English translation by G. Huguet and V. Thomson). 1930.
Before the Flowers of Friendship Faded Friendship Faded. 1931.
How to Write. 1931.
Operas and Plays. 1932.
A Long Gay Book. 1932.
The Autobiography of Alice B. Toklas. 1933.
Four Saints in Three Acts. 1934.
Portraits and Prayers. 1934.
Chicago Inscriptions. 1934.
Lectures in America. 1935.
Narration: Four Lectures. 1935.
The Geographical History of America. 1936.
Is Dead. 1937.
Everybody's Autobiography. 1937.
A Wedding Bouquet. 1938.
Picasso. 1938.
The World Is Round. 1939.
Prothalamium. 1939.
Paris France. 1940.
What Are Masterpieces. 1940.
Ida. 1941.
Wars I Have Seen. 1945.

Brewsie and Willie. 1946.
Selected Writings. Ed. Carl Van Vechten. 1946.
The First Reader and Three Plays. 1946.
In Savoy. 1946.
Four in America. 1947.
Kisses Can. 1947.
The Mother of Us All (with Virgil Thomson). 1947.
Literally True. 1947.
Two (Hitherto Unpublished) Poems. 1948.
Blood on the Dining-Room Floor. 1948.
Last Operas and Plays. Ed. Carl Van Vechten. 1949.
Things as They Are. 1950.
Unpublished Work (Yale ed., 8 vols.). 1951–58.
In a Garden. 1951.
Absolutely Bob Brown; or, Bobbed Brown. 1955.
On Our Way (with Alice B. Toklas). 1959.
Writings and Lectures 1911–1945. Ed. Patricia Meyerowitz. 1967.
Lines. 1967.
Lucretia Borgia. 1968.
Motor Automation. 1969.
A Christmas Greeting. 1969.
Selected Operas and Plays. Ed. John Malcolm Brinnin. 1970.
Gertrude Stein on Picasso. Ed. Edward Burns. 1970.
I Am Rose. 1971.
Fernhurst, Q. E. D., and Other Early Writings. 1971.
Sherwood Anderson/Gertrude Stein: Correspondence and Personal Essays. Ed. Ray
    Lewis White. 1972.
Why Are There Whites to Console. 1973.
Reflection on the Atomic Bomb. Ed. Robert Bartlett Haas. 1973.
Money. 1973.
How Writing is Written. Ed. Robert Bartlett Haas. 1974.
Last Will and Testament. 1974.
Dear Sammy: Letters from Gertrude Stein and Alice B. Toklas. Ed. Samuel M.
    Steward. 1977.

JUI JIN FAR or EDITH EATON
1865-1914

SUI SIN FAR was born Edith Eaton in England in 1865, the eldest daughter of an English-educated Chinese mother, Lotus Blossom Trufusis, and an English father, Edward Eaton. In 1873 the family (including Sui Sin Far's younger sister Winnifred, also a writer) emigrated to Canada and settled in Montreal, where Sui Sin Far received her education and where she began her career as a writer. Between 1898 and 1912, she traveled through the United States working as a journalist, stenographer, and writer of short fiction. Her collection of short stories, *Mrs. Spring Fragrance* (1912), is commonly held to be the first book-length collection by a North American writer of Chinese descent.

Curiously, Sui Sin Far's sister also chose a pseudonym for herself, but in creating a pen name she also created an entire fictional identity; she became Onoto Watanna, a Japanese noblewoman. By choosing a Japanese identity, Winnifred Eaton capitalized on the favored status of the Japanese, who were seen by Americans and Canadians to be the "good Orientals," and were regarded with less suspicion than the Chinese. The difference in perceptions of the Chinese and Japanese was due, in part, to the fact that there were few Japanese in the United States at the turn of the century, and therefore they posed much less of a threat to the white labor force than did the Chinese. In choosing a Chinese pseudonym, therefore, Sui Sin Far made it her life's work to defend her mother's maligned race.

In 1896, Sui Sin Far published an open letter in a Canadian newspaper that explicitly detailed the discriminatory practices used against the Chinese in Canada. Titled "A Plea for the Chinaman," the article argues against a proposed five-hundred-dollar head tax for Chinese-American immigrants. In another article a year later, called "The Chinese Woman in America," she described the double bind trapping many Chinese women, who were faced with the archaic sexism of their Chinese husbands and the rampant racism of the white North Americans. She chronicles some of her own experiences with racism and sexism in an article published in 1909, "Leaves from the Mental Portfolio of an Eurasian." The piece anticipates much of the writing done later in the century by other Chinese American writers like Maxine Hong Kingston and Amy Tan.

Mrs. Spring Fragrance combines stories for children and stories about a Chinese woman, her husband, and their community. The book challenges the "yellow peril" images of the Chinese that were prevalent in the popular literature of the time; there are no opium smokers, rat eaters, or hatchet wavers in these stories. Instead we encounter characters who play baseball, go to church, learn English, and have a sense of humor. The children's stories are less stories for children than they are about children. They are not concerned with contemporary social or political problems but are structured like parables, instructional tales with a moral. Sui Sin Far never married. She died of a heart failure at the age of 49 in Montreal, where she is buried in the Eaton family plot.

CRITICAL EXTRACTS

S. E. SOLBERG

As a Chinese-American writer, ⟨. . .⟩ Sui Sin Far had to find a mode that would enable her to deal with her own experience (as the classic editorial injunction has it), but to do that meant to fall outside the boundaries of any of the "main-currents" of American writing. She was not a regionalist nor nationalist. If anything, she was an internationalist, but hardly of the Henry James school, though some of what is interesting in her work lies in the subtleties that are apt to be lost on the untrained casual reader. She is not naturalist or local colorist, and her essays at humor, which tend to fall short of the mark in any case, can hardly be looked upon as falling in the Mr. Dooley or Mark Twain "native American" styles. She was trapped by experience and inclination into working within a sub-genre of American prose: what, for lack of a better term, we might call Chinatown Tales. Such classification by subject matter (Chinatown, or more broadly, the Chinese in America) breaks down an established literary form, the novel, into sub-genres defined by content, not form or stylistic skill. Eaton, by choosing to identify with and write about the Chinese, found herself alone in an essentially formless field. There had been fifty years of writing about the Chinese in America, but out of that writing no clear literary form had evolved. ⟨. . .⟩

Fiction, drama, and verse, each with a sub-genre which exploits the "Chinese as a rich source of color." This gave Eaton little enough to build on, for her intent was certainly not to exploit, but rather to record, explain, and somehow give meaning to the experience of the Chinese in America. Fenn's 1933 summing up is interesting, for he had considered two of Eaton's stories in his summary, though his bibliography does not list her collection, *Mrs. Spring Fragrance*.

> Such, then, is the literature of Chinatown—no poems, no plays, but possibly half a dozen short stories worth remembering. And Chinatown will never be adequately described by anyone who fails to see in it something more fundamental than the superficial barbarity and high coloring which have been almost the only appeal so far. . . . The real Chinatown that is worth preserving lies beneath the surface color, among the deeper currents.

I would argue that Edith Eaton as Sui Sin Far did manage to dip into those deeper currents beneath the surface color, but no matter what she saw and understood, there was no acceptable form to shape it to. Had she been physically stronger and had a more sophisticated literary apprenticeship, she might have been able to create that new form. As it was, she was defeated, for in that "glorious process of exploding old myths and of creating new ones," as Fenn puts it, "the Chinamen were bound to suffer."

Fictional stereotypes for the Chinatown tales had been established, and it was difficult for anyone, even of a strongly independent mind, to ignore them. No matter how frank and open Eaton might have been in a memoir such as "Leaves from the Mental Portfolio of an Eurasian," when she turned her hand to fiction the possible was limited by the acceptable. She was modest about her work. In acknowledging permissions to reprint previously published stories in *Mrs. Spring Fragrance* she writes: "I wish to thank the Editors . . . who were kind enough to care for my children when I sent them out into the world, for permitting the dear ones to return to me to be grouped together within this volume."

Even at the outset there were those who appreciated her difficulties and her attempts to create authentic characters. Said the editor of *Land of Sunshine*, a California magazine, in 1887:

> [her stories are] all of Chinese characters in California or on the Pacific Coast; and they have an insight and sympathy which are probably unique. To others the alien Celestial is at best mere "literary material": in these stories, he (or she) is a human being.

That her contemporaries saw Sui Sin Far's writing as an attempt to speak for Chinese-Americans is borne out by the review of *Mrs. Spring Fragrance* in the *New York Times Book Review* of July 7, 1912.

> Miss Eaton has struck a new note in American fiction. She has not struck it very surely, or with surpassing skill, but it has taken courage

to strike it all, and, to some extent, she atones for lack of artistic skill with the unusual knowledge she undoubtedly has of her theme. The thing she has tried to do is to portray for readers of the white race the lives, feelings, sentiments of the Americanized Chinese of the Pacific Coast, of those who have intermarried with them and of the children who have sprung from such unions. It is a task whose adequate doing would require well nigh superhuman insight and the subtlest of methods.

The review had more insight that the publisher who inserted an advertisement on the same page; the advertisement reads in part: "Quaint, lovable characters are the Chinese who appear in these unusual and exquisite stories of our Western Coast. . . . Altogether they make as desirable reading as the title suggests." Taken out of context, what does the title suggest? Perhaps the exotic, that could be traded on, at worst, the quaint, but hardly the struggle toward realism that is found in the pages.

—S. E. Solberg, "Sui Sin Far/Edith Eaton: First Chinese-American Fictionist," *Melus* 8, no. 1 (Spring 1981): 32–34

AMY LING

In 1912, when MRS. SPRING FRAGRANCE was published, since only six states had granted women the vote, the women's suffrage movement was still going strong. During this era, anarchist, feminist Emma Goldman was lecturing on birth control and being arrested for spreading such godless views. With foresight, however, Goldman separated women's liberation from women's vote, asserting rightly that the vote alone would not make women free: "I do not believe that woman will make politics worse; nor can I believe that she could make it better." Furthermore, she contended, suffragettes were middle-class women seeking equal rights to secure their property while working-class women, Goldman's main concern, had no property to secure. Eloquently, she expanded on the meaning of true liberation for women, blasting sacred cows women today are still wrestling with:

Woman's development, her freedom, her independence, must come from and through herself. First, by asserting herself as a personality, and not as a sex commodity. Second, by refusing to bear children unless she wants them; by refusing to be a servant to God, the State, society, the husband, the family, etc., by making her life simpler, but deeper and richer. That is, by trying to learn the meaning and substance of life in all its complexities, by freeing herself from fear of public opinion and public condemnation. Only that, and not the ballot, will set woman free, will make her a force hitherto unknown in the world, a force for real love, for peace, for harmony; a force of divine fire, of life-giving; a creator of free men and women.

Whether Edith Eaton knew Emma Goldman's work or heard her speeches we do not know, but Eaton's purposeful, single life and several of her stories reveal feminist beliefs and particularly reflect Goldman's views. The most notable of these stories is the ironic and amusing "The Inferior Woman." Will Carman, son of Mrs. Spring Fragrance's neighbor, is in love with Alice Winthrop, whom his mother considers an inferior woman because she has come from a poor family, has had little formal education, began work at fourteen and now holds a position "—private secretary to the most influential man in Washington—a position which by rights belongs only to a well-educated young woman of good family." Mrs. Carman prefers Ethel Evebrook, a well-educated suffragist, and daughter of her friend. Ethel Evebrook, however, admires Alice and invites her to speak at a suffragist meeting Ethel has organized. Alice writes to say that though she would like to help Ethel's cause, she is afraid that her experiences may not be what Ethel is looking for because the men she has worked for, far from corrupting her mind and her morals, have helped, inspired, and advised her.

The proud Alice will not have Will if his mother looks down on her. With the help of Mrs. Spring Fragrance, who by unlikely coincidence overhears the Evebrooks speak well of Alice Winthrop and relays their opinion to her neighbor, Mrs. Carman learns that Alice is not to be despised but admired for what she has attained through her own efforts. After Will has an accident and asks for Alice, Mrs. Carman comes to the young woman's house and finally accepts her as her son's choice.

Though Mrs. Spring Fragrance's rather busybody role is awkwardly woven into this tale of white people, and though Eaton's feminism, as expressed in Alice's defense of the men she has worked with, may be somewhat unorthodox, Eaton's sympathy for the self-made woman of intelligence and talent rather than the well-born and -bred woman of high social class is readily apparent. This is a theme Emma Goldman would have approved.

Two of Eaton's stories deal with the close bond of friendship between women. In one of her children's tales, "The Heart's Desire," a princess who has all the material advantages of wealth is nonetheless unhappy. Thinking she needs company, her courtiers bring her successively a father, a mother, and a little brother, but none of these make her happy. Finally, Princess O'Yam herself sends a note, carried by a dove, to a poor, hungry girl, Ku Yum, who comes to the palace. O'Yam is finally satisfied and announces to all her people, "Behold, I have found my heart's desire—a little sister." In "The Chinese Lily" a character surprisingly named Sui Sin Far befriends a young crippled woman whose only contact with the world had been the daily visits of her brother, Lin John. One evening, when the brother fails to come, Sin Far, hearing her neighbor crying, knocks on the door and visits with the crippled Mermei. Mermei discovers "one can't talk to a man, even if he is a brother, as one can to one the same as oneself." Sin Far agrees that "The woman must be the friend of the woman." One night their building catches fire; the brother, who has since fallen in love with Sin Far, climbs the ladder in time to save only one life. While each woman urges the other to go with him, Lin John selects his sister. This story of love as sacrifice may be seen as a version of "Greater love hath no man than this, that a man lay down his life for his friends." But it is also a story of filial duty, for Lin John is the same man, mentioned earlier, who worked for three years for another sister's freedom only to have her steal his savings.

The sorrowful note sounded in Eaton's first published piece about spring recurs throughout her stories. Those urging cheerfulness and happiness are generally the children's tales. The adult stories show the "melancholy deep of life" which she already knew at age twenty-three. Several of her heroines— Alice Winthrop, the "inferior woman," and Pan, the Eurasian deceived by a white journalist—are "born . . . Bohemian, exempt from the conventional restrictions imposed upon either the white or Chinese woman" (p. 86). Eaton herself, with an unsuccessful painter father and a mother who had once been a tightrope dancer, must have felt keenly her rejection by society—because of her Bohemian background as well as the racial mix within her. One of her characters, Tian Shan, learns "to reject realities and accept dreams as the stuff upon which to live. Life itself was hard, bitter, and disappointing. Only dreams are joyous and smiling" (p. 234). These stories are Eaton's dreams, some joyous and smiling because she wills them so, once or twice imposing a happy ending at the expense of credibility. Nonetheless, the sad notes, certain melodies in minor keys, are inevitable because she is honest and sees clearly.

—Amy Ling, "Edith Eaton: Pioneer Chinamerican Writer and Feminist," *American Literary Realism* 16, no. 2 (Autumn 1983): 295–97

ANNETTE WHITE-PARKS

To appreciate the immensity of her achievement, whatever its quantity, it is essential to recall the social-political environments in which she was writing. Consider that Sui Sin Far's first known publication appeared 15 years after the Chinese Exclusion Act of 1882 had barred all Chinese women except the wives of Chinatown merchants from entering the US, a decade after witch-hunts in California and Washington, both states where she was writing, had burned Chinese immigrants from their homes, sheared their queues, massacred many and forced others onto ships for deportation. "Chinese Women in America" came before the eyes of the American reading public only a year in advance of the Philippine-American War and the United States's annexation of Hawaii, with the accompanying "little brown brother" rhetoric and actions to match toward anyone who appeared Asian. Sui Sin Far herself looked so fully European that friends advised her to "pass," a stance which she shunned but which may have promoted the particular mediator role she had chosen. Her disregard for national barriers is typified in the statement, "I have no nationality and am not anxious to claim any" ("Leaves" 132),a perspective allowing her fiction to slip between Chinatown settings so quietly we are often unaware of where a story is located. Yet any reader aware of the history of immigration laws in respect to persons with Chinese blood in both the US and Canada suspects that the crossings of borders by Sui Sin Far in her life may have been undertaken with as much skill as her style in a short story.

The considerable range of this style may be observed through the variety of stories in Mrs. Spring Fragrance, running the spectrum from myths and fairy-tales of old China, ostensibly intended for children, to depictions of stark immigrant experiences wherein Chinese, especially women, confront the dual challenge of adjusting to a new, foreign environment and maintaining cultural integrity. Even the tales, though, express more than that which appears on the surface, frequently weaving a rich underlayer for themes that will develop through more complex stories. "Misunderstood," for example, describes the ritual of the Ceremony of the Moon, during which the foundation for a boy baby's queue and his future is laid. This image recurs when we see her son's "little queued head" resting on Pau Lin's shoulder as they sit in the steamer await-ing the father and husband who has preceded them to America by seven years in "The Wisdom of the New." ⟨. . .⟩ Thus, when little Yen later comes running in, snatches his cap from his head, and announces: "'See, mother . . . I am like father now. I wear no queue,'" the enormity of Pau Lin's feelings, as she lays her son's queue in her trunk, is indisputable. "Wisdom," moreover, sets up sev-eral elements of a typical immigrant situation, as Sui Sin Far depicts it: the hus-band who has come to America first and presses the wife to become instantly Americanized, which she defies; the contention between husband and wife (and symbolically between cultures) which comes to rest in the child; the interference of the white women whom Pau Lin suspects instantly, for she "had come from a land where a friendship between a man and a woman is almost unknown." The white women, as is often the case, seem kind, friendly, eager to help. Pau Lin is not persuaded. They come from a culture that has taken her husband, has potential for taking her child. This theme is illustrated in other stories such as "The Land of the Free," when another recent immigrant, Lae Choo, reaches for the baby who has been taken from her and put in a white boarding school, only to have him pull away and cling to the white woman's skirts. Thus when, at "Wisdom's" climax, Pau Lin smiles and says of her son: "He is saved," she understands what the white reader may not, but what Sui Sin Far strives to make clear. As with the black mother who kills her daughter to save her from being returned to slavery in Toni Morrison's *Beloved*, in a dire situation the strength of the mother's own will seizes what she sees as a last margin of hope for retaining her child.

That Sui Sin Far's fiction succeeded in gaining mainstream attention in its own era is demonstrated by such notice as a review in *The New York Times* (7 July 1912) applauding Mrs. *Spring Fragrance* for depicting the unique view of Chinese American families. In recent years Sui Sin Far has been noticed as the only writer to present pre-World War I Chinatowns in North America from an "insider" perspective, and Frank Chin credits her with founding an authentic Chinese American fiction, in contrast to the "white tradition of Chinese novelty literature," which was the trend in her lifetime (Chin xvii). Charles Lummis, editor of *Land of Sunshine*, had made this distinction when he writes, "To others the alien Celestial is at best mere 'literary material'; ⟨. . .⟩ in these stories he (or she) is a human being" (Lummis 336).

Though not one of the Chinese she writes of, per se (the sea she sailed to North America was, after all, not the Pacific but the Atlantic) and feeling, in many ways, as much an outsider to Chinese as to Anglo society, Sui Sin Far devoted her fiction to creating a style that would shatter the "alien Celestial" stereotype by tapping universal emotions. Hers was the middle stance, the mediator role Mary Dearborn describes for women writers of dual parentage. Yet despite her sense of belonging nowhere, Sui Sin Far in fact belongs everywhere, bringing us an angle of vision which encompasses a true intercultural perspective.

—Annette White-Parks, "Introduction," "'The Wisdom of the New' by Sui Sin Far," *Legacy* 6, no. 1 (Spring 1989): 35–36

ELIZABETH AMMONS

A major problem in ⟨. . .⟩ Mrs. *Spring Fragrance*, is Sui Sin Far's idealization of Chinese men. Wou Sankwei's overnight reform into a sensitive, understanding husband who contritely forgives his wife for the murder of their son is not believable. The characterization suggests that Sui Sin Far is as romantic and out-of-touch in her perspective on Chinese men as the do-gooder white women she attacks in her stories. If Chinese men are so miraculously forgiving and caring, why do Chinese women in Sui Sin Far's fiction—or in real life—have any problems?

How aware of it she was we cannot say, but Sui Sin Far's dilemma as a writer is not hard to imagine. It is a dilemma constantly faced by women of color in the United States. At the turn of the century the dominant culture was filled with vicious, racist stereotypes of Chinese men. To admit any flaws in them beyond the most minor foibles was to give the racist script credibility. Yet to say that they had no significant flaws was to cooperate in Chinese women's oppression. Sui Sin Far's negotiation of this minefield was not always successful. Ironically, it can be argued that her own "Americanization"—her distance from the day-to-day lives of Chinese women in the United States— in combination with her desire to counteract racist stereotypes of Chinese men as tyrants and brutes led her to exaggerate in the opposite direction. Too often she presents unrealistically ideal male characters and, therefore, an inaccurately "benevolent" view of gender relations in the Chinese community.

However, if the argument of Wou Sankwei's story in "The Wisdom of the New" is hard to accept, the meaning of Pau Lin's is not. As a story about creativity, silencing, and death, "The Wisdom of the New" is also about art. Denied voice, Pau Lin murders her son, her most wonderful creation; she renders herself barren, without offspring. It is more than accidental here, I think, that Sui Sin Far, in her acknowledgment to *Mrs. Spring Fragrance*, speaks with great tenderness of her stories as her "children" whom she sent "out into the world," her "dear ones" who have been allowed to live in magazines and are now returning to her "to be grouped together within this volume" (*MSF*, p. vii). If we extend this metaphor, we can think not only of Sui Sin Far's art as her children, the products of her flesh and blood that are mercifully allowed to live and come home to her, but also, conversely, of Pau Lin's child as her art, the product of her flesh and blood that, cruelly, is allowed to live only if it is so transformed and deformed that it turns against rather than expresses its creator. That is, the murder of the child in "The Wisdom of the New," in addition to signifying a real death, represents as well the murder of Chinese women's art in America. Using a white American woman artist as foil, Adah Charlton, the story speaks of the deathly, "barren," deeply unnatural silence into which potential artists like Pau Lin have been plunged by a racist, sexist culture.

Voice and voicelessness, speech and silence, who has the authority to name and shape the Chinese American woman's experiences and who does not—these are the issues that open *Mrs. Spring Fragrance*. Sui Sin Far's method is cautious and indirect. As people in risky situations often must, she uses humor and allegory to suggest her meaning, to assert her claim to authority in a hostile environment. Assert it she does, however, and the volume's subsequent stories branch out in various directions. The remaining stories in the first half of the "MRS. SPRING FRAGRANCE" section continue to examine relationships between Chinese Americans and Caucasian Americans and to concentrate on women's experiences.

In "Its Wavering Image" a young woman of mixed Asian and white parentage embraces her Chinese ancestry and cultural identity after being exploited and betrayed by a young white newspaperman who prints information that she gave him confidentially about the Chinese community. "The Gift of Little Me" praises the devotion of a white American woman who lives and works in Chinatown as a schoolteacher and is wrongfully accused of kidnapping a Chinese baby. "The Story of One White Woman Who Married a Chinese" develops openly Sui Sin Far's criticism of white middle-class feminism, portraying it as a culturally and class-biased ideology that is arrogant and authoritarian in its ethnocentricity (in fact, the story identifies white middle-class feminism as a male rather than a female political project). Its sequel, "Her Chinese Husband," also flies in the face of stereotypes. Painting a very positive picture of a Chinese American man, it shows that a young white woman enjoys more true freedom, as well as an undemeaning dependence, in her marriage to him than she did in her earlier marriage to a supposedly emancipated white American man. Rather than expect her to masculinize herself, as her first husband had demanded, the young woman's Chinese husband respects and shares with her values and activities that are denigrated in the dominant culture as feminine: cooking, sewing, being with children, talking about feelings. Sexual passion, frequently the pretext for the sexual domination and exploitation of women in hierarchical heterosexual society, does not constitute the center of their relationship. Instead, at the heart of their bond is a genuine emotional compatibility and rapport. The last story in this first section, "The Americanizing of Pau Tsu," reiterates the theme of "The Wisdom of the New," but does not end in death. Both the Americanized Chinese husband and his friend, the modern young white woman, come to realize how their friendship wounds and renders invisible the Chinese wife who is not included in it.

The nine stories that complete the "MRS. SPRING FRAGRANCE" section of the book also deal with discrimination and Anglo-Asian conflicts and problems, but they generally focus on relationships among Chinese Americans. "The Chinese Lily" celebrates the loyalty of a brother to his sister and the heroic sacrifice made for her by the woman he loves. "The God of Restoration" shows the betrayal of trust between cousins in America and supports the traditional Chinese idea that romantic love is not sufficient reason to ignore family duties. "The Smuggling of Tie Co" and "Tian Shan's Kindred Spirit" are both love stories set against the backdrop of illegal border crossings and the threat of deportation. In one story a young woman dressed as a man sacrifices herself to protect the smuggler she secretly loves; in the other a young woman (also dressed as a man) gets herself caught by border police in order to be deported with the man she loves. "The Sing Song Woman" shows the generous friendship of an unrespectable woman for another woman. "The Three Souls of Ah So Nan" illustrates the wisdom of not following traditional customs if no one is hurt by the deviation. "The Prize China Baby" tells of a poor and powerless woman's decision to enter her child in a mission contest in an effort to gain control over her life and keep her baby, whom her husband plans to give away. "Lin John" records a brother's labor to make enough money to buy his sister out of concubinage, only to learn that she has no desire to be liberated. "In the Land of the Free" relates in depressing detail a Chinese couple's fight to get their baby out of a United States government immigration detention orphanage.

Thematically, these stories present a range of issues and perspectives. Some address white manipulation and exploitation of Chinese people in the United States. Others show friendships between white people and Chinese people. Still others show friendships, but the emphasis falls on how problematic such bonds are. Certain stories celebrate immigrant life in the United States (the Spring Fragrances' happiness), and certain stories dramatize a strong yearning to return to China—to leave North America forever. There is rage at U.S. government policies in the fiction. There is hope that the Chinese family can survive the pressures of dissolution in the New World. There is also hope that the family will adapt and change in some ways. Contempt for stereotypes is a frequent theme—and yet often rising out of that contempt are characterizations of Chinese men that, ironically, err in the opposite direction. Frequently there is anger at middle-class white feminism. Just as frequently, there is pride in Chinese American women's own strength and courageous self-definitions.

Perhaps most fascinating, however, are Mrs. Spring Fragrance's images of female cross-dressing, rebellion, and secret, subversive writing that invite us to reflect on Sui Sin Far's own story as the first woman of Chinese heritage in the United States to publicly and successfully make writing about Chinese American experiences her life's work. Composed of many pieces, the panorama of Mrs. Spring Fragrance is sweeping and evocative. The book constantly shifts its focus rather than concentrate in depth on one individual's experience. What Sui Sin Far offers is a collection of lives, not an intensive anatomy of one life.

—Elizabeth Ammons, *Conflicting Stories: American Women Writers at the Turn into the Twentieth Century* (New York: Oxford University Press, 1992): 114–16

JAMES DOYLE

In spite of her insistence in the *Montreal Star* article on the integration of the Chinese into North American life, Edith Eaton's early fictions tended to exploit exotic and melodramatic images of her mother's people. Her story "The Gamblers," in the *Fly Leaf* (Feb. 1896), is about intrigue and murder in a gambling and opium den. "The Story of Iso" and "A Love Story of the Orient" in the *Lotus* (Aug. and Oct. 1896) involve star-crossed love and generational conflict in China. "A Chinese Ishmael" (*Overland Monthly* July 1899) is also a melodrama of tragic love, related to the Chinese inability to adapt to the West. In "The Smuggling of Tie Co," (*Land of Sunshine*, July 1990; included in *Mrs. Spring Fragrance*), a Chinese woman disguised as a man dies rather than betray the European-American man who helps her enter the United States illegally from Canada.

But behind the melodrama are indications of Eaton's serious concerns for a subject very close to her own experience, as she revealed in an article for the *Land of Sunshine* (Jan. 1897), "The Chinese Woman in America." Eaton was concerned that women of her ethnicity, when they were able to get into Canada and the United States at all, were frequently subjected to the double discrimination of the archaic domestic attitudes of Chinese men and the racism of European North Americans. The idea of a woman caught between two worlds and unable to participate fully in the lives of either is repeated in much of her fiction.

The stereotyped images and plot devices in Eaton's stories recall similar elements in the fiction of Euro-American writers who occasionally wrote about the Chinese, such as Bret Harte and Ambrose Bierce. With its use of the transvestite disguise, for instance, "The Smuggling of Tie Co" is notably like Ambrose Bierce's "The Haunted Valley," in his story collection *Can Such Things Be?* (1893). The most significant of Eaton's affinities, however, is not with a United States author, but with another Canadian, Pauline Johnson (1861–1913). Indeed, the lives and literary careers of the two Canadians are remarkably parallel. Both were born in the 1860s of ethnically mixed parentage (Johnson's mother was anglo-American, and her father a Mohawk chieftain with some European ancestry); both began publishing professionally in Canadian magazines in the 1880s; and both used stereotyped images of their minority heritage to gain attention and sympathy for serious social and moral problems relating to those minorities. The affinity between Eaton and Johnson is dramatically indicated by their public images. Both adopted ethnic pseudonyms, but were known publicly by their European birth names as well as their pseudonyms. In their literary and other presentations of themselves they emphasized the coexistence of their European and non-European heritages. Eaton saw herself simultaneously as the anglo-Canadian Edith Eaton and the Chinese/Eurasian Sui Sin Far. Johnson similarly presented herself as Tekahionwake, the half-mythical "Mohawk Princess" of the Six Nations, and a conventional Victorian anglo-Canadian woman from Brantford, Ontario.

Analogies are evident also in their writings. It is not certain that they were familiar with each other's work; it seems likely that Eaton would know something of Johnson after 1900, as Johnson's fame grew from her stage recitations and her books of poems and Indian legends. But the two writers expressed in similar terms the feelings of alienation and the determination to survive of the human being suspended between two cultures. Unlike Eaton, Johnson avoided explicit autobiography, but some of her short stories collected in *The Moccasin Maker* (1913) are obviously based on her own and her family situations. "My Mother" dramatizes the discrimination experienced by Johnson's mother from both her English and Indian connections as a result of her marriage. "As It Was in the Beginning" tells the story of an Indian child separated from her traditions and language and forcibly introduced into white Christian culture.

Eaton's article, "Leaves from the Mental Portfolio of an Eurasian" (*Independent* 21 Jan. 1909), chronicles more directly her experiences of alienation and sorrow. "I have come from a race on my mother's side which is said to be the most stolid and insensible to feeling of all races," she wrote, yet I look back over the years and see myself so keenly alive to every shade of sorrow and suffering that it is almost a pain to live" (127). Focussing on her peregrinations between nations and cities, as a child with her parents and as an adult trying to establish herself as a writer, she conveys the rootlessness and isolation of the person of mixed European and Asian ethnicity. ". . . I roam backward and forward across the continent. When I am East my Heart is West. When I am West, my heart is East" (132). In eastern Canada and in the western U.S., she encounters hostility from people of both Chinese and European origin. "After all I have no nationality and am not anxious to claim any," she concludes (133).

—James Doyle, "Sui Sin Far and Onoto Watanna: Two Early Chinese-Canadian Authors," *Canadian Literature* 144 (Spring 1994): 52–54

AMY LING AND ANNETTE WHITE-PARKS

Mrs. Spring Fragrance, Sui Sin Far's only published volume, had a modest initial run of twenty-five hundred copies in 1912 and to our knowledge was not reprinted. Nevertheless, *Mrs. Spring Fragrance* is a seminal work, a foundation piece not only for Asian North American literature but also for a multicultural understanding of Canada and the United States. The original edition was divided between "Mrs. Spring Fragrance" and "Tales of Chinese Children"; almost two-thirds of the stories reprinted in this volume are from the first section. Some present-day readers may consider the somewhat flowery style of these stories dated. Others may take issue with a certain "orientalism" in the author's tone and with the feeling that she is as much outsider as insider to the Chinese North American community. In "Leaves," for example, the statement "the white blood in our veins fights valiantly for the Chinese half of us" may be interpreted to confer greater valor to and passion for her "white blood," as Lorraine Dong and Marlon K. Hom have pointed out. We must remember, however, that being half English, educated entirely in English and English

Canadian schools, and growing to maturity among English and French Canadians, Sui Sin Far—as Edith Eaton—could not help but imbibe some of the orientalist notions and terms of her place and time. What is significant is not that she occasionally lapsed (from our vantage point of hindsight) into the stereotypes of her day but that she was clear-sighted enough to recognize current national policies and social valuations as prejudicial and unjust and was courageous enough to speak out against them. Furthermore, she turned around the very thing that has been held against her—an English training—to give voice to a people who had no voice. We must also remember that Sui Sin Far was a writer of multilayered visions, all frequently operating at once. Nothing she writes should be interpreted in the absence of context or taken only at its surface, literal level.

Sui Sin Far's stories are significant in many respects. First, they present portraits of turn-of-the-century North American Chinatowns, not in the mode of the "yellow peril" or zealous missionary literature of her era but with well-intentioned and sincere empathy. Second, the stories give voice and protagonist roles to Chinese and Chinese North American women and children, thus breaking the stereotypes of silence, invisibility, and "bachelor societies" that have ignored small but present female populations. Finally, in a period when miscegenation was illegal in nearly half the United States, Sui Sin Far's stories are the first to introduce the plight of the child of Asian and white parents. In making public her ambiguous position between worlds, Sui Sin Far initiated a dialogue between Chinese and European North Americans and their multicultural, multiracial descendants. In giving her "right hand to the Occidentals" and her "left to the Orientals," she not only speaks for Eurasians but also articulates the position of generations of bicultural Asian Americans and Asian Canadians and anticipates that of Asian adoptees into Caucasian families. Many themes that Sui Sin Far's writings introduced a hundred years ago continue to be relevant today: the need for interracial understanding and self-affirmation; the balancing of individual and community needs; the clash between tradition and change in recent immigrant experience; and the between-worlds plight of the racially or culturally mixed person.

    —Amy Ling and Annette White-Parks, "Introduction," *Mrs. Spring Fragrance and Other Writings* by Sui Sin Far (Urbana, IL: University of Illinois Press, 1995), 5–6

AMY LING

If we set Sui Sin Far into the context of her time and place, in late nineteenth-century sinophobic and imperialistic Euro-American nations, then we must admit that for her, a Eurasian woman who could pass as white, to choose to champion the Chinese and working-class women and to identify herself as such, publicly and in print, was an act of great determination and courage. Addressing a predominantly white readership, she had the audacity (to borrow Ammons's word) to tell them, in such stories as "In the Land of the Free" and "'Its Wavering Image,'" that they were racially prejudiced and abused the Chinese and, in such stories as "The Wisdom of the New" and "Pat and Pan," that, though well-meaning, their interference sometimes had tragic consequences.

But most of the stories in Mrs. Spring Fragrance sought to counter the prevailing notions that the Chinese were heathen, unassimilable, hatchet-waving rat eaters and pipe-smoking opium addicts who had no right to live in the United States or Canada. In the title story of the collection, she shows that Chinese have a sense of humor and a liveliness of spirit, that they can play baseball, sing "Drink to Me Only with Thine Eyes," and learn English well enough to dare, as in the story "The Inferior Woman," to write a book about white Americans—a mirror image of what Sui Sin Far herself was doing. She even dared to express the opinion that the Chinese custom of arranged marriages can be a good thing. In such stories as "The God of Restoration" and "Lin John," she demonstrates that the Chinese are capable of incredible patience and hard work. In "The Wisdom of the New," "The Smuggling of Tie Co," and "The Chinese Lily" she writes about Chinese women who make the ultimate sacrifice, which, as Jane Tompkins points out, is the "supreme act of heroism" in the Christian faith and the most powerful act available to the poor and powerless. In defiance of the antimiscegenation laws then common in many states, Sui Sin Far's "Story of One White Woman Who Married a Chinese" and "Her Chinese Husband" lead the reader through the experience of an interracial romance, emphasizing spiritual values and respect for human dignity over insignificant racial differences. "Her Chinese Husband" makes a plea for the social acceptance of Eurasians and stresses the critical importance of their maintaining pride in both halves of their ancestry. The story also shows that the Chinese, too, can be narrow-minded and "hate with a bitter hatred all who would enlighten or be enlightened," for it is Chinese men who kill the story's hero.

"The Wisdom of the New" and "The Americanization of Pau Tsu" are contrasting stories about the adjustment of Chinese wives who, after years of separation, join their Americanized husbands in the United States. In the first, the husband is insensitive to his wife's jealousy of a young, white American woman, Adah Charleton—with tragic results. In the second, the husband understands his wife's reaction to his friendship with a young, white American woman, Adah Raymond, and, protecting his wife, he distances himself from his friend—with, presumably, happy results. That the white women have the same first name, that Adah was the name Winifred gave Edith in Marion: The

Story of an Artist's Model (which is a slightly fictionalized biography of their sister and the Eaton family), that the stories are almost identical except for their endings, and that Edith Eaton/Sui Sin Far taught English in Chinatown lead to speculations about the possible autobiographical nature of this story, but, unfortunately, we have no way of verifying such a hypothesis. Many of these stories have tantalizing depths that remain unplumbed: the cross-dressing theme in "The Smuggling of Tie Co," "Tian Shan's Kindred Spirit," and "A Chinese Boy-Girl"; the self-sacrificial element of "The Chinese Lily," "The Story of a Little Chinese Seabird," and "Lin John"; and the nature of friendship between women in "A Chinese Lily" and "The Sing Song Woman."

    —Amy Ling, "Introduction to Part 1," *Mrs. Spring Fragrance and Other Writings* by Sui Sin Far (Urbana, IL: University of Illinois Press, 1995), 13–14

ANNETTE WHITE-PARKS

It is worth noting that these two articles ("Girl Slave in Montreal: Our Chinese Colony Cleverly Described," 1894, and "Half-Chinese Children: Those of American Mothers and Chinese Fathers," 1895) plus "A Plea for the Chinaman: A Correspondent's Argument in His Favor," published in the *Montreal Daily Star* in 1896, were written during an era of severe Chinese witch-hunts in both Canada and the United States, after each nation had completed the transcontinental railroad. While it was being built, labor contractors had urged people from China to migrate for work, but as soon as their work was finished, there was a flurry of racist laws and social abuse to drive Chinese immigrants out of North America. The 1890s saw the second decade of the Chinese Exclusion Act, passed by the United States government in 1882 to prevent Chinese from entering the country. It also saw the gradual increase in head taxes, initially imposed by the Canadian Parliament in 1885 on Chinese seeking to enter Canada. At the time of "A Plea," there was a petition to increase the tax to five hundred dollars.

    Sui Sin Far's "Plea," cast in letter form but indeed her most persuasive essay, protests this increase and points out the injustice, illogic, and inconsistency when a nation uses the rhetoric of equality yet persecutes people because of their race. Responding to a Mr. Maxwell, the representative of a commission from British Columbia who is pushing the tax, her argument is classic and brilliantly tongue-in-cheek. This writing dramatically illustrates her claim in "Leaves" to have fought the battles of the Chinese in the papers. It is also significant because it is the first located writing where she openly speaks in her own name for the Chinese. Her tone is that of the sympathetic outsider, and she signs the letter "E.E.," initials that stand for "Edith Eaton," the name she is known by professionally; the piece is written while she still lives with her parents and is generally seen as an "English woman." Desmond Wu translated the piece into Chinese in 1992, when approximately three hundred Chinese Canadians rallied on Ottawa's Parliament Hill demanding restitution for the head tax against which "E.E." had protested. The inspiration this letter offered the protesters almost one hundred years after it was originally written testifies to Sui Sin Far's contemporaneity and the continuance of her dream to fight the battles of the Chinese in print.

To appreciate the evolution of Sui Sin Far's ethnic-racial identification, we can compare this letter with "Spring Impressions: A Medley of Poetry and Prose," the seventh in a series of eight sketches she wrote between 1888 and 1890 for the Canadian *Dominion Illustrated*, all signed "Edith Eaton" and with English and French Canadian subjects and settings. Though in these pieces the author shows no literal awareness of the Chinese Canadians and Chinese Americans to whose voices her future writings would be dedicated, there is a continuity in language and theme between these pieces and her later work. Amy Ling interprets "Spring Impressions" as "key to Sui Sin Far's later work," for here the phrase that entitles her 1912 book is first introduced: "When the spring fragrance and freshness fill the air." Further, her empathetic stance toward "those who have suffered wrongs, perchance beyond the righting," anticipate her dedication to a cause larger than herself.

—Annette White-Parks, "Introduction to Part 2," *Mrs. Spring Fragrance and Other Writings* by Sui Sin Far (Urbana, IL: University of Illinois Press, 1995), 171–72

ANNETTE WHITE-PARKS

While reflecting the benign Orientalism emphasized by *Mrs. Spring Fragrance*, reviewers recognized that this author was doing something different from simply offering stereotyped portraits of Chinese immigrant life. The first review, which Sui Sin Far wrote to Charles Lummis "was good to read," appeared on 22 June 1912 in the *Montreal Weekly Witness*. In a response that combined recognition of the volume's Orientalism and "book beautiful" design, the reviewer highlighted the writer's pluralistic identity: "One of the charming gift books of the season comes from the pen of a Canadian Chinese, or half Chinese, woman, whose sympathies range her on the side of the Chinese mother rather than of the English father. 'Mrs. Spring Fragrance,' by Sui Sin Far (Edith Eaton) . . . is a collection of short sketches of Chinese life in the United States and Canada." The words "rather than" emphasize the divisive stance that society has always imposed on Sui Sin Far because of her dual racial parentage. They are prefatory to presenting her as a "Chinese" insider: "Naturally Sui Sin Far can enter into the Chinese thoughts, prejudices, emotions and grievances as no foreigner could do, and yet she understands the friendly attitude of many individuals in the two countries of their adoption towards the Chinese immigrants in contrast with the unfriendly and often heartless treatment meted out to them by the representatives of both governments." The phrase "yet she understands" reinforces the reviewer's point that this Sui Sin Far, understanding of Chinese immigrants though she might be, remains safely in sympathy with the white cultures dominant in both Canada and the United States, if not with the government policies in those countries. It is also apparent that, in contrast to the three U.S. reviewers who claimed Sui Sin Far's sources, inspiration, and identity as part of their nation, the *Montreal Weekly Witness* presented the author of *Mrs. Spring Fragrance* as "a Canadian Chinese, or half Chinese woman."

The second review to appear, on 29 June 1912 in the *Boston Globe*, gave the book three paragraphs. This reviewer also leaned on Orientalist rhetoric in describing the title character Mrs. Spring Fragrance as "that delicious Americanized person" but also recognized that Sui Sin Far's perspective and themes ran counter to literary representations of Chinese or Chinese Americans as alien and threatening: "The tales are told with a sympathy that strikes straight to one's heart; to say they are convincing is weak praise, and they show the Chinese with feelings absolutely indistinguishable from those of white people—only the Chinese seem to have more delicate sensibilities, and more acute methods of handling their problems."

On 7 July 1912 the *New York Times Book Review* devoted one long, substantial paragraph to the book. The reviewer wasted no words on the exotic but rather singled out Sui Sin Far's emphasis on "the lives, thoughts and emotions of the Chinese women who refuse to be anything but intensely Chinese, and . . . the characters of the half-breed children." Despite use of stereotyped language ("half-breed children") and a lack of sensitivity to the complexity of her woman characters (they do not "refuse to be anything but intensely Chinese"), the *Times* review was most astute at observing the unique interracial dialogue opened up by Sui Sin Far's work and its broader significance to literature: "Miss Eaton has struck a new note in American fiction. The thing she has tried to do is to portray for readers of the white race the lives, feelings, sentiments of the Americanized Chinese of the Pacific Coast, of those who have intermarried with them and of the children who have ⟨sprung⟩ from such unions."

The *Independent*, whose editor Sui Sin Far had explicitly acknowledged in both the *Globe* article and a letter to Lummis, did not comment on the book until 15 August 1912, and the comments were only two sentences long:

> Our readers are well acquainted with the dainty stories of Chinese
> life written by Sui Sin Far (Miss Edith Eaton) and will be glad to
> know that those published in THE INDEPENDENT as well in other
> periodicals have been brought together in a volume entitled *Mrs.
> Spring Fragrance* (McClurg; $1.40). The conflict between occidental

and oriental ideals and the hardships of the American immigration
laws furnish the theme for most of the tales and the reader is not only
interested but has his mind widened by becoming acquainted with
novel points of view.

As we might expect from this journal, the remarks clearly recognize the ideological content of the volume, although the reviewer's patronizing assumptions about Chinese immigrants ("novel points of view") and women writers
("dainty stories of Chinese life") are evident.

Even with skillful marketing and positive reviews, it is unlikely that *Mrs.
Spring Fragrance* brought in many financial dividends for either the author or
her publishers. Sui Sin Far's remarks about the book in a 23 March 1912 letter
to Lummis—"I am very tired and hoped to have got some money for it by this
time"—suggest her feelings of continuing financial pressure, as does her wish
regarding her benefactors expressed in the *Globe* article: "I hope soon to be in
a position to repay them." The *Independent's* listed price of $1.40 tells us what
Mrs. Spring Fragrance sold for, but we do not know the author's royalties.
McClurg's initial pressrun consisted of only twenty-five hundred copies, and
there is no evidence of further editions. Part of the reason for the apparently
poor sales was probably that collections of short stories, then as now, were
risky ventures. The deeper reason, I suspect, lay in the nature of *Mrs. Spring
Fragrance's* contents, radical far beyond the ability of its Orientalist frosting to
camouflage or its reviewers to recognize.

—Annette White-Parks, *Sui Sin Far: A Literary Biography* (Urbana, IL: University of Illinois
Press, 1995), 200–2

ANNETTE WHITE-PARKS

To interpret the critical questions of race as Sui Sin Far—and any writer of
non-European heritage—must have encountered them in the imperialist-racist
climate of North America at the turn-of-the-century, we must look at the
options such writers were faced with: 1) to climb into the Procrustean bed the
dominant, European-based culture defined for them, be assimilated and give
up traditional cultures, or 2) to fight back against the discriminatory laws and
attitudes these writers lived with daily as individuals and took stands on as
artists. Sui Sin Far seems never to have doubted that her choice was to fight.
From early childhood, she recalls street battles with other children who
malign her and her siblings for being Eurasian, and writes: "I glory in the idea
of dying at the stake and a great genie arising from the flames and declaring
to those who have scorned us: 'Behold, how great and glorious and noble are
the Chinese people!'" ("Leaves" 127). As an adult, Sui Sin Far relates an actual
confrontation with her dream and tells how she responded. It happened in "a
little town away off on the north shore of a big lake" in the "Middle West,"

when she was lunching with White American acquaintances, including her employer, who perceived her as being racially the same as themselves. Conversation turns to the "cars full of Chinamen that past [sic] that morning" by train, leading to her companions' observations that "I wouldn't have one in my house," and "A Chinaman is, in my eyes, more repulsive than a nigger," and "I cannot reconcile myself to the thought that the Chinese are human like ourselves . . . their faces seem to be so utterly devoid of expression that I cannot help but doubt" ("Leaves" 127).

"A miserable, cowardly feeling keeps me silent," Sui Sin Far recalls, leading us through the agony of her tension as she considered the "strong prejudices against my mother's countrymen," knowing that, if she spoke, "every person in the place will hear about it the next day." She also admitted that "I have no longer an ambition to die at the stake" ("Leaves" 129). Then she lifted her eyes and addressed her employer: "The Chinese may have no souls, no expression on their faces, be altogether beyond the pale of civilization, but whatever they are, I want you to understand that I am—I am a Chinese."

The people at this luncheon table reflect the society in which they are living. It is the decade of the annexation of Hawaii, when America hovers on the verge of a war with the Philippines, a period during which, Ron Takaki observes, racism and expansionism joined hands and climaxed in the Spanish-American War. Value to humans is not assigned by ethnicity, but by such physical features as eye shape and hair texture and skin color—and a religious background that Christian missionaries labeled as "heathen." It is a scene Sui Sin Far, whose Chinese mother had been educated by English missionaries and later married her British father in Shanghai, knew very well. She had played it in England, being pulled aside as a toddler by "a white haired old man" who surveyed her through his eyeglasses and said: "Ah, indeed . . . now I see the difference between her and other children." She had played it in New York, fighting against taunts of "Chinky, Chinky, Chinaman, yellow-face, pig-tail, rat-eater." She had played it in Montréal, where people gazed at her and thirteen brothers and sisters as they "gaze upon strange animals in a menagerie," and the children "seldom leave the house without being armed for conflict." "Why is my mother's race despised?" she had asked, watching her mother and father. "Is she not every bit as good and dear as he?" ("Leaves" 130).

The incomprehensibility of racism was the problem that would pervade Sui Sin Far's fiction. Binding in common all regions that she traversed—England, Canada, the United States—was a ruling Anglo majority in whose eyes words like "freedom," "equality," even "humanity" did not apply to people with skins darker than their own. ⟨. . .⟩

In "The Land of the Free," money becomes the great mediator. Written during an era when the words on the Statue of Liberty grated against the rapacious ethic of laissez-faire in society and naturalism in literature, the title in this story resonates with irony: "Sure, anyone can pull himself up by the boot-straps if he's got what if takes." And part of what it took, Sui Sin Far's fictions pointedly notice, was having a gender and a complexion to match that of members of the Supreme Court. Time moves, at this moment, between the Chinese Exclusion Act of 1882, which bars most Chinese from legally migrat-ing to the United States, and the Alien Land Laws which have been gradually creeping across this nation since 1889, prohibiting Asian immigrants from owning land. In 1903 the Dominion Parliament passed a requirement of $500 in head tax, plus $200 in cash, on most Chinese who wish to get into Canada. In two societies that laud free opportunity, equality is racially qualified and laws are constructed through prejudice.

Repeatedly, in Sui Sin Far's stories, characters from the two races, Chinese and White, act out the drama. The pattern that begins to unfold reveals that it is not only "the law" with which Chinese immigrants to North America must contend, but also the double standard in attitude existing at all personal lev-els. This is illustrated in the short story "Mrs. Spring Fragrance," when Mr. Spring Fragrance, a Chinese-American "curio merchant" who has lived in Seattle for many years, engages in dialogue with his White American neigh-bor: "Haven't you ever heard that all Americans are princes and princesses, and just as soon as a foreigner puts his foot upon our shores, he also becomes of the nobility?" asks the neighbor. "What about my brother in the Detention pen?" retorts Mr. Spring Fragrance. But, the neighbor asserts, "we . . . real Americans are up against that—even more than you. It is against our princi-ples." "I offer the real Americans my consolations that they should be com-pelled to do that which is against their principles," Mr. Spring Fragrance replies.

With paired terms such as "foreigner" and "real Americans," "you" and "our principles," "I" and "their principles," the "us-them" situation becomes clear and provocative. The story's language reflects core and even unconscious differ-ences between these two neighbors, one Chinese and one White, and reveals the lack of understanding in the mouth of the latter. The fact that this young man, "a star student at the University of Washington," sees himself as the Spring Fragrances' friend furthers the irony. Whites, even when well-intended, fail to recognize Chinese as a "real" part of the nation both occupy. Moreover, we notice, Mr. Spring Fragrance is the character with superior knowledge, or insight into the dramatic irony being employed. Even when Whites and Chinese appear to converse, they speak from different sets of assumptions.

—Annette White-Parks, "A Reversal of American Concepts of 'Otherness' in the Fiction of Sui Sin Far," *Melus* 20, no. 1 (Spring 1995): 18–19, 24–25

BIBLIOGRAPHY

Mrs. Spring Fragrance. 1912.
Mrs. Spring Fragrance and Other Writings (edited by Annette White-Parks). 1995.

EUDORA WELTY
1909-

EUDORA WELTY was born on April 13, 1909, in Jackson, Mississippi, where she lives to this day, having left for only a few years (to get her B.A. from the University of Wisconsin in 1929 and then to take advertising courses at Columbia University). Her first and last job before becoming a a self-supporting author was as a publicity agent for the Works Progress Administration (WPA). Welty's first collection of short stories, *A Curtain of Green* (1941), reflects some of what would become enduring themes in her fiction: an emphasis on people who are "outsiders" either physically or mentally, a concern with the South and its traditions, and an awareness of the complex emotional currents than run through all families. These short stories led many readers and reviewers to compare Welty with Faulkner, just as later they would connect her with O'Connor, on the basis of each writer's use of the grotesque, the Gothic, and dark humor. Ironically, Welty rejects such labels, insisting that such categories are overly simplified and limiting.

Much of Welty's subsequent fiction, both short stories and novels, reflects her interest in classical mythology. Her 1942 novella, *The Robber Bridegroom*, is a light piece that experiments with blending fairy tales, legends, and history. She continued with this theme in a later collection of stories, *The Golden Apples* (1949). The family takes center stage in many of Welty's novels, particularly *Delta Wedding* (1946), one of her best-known novels. This novel, which depicts the events preceding a wedding in a large southern family, illustrates Welty's concern with the oral tradition, particularly the way family stories are passed on. *Delta Wedding* also reveals the precision with which Welty renders southern dialects, and her unerring eye for detail. This same precision and eye for detail can be seen visually in the book of photographs she published in 1989, the culmination of a life-long passion for photography.

After publishing a novella, *The Ponder Heart*, in 1954, and a collection of stories in 1955, Welty published almost nothing for the next fifteen years. Her time was, for the most part, occupied with caring for her sick mother, who died in 1966 after a long illness. Her 1972 novel, *The Optimist's Daughter*, which won the Pulitzer Prize, is her most autobiographical work. She is, however, an intensely private person, who has not yet authorized a biography or released her personal papers, claiming that she wants to be judged on her work alone.

Welty did not often address the racial unrest that plagued the country during the Civil Rights era. She wrote in an essay that the fiction writer's job is to reveal in fiction life as it is, rather than pontificate about life as it should be. In 1963, however, after Medgar Evers was shot in Jackson, Mississippi, Welty wrote several short stories ("Where Is the Voice Coming From?" and "The Demonstrator," among others) that revealed not only her horror at the assassination but also the terrifying and distorted logic that fuels racism and bigotry. As a result of her achievements in fiction, Welty has been awarded almost every major literary prize, including several Guggenheim Fellowships, the President's Medal of Freedom, the National Institute of Arts and Letters Gold Medal, and the National Medal for Literature. She was also awarded France's highest award for a writer, the Chevalier de l'Ordre des Arts and Lettres.

CRITICAL EXTRACTS

KATHERINE ANNE PORTER

Not being in a hurry, Miss Welty was past twenty-six years when she offered her first story, "The Death of a Traveling Salesman," to the editor of a little magazine unable to pay, for she could not believe that anyone would buy a story from her; the magazine was *Manuscript*, the editor John Rood, and he accepted it gladly. Rather surprised, Miss Welty next tried the *Southern Review*, where she met with a great welcome and the enduring partisanship of Albert Erskine, who regarded her as his personal discovery. The story was "A Piece of News" it was followed by others published in the *Southern Review*, the *Atlantic Monthly*, and *Harper's Bazaar*.

She has, then, never been neglected, never unappreciated, and she feels simply lucky about it. She wrote to a friend: "When I think of Ford Madox Ford! You remember how you gave him my name and how he tried his best to find a publisher for my book of stories all that last year of his life; and he wrote me so many charming notes, all of his time going to this little brood of promising writers, the kind of thing that could have gone on forever. Once I read in the *Saturday Review* an article of his on the species and the way they were neglected by publishers, and he used me as the example chosen at random. He ended his cry with 'What is to become of both branches of Anglo-Saxondom if this state of things continues?' Wasn't that wonderful, really, and typical? I may have been more impressed by that than would other readers who knew him. I did not know him, but I knew it was typical. And here I myself have turned out to be not at all the martyred promising writer, but have had all the good luck and all the good things Ford chided the world for withholding from me and my kind."

But there is a trap lying just ahead, and all short-story writers know what it is—The Novel. That novel which every publisher hopes to obtain from every short-story writer of any gifts at all, and who finally does obtain it, nine times out of ten. Already publishers have told her, "Give us first a novel, and then we will publish your short stories." It is a special sort of trap for poets, too, though quite often a good poet can and does write a good novel. Miss Welty has tried her hand at novels, laboriously, dutifully, youthfully thinking herself perhaps in the wrong to refuse, since so many authoritarians have told her that was the next step. It is by no means the next step. She can very well become a master of the short story, there are almost perfect stories in this book. It is quite possible she can never write a novel, and there is no reason why she should. The short story is a special and difficult medium, and contrary to a widely spread popular superstition it has no formula that can be taught by correspondence school. There is nothing to hinder her from writing novels if she wishes or believes she can. I only say that her good gift, just as it is now, alive and flourishing, should not be retarded by a perfectly artificial demand upon her to do the conventional thing. It is a fact that the public for short stories is smaller than the public for novels; this seems to me no good reason for depriving that minority. I remember a reader writing to an editor, complaining that he did not like collections of short stories because, just as he had got himself worked into one mood or frame of mind, he was called upon to change to another. If that is an important objection, we might also apply it to music. We might compare the novel to a symphony, and a collection of short stories to a good concert recital. In any case, this complainant is not our reader, yet our reader does exist, and there would be more of him if more and better short stories were offered.

These stories offer an extraordinary range of mood, pace, tone, and variety of material. The scene is limited to a town the author knows well; the farthest reaches of that scene never go beyond the boundaries of her own state, and many of the characters are of the sort that caused a Bostonian to remark that he would not care to meet them socially. Lily Daw is a half-witted girl in the grip of social forces represented by a group of earnest ladies bent on doing the best thing for her, no matter what the consequences. Keela, the Outcast Indian Maid, is a crippled little Negro who represents a type of man considered most unfortunate by W. B. Yeats: one whose experience was more important than he, and completely beyond his powers of absorption. But the really unfortunate man in this story is the ignorant young white boy, who had inno-

cently assisted at a wrong done the little Negro, and for a most complex reason, finds that no reparation is possible, or even desirable to the victim. . . .
The heroine of "Why I Live at the P. O." is a terrifying case of dementia prae-
cox. In this first group—for the stories may be loosely classified on three separate levels—the spirit is satire and the key grim comedy. Of these, "The
Petrified Man" offers a fine clinical study of vulgarity—vulgarity absolute,
chemically pure, exposed mercilessly to its final subhuman depths. Dullness,
bitterness, rancor, self-pity, baseness of all kinds, can be most interesting material for a story provided these are not also the main elements in the mind of
the author. There is nothing in the least vulgar or frustrated in Miss Welty's
mind. She has simply an eye and an ear sharp, shrewd, and true as a tuning
fork. She has given to this little story all her wit and observation, her blister-
ing humor and her just cruelty; for she has none of that slack tolerance or sentimental tenderness toward symptomatic evils that amounts to criminal
collusion between author and character. Her use of this material raises the
quite awfully sordid little tale to a level above its natural habitat, and its realism seems almost to have the quality of caricature, as complete realism so
often does. Yet, as painters of the grotesque make only detailed reports of
actual living types observed more keenly than the average eye is capable of
observing, so Miss Welty's little human monsters are not really caricatures at
all, but individuals exactly and clearly presented: which is perhaps a case
against realism, if we cared to go into it. She does better on another level—
for the important reason that the themes are richer—in such beautiful stories
as "Death of a Traveling Salesman," "A Memory," "A Worn Path." Let me admit
a deeply personal preference for this particular kind of story, where external
act and the internal voiceless life of the human imagination almost meet and
mingle on the mysterious threshold between dream and waking, one reality
refusing to admit or confirm the existence of the other, yet both conspiring
toward the same end. This is not easy to accomplish, but it is always worth
trying, and Miss Welty is so successful at it, it would seem her most familiar
territory.

—Katherine Anne Porter, *A Curtain of Green*: "Introduction," *A Curtain of Green* by Eudora
Welty (New York: Doubleday: 1941), excerpted in *Modern Critical Views: Eudora Welty*, ed.
Harold Bloom (New York: Chelsea House Publishers, 1986), 14–16

JOHN EDWARD HARDY

The reputation of Eudora Welty is beginning to outrun criticism of her work.
We need something comprehensive in the way of a study, something less hasty
than the review and something at once more objective and not so essentially
condescending as the *bon voyage* essay. Wherever it was she was going, I think

it will be generally agreed that Miss Welty has by now arrived—perhaps for the second or third time—and it would be no longer very discerning to treat the seasoned traveler as if she were the young Isabel Archer.

But, such is the nature of her work itself, a study that is to be really comprehensive must be most particular. We will have to take one thing—or one thing at a time, anyway. The Welty reader too should be lessoned with the characterizing refrain-phrase of E. M. Forster's little essay on Virginia Woolf—"one thing—one." And the one thing I want to consider here is *Delta Wedding*. A great many critics seem to think that Miss Welty is at her best in the shorter forms; and perhaps she feels so too, to judge from the continued emphasis of her work. But this novel, it seems to me, is not only still the biggest thing, but still the most rigidly restricted, disciplined. It has most characteristically developed that sense of the symbolic particularity of things, of a place and a time and people, which can make the good regionalist the most universal of artists—or of novelists, at any rate. It is the most "one"—whole.

I mean to suggest, then, that the most important thing about the novel is its formal structure. But if the nature of its design has, perhaps, escaped many readers, the reasons are not hard to find. There is considerable prejudice against a "serious" novelist's treating material of this kind with such an attitude of sympathy as Miss Welty assumes. Certainly it was obvious from the start, to a reader with any sensitivity at all, that *Delta Wedding* was not simply another Mississippi plantation, "historical" novel, designed for a bosom-and-columns dust jacket. But, if the author's irony is felt from the first sentence, its essence is very subtle. And the patience of a good many of the liberal reviewers a few years ago was pretty short.

If Miss Welty wasn't starry-eyed in quite the usual way about "the South," she wasn't indignant either, or even decently tough and realistic now and again. She had distinctly her own version of what Wyndham Lewis called Faulkner's "whippoorwill tank"; but it might have seemed only unfortunately less manageable than his. The novel *was*, after all, historical—that its time was only about twenty and not seventy-five or a hundred years past was calculated to allay suspicion only slightly. Few eyebrows were raised particularly over the treatment of the Negroes in the novel; but they might well have been. The darkies were sometimes just a little too charmingly typical. And where the attitude went beyond one of placid acceptance—this remains, I think, one of the most genuinely distressing flaws of the novel—it often became only half-heartedly apologetic, with a rather strong suggestion of the old "well, at least they had *status*" routine. What Miss Welty could do with Negroes at her best in some of the short stories seemed rather sadly absent here. And one could go only so far in justifying it on grounds of dramatic propriety, that the author was bound to the point-of-view of the white characters of the story; simply for purposes of realism, it might easily have been made a little *more* apparent how severely restricted that outlook was in this regard.

And yet the immediate inferences from all this are, clearly, not correct. And perhaps the best way of getting at *why* they are not correct is simply to allow the novel to establish for itself the perspective in which we are to look at its features.

One has first to see that Miss Welty is not taking *any* attitude toward "the South." The story is about the Delta, at the most—not the South, not even Mississippi. Yankees, of course, are unthinkable; but Ellen, the Virginian, is acutely conscious all her life of *her* difference from the Delta family she mothers. And the circle is drawn even closer; Troy Flavin, who is largely responsible for the significance of the wedding as a symbol of threatened disruption, is alien by virtue of being a *hill-country* Mississippian. And (disregarding for the moment Laura McRaven, whose case is rather special), Robbie Reid, whom the family wisely regard as a far greater threat to the insularity of their world even than Troy, is foreign as a native of the *town* of Fairchilds, as distinguished from the plantation.

The psychological basis of the relationship of the characters one to another here is simple enough, of course. The barrier between Robbie Reid and the Fairchilds is greatest for several reasons—simply that she is a woman, that she is the unworthy wife of the darling of the family, but most important of all, that she *is* a lifelong near neighbor. In any society, of course, class distinctions are always, though ironically, most keenly appreciated by native members of the immediate community. Troy Flavin, not so much out of mere stupidity as simply because his origins are more remote, finds nothing so terribly formidable in the family he is "marrying into"—as he puts it with a confidence which dismays and amuses those who know the Fairchilds. And in the face of his naïve assurance, the family are fairly constrained to be gentle with him, though they make little effort to hide their feelings from Dabney. But the point I want to make just now is that this narrowing of the circle is carried so far that it finally excludes emphasis upon the kind of typicality, the true provincialism, in character and situation, which is characteristic of the commonplace regional novel. The Fairchilds are finally most typical, if at all, in their very singularity. And it is at this point that the principle of exclusiveness almost ceases, or for the readers purposes in understanding the novel ought almost to cease, to be social principle at all. It becomes, rather, the *formal* principle, and the principle of sensibility, in a version of pastoral which has been before only vaguely hinted at in the Southern novel.

Miss Welty's awareness of the classic elements of pastoral in the situation she is dealing with is quite evident. One may take as an initial statement of the conventional "paradox" of pastoral, the familiar principle of inversion of values, one of Laura's early reflections—"Jackson was a big town, with twenty-five thousand people, and Fairchilds was just a store and a gin and a bridge and one big house, yet she was the one who felt like a little country cousin when she arrived."

But it is just the awareness it reveals which is most important about a passage like this. What it says, the statement of the pastoral "formula" in these terms, is only a starting point. The tradition of the Southern novel has been all but exclusively pastoral from the start, of course—and in a great many different ways, both naturalistic and romantic. But there has been before no such fully *conscious* exploring of the implications of the mode as Miss Welty's, an insight which finally carries beyond the significance of the form for the *mores* of the society which produced it.

—John Edward Hardy, "*Delta Wedding* as Region and Symbol," *The Sewanee Review* 60, no. 3 (Summer 1952), excerpted in *Modern Critical Views: Eudora Welty*, ed. Harold Bloom (New York: Chelsea House Publishers, 1986), 29–31

ROBERT PENN WARREN

If this general line of interpretation is correct, we find that the stories represent variations on the same basic theme, on the contrasts already enumerated. It is not that there is a standard resolution for the contrasts which is repeated from story to story; rather, the contrasts, being basic, are not susceptible of a single standard resolution, and there is an implicit irony in Miss Welty's work. But if we once realize this, we can recognize that the contrasts are understood not in mechanical but in vital terms: the contrasts provide the terms of human effort, for the dream must be carried to, submitted to, the world, innocence to experience, love to knowledge, knowledge to fact, individuality to communion. What resolution is possible is, if I read the stories with understanding, in terms of the vital effort. The effort is a "mystery," because it is in terms of the effort, doomed to failure but essential, that the human manifests itself as human. Again and again, in different forms, we find what we find in Joel of "First Love": "Joel would never know now the true course, or the true outcome of any dream: this was all he felt. But he walked on, in the frozen path into the wilderness, on and on. He did not see how he could ever go back and still be the boot-boy at the Inn."

It is possible that, in trying to define the basic issue and theme of Miss Welty's stories, I have made them appear too systematic, too mechanical. I do not mean to imply that her stories should be read as allegories, with a neat point-to-point equating of image and idea. It is true that a few of her stories, such as "The Wide Net," do approach the limit of allegory, but even in such cases we find rather than the system of allegory a tissue of symbols which emerge from, and disappear into, a world of scene and action which, once we discount the author's special perspective, is recognizable in realistic terms. The method is similar to the method of much modern poetry, and to that of much modern fiction and drama, but at the same time it is a method as old as fable, myth, and parable. It is a method by which the items of fiction (scene, action, character, etc.) are presented not as document but as comment, not as a report but as a thing made, not as history but as idea. Even in the most realistic and reportorial fiction, the social picture, the psychological analysis, and the pattern of action do not rest at the level of mere report; they finally operate as expressive symbols as well.

Fiction may be said to have two poles, history and idea, and the emphasis may be shifted very far in either direction. In the present collection the emphasis has been shifted very far in the direction of idea, but at the same time there remains a sense of the vividness of the actual world: the picnic of "The Wide Net" is a real picnic as well as a "journey," Cash of "Livvie" is a real field hand in his Easter clothes as well as a field god. In fact, it may be said that when the vividness of the actual world is best maintained, when we get the sense of one picture superimposed upon another, different and yet somehow the same, the stories are most successful.

The stories which fail are stories like "The Purple Hat" and "Asphodel," in which the material seems to be manipulated in terms of an idea, in which the relation between the image and the vision has become mechanical, in which there is a strain, in which we do find the kind of hocus-pocus deplored by Diana Trilling.

And this brings us back to the criticism that the volume "has tremendous emotional impact, despite its obscurity," that the "fear" it engenders is "in inverse ratio to its rational content." Now it seems to me that this description does violence to my own experience of literature, that we do not get any considerable emotional impact unless we sense, at the same time, some principle of organization, some view, some meaning. This does not go to say that we have to give an abstract formulation to that principle or view or meaning before we can experience the impact of the work, but it does go to say that it is implicit in the work and is having its effect upon us in immediate aesthetic terms. Furthermore, in regard to the particular work in question, I do not feel that it is obscure. If anything, the dreamlike effect in many of the stories seems to result from the author's undertaking to squeeze meaning from the item which, in ordinary realistic fiction, would be passed over with a casual glance. Hence the portentousness, the retardation, the otherworldliness. For Miss Welty is like the girl in "A Memory":

> from any observation I would conclude that a secret of life had been nearly revealed to me, and from the smallest gesture of a stranger I would wrest what was to me a communication or a presentiment.

In many cases, as a matter of fact, Miss Welty has heavily editorialized her fiction. She wants us to get that smallest gesture, to participate in her vision of things as intensely meaningful. And so there is almost always a gloss to the fable.

One more word: it is quite possible that Miss Welty has pushed her method to its most extreme limit. It is also possible that the method, if pursued much farther, would lead to monotony and self-imitation and merely decorative elaboration. Perhaps we shall get a fuller drama when her vision is submitted more daringly to fact, when the definition is plunged into the devouring river. But meanwhile Miss Welty has given us stories of brilliance and intensity; and as for the future, Miss Welty is a writer of great resourcefulness, sensitivity, and intelligence, and can probably fend for herself.

—Robert Penn Warren, "Love and Separateness in Eudora Welty," *Selected Essays* (New York: Random House, 1958), excerpted in *Modern Critical Views: Eudora Welty*, ed. Harold Bloom (New York: Chelsea House Publishers, 1986), 26–28

JOYCE CAROL OATES

In "The Demonstrators"—the O. Henry First Prize story of 1968—the lonely consciousness of an ordinary, good man is seen in a context of greater, more violent loneliness, the terrible general failure of mankind. The demonstrators themselves, the civil rights agitators, do not appear in the story and need not appear; their intrusion into the supposedly placid racist society of this small Southern town is only symbolic. They too are not to be trusted, idealistic as they sound. Another set of demonstrators—demonstrating our human powerlessness as we disintegrate into violence—are the Negroes of the town, a choral and anonymous group with a victim at their theatrical center, one of themselves and yet a curious distance from them, in her death agony.

The story begins with the semi-colloquial "Near eleven o'clock" and concerns itself at first with the forceful, colorful personality of an aged woman, Miss Marcia Pope. Subject to seizures as she is, crotchety and wise in the stereotyped manner of such old dying ladies, she is nevertheless the only person in town "quite able to take care of herself," as the doctor thinks at the conclusion of the story; a great deal has happened between the first and last paragraphs. The doctor's mission is to save a young Negro woman, who has been stabbed by her lover with an ice pick; his attempt is hopeless, the woman is bleeding internally, too much time has been wasted. And so she dies. The doctor goes home and we learn that he himself is living a kind of death, since his wife has left him; his wife left him because their thirteen-year-old daughter, an idiot, had died. . . . everything is linked to everything else, one person to another, one failure to another, earlier, equally irremediable failure. The doctor is "so increasingly tired, so sick and even bored with the bitterness, intractability that divided everybody and everything." The tragedy of life is our permanence of self, of Ego: but this is also our hope, in Miss Welty's phrase our "assault of hope," throwing us back into life.

The next morning he reads of the deaths of the Negro lovers, who managed to kill each other. The homespun newspaper article concludes, "No cause was cited for the fracas." The doctor had not failed to save the Negro woman and man because there was never the possibility of their being saved. There was never the possibility of his daughter growing up. Of the strange failure of his marriage nothing much is said, yet it too seems irreparable. But, as he looks into the garden, he distinguishes between those flowers which are "done for" and those which are still "bright as toys." And two birds pick in the devastation of leaves, apparently permanent residents of the garden, "probing and feeding."

"The Demonstrators" resists analysis. It is a small masterpiece of subtlety, of gentleness—a real gentleness of tone, a reluctance to exaggerate or even to highlight drama, as if sensing such gestures alien to life. We are left with an unforgettable sense of the permanence and the impermanence of life, and especially of the confused web of human relationships that constitute most of our lives. The mother of the dying Negro girl warns her, "I ain't going to raise him," speaking of the girl's baby. Of course she is going to raise him. There is no question about it. But the warning itself, spoken in that room of unfocussed horror, is horrible; the grotesque has been assimilated deftly into the ordinary, the natural.

It is an outstanding characteristic of Miss Welty's genius that she can write a story that seems to me, in a way, about "nothing"—Flaubert's ideal, a masterpiece of style—and make it mean very nearly everything.

—Joyce Carol Oates, "The Art of Eudora Welty," *Shenandoah* 20 (Spring 1969), excerpted in *Modern Critical Views: Eudora Welty*, ed. Harold Bloom (New York: Chelsea House Publishers, 1986), 72–74

REYNOLDS PRICE

⟨Reynolds Price⟩ Are you aware, as you turn from writing fiction to prose essays, of different problems? Are they two entirely different processes for you?

⟨Eudora Welty⟩ I think of writing stories as going *south* and writing essays as going *north*.

R.P. Against the wind?

E.W. No, just two different directions—upstream and downstream. I can't work on them simultaneously. I like both. I think it's more natural to me to write stories, but I like writing essays. I think I'm not a born critic, but I may be a born appreciator. I like to write about things I like.

R.P. The liking is steadily reflected in this present selection from nearly 35 years of essays and reviews. With the single exception of your review of a biography of Ford Madox Ford (a writer you do admire), you haven't written about any writer or any thing that you haven't at least 90 percent liked. Has that been a conscious choice?

E.W. Yes, it has. I don't accept the review of a book that I know I'll dislike. I don't enjoy it. I really write for pleasure in reviewing as much as I write for pleasure in writing stories. I like the work of doing it, so I prefer to write about something that strikes my imagination or that I can admire. I felt at one time that I should have written a preface to this book to say that the essays and reviews weren't written with a whole in mind—since I'm not a professional critic, I don't write to compare one person with another person. I write each one only about that subject. I wasn't setting out to put Willa Cather and Jane Austen into their related levels of excellence.

R.P. Some hierarchy of genius.

E.W. That is not my way of reading or thinking or anything else. I like each thing for what it is. But I didn't think it was necessary to explain that; anyone would see it if they began to read. I only regret, even though I chose these out of a great number, that I'd never written some that I wish I had—on P. G. Wodehouse, V. S. Pritchett, Edward Lear, travel books about places that I love. I wish I could have written more; I still intend to just because I love them.

R.P. Have you ever wished you could make a statement against a book? Have you ever felt that a book was dangerous and should be combatted?

E.W. I don't feel like setting up as a moral judge of anything—no, I don't. I never felt that any book was dangerous, that I can think of right off the bat. (However, my mother thought that the Elsie Dinsmore Series books would be dangerous for me and forbade them to me as a child.) I don't feel that it's up to me to pronounce judgment on whether somebody should have *written* a book; *that* would be dangerous. It's O.K. with me for people to write anything; I don't have to read it or *agree* with a word.

R.P. Whenever I read a book by a good writer, I'm always fascinated when I think I begin to discover the one word that's recurring, almost unconsciously, as a kind of secret motto or emblem for the book. The word I noticed most frequently, even in this selection from years of work, is *radiance* in its various forms. It recurs a dozen or so times and clusters round the writers who seem closest to you, both as reader and writer—Jane Austen, Chekhov, Willa Cather, E. M. Forster, Katherine Anne Porter, Henry Green, Elizabeth Bowen. And it seems to me that the word contains and summarizes an important theme of all the essays—that the writer *is* a visionary, whose gift is a gift of actual and internal vision; that the writer is someone who both sees and radiates. Well, the point of the speech I seem to be making is this—have you found in your own writing of fiction that a story comes to you entire or do you find that you get a piece, a *glimpse*, and that the story radiates from there; that it manufactures itself around a fragment of vision?

E.W. I never had thought about it as seeing it from a *piece*, but of course that may precede the way I think of myself as seeing it. I do *see* a story, feel a story, as a whole before I ever begin the process of thinking how to work it out; and, as you know, I do a lot of revision, but it's always toward getting closer to the original—I hate to use the word *vision* in relation to my process of writing—the original perception of what it is I want to do. It *is* a whole, but also, if it has any vitality, it allows changing in working toward it. It has to be flexible. To be alive it has to remain always capable of moving and growing itself, in the work. I didn't know I used the word *radiance* all the time; but I can understand why I might have—having a visual mind (literally visual) and a pretty good observing eye, through having trained it over the years. But the way of perception, that a writer must learn, is also an act of vision; and it's the act you can recognize in the writer you're reading—it's like visions meeting (isn't it?), which is what you seek.

R.P. Yes, and more—as your uses of *radiance* began to mount, I came to feel that the essays combined to advance a concept of the great writer as a kind of nuclear power plant, a large center of energy, radiating for us; and that the nuclear fuel is love, a deep tender fascination with human life.

E.W. That *is* what it is. It goes to the center of my being, my feeling for what I've read. It's a *vital* force.

R.P. Well, you know I agree; but it's worth considering that there almost always have been sizable writers who could hardly be said to work out of love for the human species and that there are many such younger writers working today. Perhaps you and I and certain writers in older traditions had kinds of *luck* which made tenderness come more naturally to us than it does to young people today.

E.W. I think that's absolutely true. I don't think we ever questioned it. What young writers are doing today is questioning. They tend to doubt the truth of something that doesn't hurt pretty badly; there's a sort of distressing feeling that if you admire or like something, there's a *lie* in it somewhere—either in it or in yourself—which is such a frightening prospect when you think of all that can be missed out of life if you can't embrace a little more of it than comes in through such a narrow squint-hole, like the leper's squint in a church. Not like Swift! He hated but saw everything. I feel now sometimes that so much is being left out, and so many young writers feel that their proper place is one of isolation from what they're writing about that there's no sense of anything *joining*. I'm not saying this in a condemnatory way, but in a concerned way, though I do often get the terrible feeling "How facile!"

 —Reynolds Price, "Eudora Welty in Type and Person," *The New York Times Book Review* (7 May 1978) reprinted in *Conversations with Eudora Welty*, ed. Peggy Whitman Prenshaw (New York: Random House, 1984), 230–32

CLEANTH BROOKS

Losing Battles is Miss Welty's most profound and most powerfully moving account of the folk society. In it we listen to a whole clan gathered for the birthday of its matriarch, great-grandmother Vaughn, and we hear them talk from the dawn of one day to near midnight and later on into the afternoon of the following day. It is wonderfully rich and exuberant talk and there are a variety of voices: male and female, gentle and quiet or aggressive and domineering, querulous and argumentative or ironic and conciliatory; but they are all voices of the folk and speak the characteristic folly or wisdom, joy or melancholy, of such a community. ⟨. . .⟩

 The truth of the matter is that *Losing Battles* is in spirit a kind of Tall Tale of the Old Southwest. Indeed, the action is so violent and some of the coincidences so improbable that it needs its folk language and sayings and ways for the actions depicted to pass muster as credible. Pass muster they do, for by virtue of its folk characters and the language they speak, the novel strikes the reader as being itself a kind of folk tale—bardic, outrageously strange, almost epic in its happenings.

 A second qualification that I want to make is this: in spite of the seriousness with which Eudora Welty takes this folk culture, she does not sentimentalize it. She does not make it too good to be true. If the clan loyalties of the Beechams and the Renfros are admirable and excite the envy of us modern readers who tend to be alienated, lacking in family ties, and lonely in our unhappy self-sufficiency, Miss Welty makes it plain that the pressure of this great extended Renfro family can be suffocating. Gloria wants to have Jack to herself. During his long absence she has tried to find a little privacy in this busy, cluttered, almost too tightly related tribe. Even after she has had revealed to her that her father was a Renfro too, she yearns to get away from Jack's vast family. As the novel ends, she is still saying: "And some day, some day, yet, we'll move to ourselves. And there'll be just you and me and Lady May." Lady May is their baby girl.

This counter note, this glimpse at the other side of the matter, is the necessary pinch of salt. The strength of family ties is touching, and the loyalties of the clan may well rouse in the modern a certain homesickness for a world that many of us have lost. But Miss Welty is not writing a tract in defense of the extended family. Rather, she is dramatizing such a family, and in doing so she is telling the truth about it. The virtues are there, but the Renfros have the defects of their virtues. ⟨. . .⟩

A folk community is usually uneasy in the presence of those who exalt the written word, and in this regard Miss Welty's Banner community is not special. ⟨. . .⟩

Such is the uneasy truce that is struck between the representatives of the oral and the written traditions. And I can be sympathetic with the fears that plague the child of the oral tradition. He has good reason to guard his innocence. Thus the Renfros, who instinctively flinch from the sophistications of the great world outside, see the school teacher as the prime agent of that studiedly artificial world. As we have earlier remarked, Yeats believed that members of the unwritten oral tradition had cause to be wary in the presence of the evangelists of the printed world. But Yeats knew also that the genuine artist does not threaten the oral tradition of the folk.

The genuine artist, though aware of the limitations of the unwritten tradition, respects it. He appreciates its honesty and its other basic virtues. He knows that these virtues are not really antagonistic to the virtues of the great written tradition. He remembers that Homer, the father of the poetry of Western civilization, was himself a poet of the oral tradition, even though he was to become the very cornerstone of the written tradition.

The genuine artist not only respects and admires the oral tradition; he knows how to use it, how to incorporate it into the written, and thus how to give it an enduring life.

Eudora Welty is just such an artist, for in her work one finds a true wedding of the two diverse but not hostile traditions. It is as such an artist that I salute her on this happy occasion.

—Cleanth Brooks, "Eudora Welty and the Southern Idiom," *Eudora Welty: A Form of Thanks* (Jackson: University Press of Mississippi, 1979), excerpted in *Modern Critical Views: Eudora Welty*, ed. Harold Bloom (New York: Chelsea House Publishers, 1986), 102, 104–7

PATRICIA MEYER SPACKS

Eudora Welty, writing mainly of the experience of white Southerners, uses and merges mythologizing talk about past and present, exploiting both comic and serious possibilities. Reading through *The Collected Stories*, one encounters a series of distinctive and powerful voices, voices participating often in shifting patterns of conversation, voices that sometimes speak directly to the reader, sometimes talk to themselves. The stories contain diverse characters, settings, and events; although theme and character link some, others bear no obvious connection to one another. Yet, reading them together, one feels in touch with a community. The voices comment on one another, weaving a rich linguistic texture and affirming the necessity and the vitality and the creativity of talking about people. ⟨. . .⟩

In the culture Welty evokes, people talk constantly about one another, generating legends even of the present. Present and past often merge, for Welty as for Faulkner. Miss Katie Rainey, "the old lady that watches the turn of the road" until her death, figures in "The Wanderers" (1949) as one who not only sees but hears. The voices she hears come from her imagination. They tell contemporary truth, yet belong to the past; they speak of human recurrence. She waits for her daughter, past forty now, and she listens:

> Waiting, she heard circling her ears like the swallows beginning, talk about lovers. Circle by circle it twittered, church talk, talk in the store and post office, vulgar man talk possibly in the barbershop. Talk she could never get near now was coming to her.
> "So long as the old lady's alive, it's all behind her back."
> "Daughter wouldn't run off and leave her, she's old and crippled."
> "Left once, will again."
> "That fellow Mabry's been taking out his gun and leaving Virgie a bag of quail every other day. Anybody can see him go by the back door." . . .
> "I declare." . . .
> "Oh, sure. Fate Rainey's a clean shot, too."
> "But ain't he heard?"
> Not Fate Rainey at all; but Mr. Mabry. It was just the talk Miss Katie heard was in voices of her girlhood, and some times they slipped.

Fate Rainey is Miss Katie's dead husband; Mr. Mabry is courting her daughter. Her own experience and her daughter's merge as she listens to the voices of her community, voices of fantasy. "I been by myself all day," she tells her daughter, Virgie: yet this world hardly allows isolation. The community and its voices interpenetrate all experience. Miss Katie expresses truth to herself in the guise of imagined gossip.

The constant impingement on the individual of the community's voices and judgments becomes Virgie's preoccupation when left alone by her mother's death. The account of rituals and ceremonies surrounding the death, of people coming to the house of mourning and of what they say, occupies much of the story. Then Virgie, finally alone, drives to a neighboring village, looks at a cemetery, sits in the rain. Her meditations recall other people's insistent opinions. She remembers a man buried in the cemetery who "lived in another part of the world," leaving for a time, keeping his own secrets, yet never avoiding persistent assessment by those of his home place. Virgie avoids an encounter with Mr. Mabry, walking in the rain, who fails to see her because she wishes not to be seen. "She watched him march by. Then she was all to herself." She thinks about the extreme difficulty, perhaps the impossibility, of being all to oneself. Remembering a picture of Perseus with the head of Medusa, she thinks about that too. "Cutting off the Medusa's head was the heroic act, perhaps, that made visible a horror in love, Virgie thought—the separateness." Horror, yet also goal. With a black woman holding a hen, Virgie sits under a tree in the rain. "Then she and the old beggar woman, the old black thief, were there alone and together in the shelter of the big public tree, listening to the magical percussion, the world beating in their ears. They heard through falling rain the running of the horse and bear, the stroke of the leopard, the dragon's crusty slither, and the glimmer and the trumpet of the swan."

Both alone and together at the story's end, Virgie and the black woman "hear" natural creatures—not so natural either, in the rural South: animals of legend, rather, imaginable out of literary tradition—in much the same way that Virgie's mother has earlier "heard" voices of the community. Isolation, separation are temporary constructions at best. In fictive isolation, the woman conjures up the alternative community of an imagined animal creation. Those surrounding Virgie in her everyday life are busybodies, compulsive interferers with and talkers about others; they will not leave her alone. Yet to live alone would be, after all, a horror. The gossip that plagues Virgie, the town's compulsive interest in the affairs of others, also affirms necessary connection: an arrangement of things superior to any imaginable alternative. Even the vision of running animals in their beauty and freedom gains intensity of being shared, if only silently.

—Patricia Meyer Spacks, "Gossip and Community in Eudora Welty," *Gossip* (New York: Knopf, 1985), excerpted in *Modern Critical Views: Eudora Welty*, ed. Harold Bloom (New York: Chelsea House Publishers, 1985), 155–58

PETER SCHMIDT

These hidden sibylline powers are traditionally associated with oral rather than written authority—song rather than text, inspiration and improvisation rather than imitation. In Domenichino's most famous painting of a sibyl, for example, a new, handwritten scroll is juxtaposed against an ancient printed text. Translated, the scroll in the picture reads, "One God, Who Alone Is Supremely Great [and] Unborn." The sibyl appears to have just been inspired by these words, then to have written them down on a scroll. Although they have been received later than the bound script on which they rest, as a kind of orally dictated supplement, the sibyl's words in fact overthrow, or at least challenge, the authority of the earlier text. Representing the moment of *furor divinus* or divine inspiration, such a sibylline text overturns the traditional Western investing of greatest authority in written and codified texts. It celebrates the potentially subversive and revisionary prowess of oral discourse, seeing it as a return to the original, oral authority of God's Word. ⟨. . .⟩

At their deepest, most powerful level, the sibylline scenes of instruction in Eudora Welty's short stories teach the woman involved how to recover the lost authority of oral discourse and transcribe it into new and subversive written discourse. Characters such as Phoenix Jackson, Powerhouse, and Ruby Fisher in *A Curtain of Green* celebrate the power of oral rather than written language, and heroines like the cornet player in "The Winds," Easter in "Moon Lake," and Miss Eckhart in "June Recital" teach younger women how to identify the stereotypes that have been governing them without their knowledge—the Cinderella and Medusa "texts" promoted by the sentimental romance—and how to create a new definition of women's heroism. ⟨. . .⟩

Acts of displacement, revision, and remembering characterize the comic heroines in Welty's stories, most notably Virgie Rainey. She appropriates the role of Perseus and slays Medusa, as Miss Eckhart, Jenny, Old Addie, Clytie, and others could not. With one stroke of the imagination, she assaults Morgana's deadly, stereotypical image of a strong and independent woman as a monster. To do this, like Perseus she reflects that dangerous image *back to itself*, identifying it *as* an image, a cultural fiction, thus taking the first step towards conquering its power to dominate her. And like the Cumaean sibyl in Domenichino, Virgie meditates on how a new tradition may replace the old, in which a woman may be Perseus, not merely Medusa. Her struggle, however, will be never-ending, always a part of the on-going struggle of women's history. In Welty's words in *The Golden Apples*,

> She might be able to see it now prophetically, but she was never a prophet. Because Virgie saw things in their time, like hearing them—and perhaps because she must believe in the Medusa equally with

> Perseus—she saw the stroke of the sword in three moments, not one.
> In the three was the damnation—no, only the secret, unhurting
> because not caring in itself—beyond the beauty and the sword's
> stroke and the terror lay their existence in time—far out and endless,
> a constellation which the heart could read over many a night . . . .
>   In Virgie's reach of memory a melody softly lifted, lifted of itself.
> Every time Perseus struck off the Medusa's head, there was the beat of
> time, and the melody. Endless the Medusa, and Perseus endless. (460)

Such a passage is obviously inspired in part by Benvenuto Cellini's statue of Perseus, a reproduction of which Welty owns. Eugene MacLain in "Music from Spain" also remembers a picture on Miss Eckhart's wall, but unlike Virgie he recalls not Cellini's Perseus but a sibyl: "Eugene felt untoward visions churning, the Spaniard with his great knees bent and his black slippers turning as if on a wheel's rim, dancing in a red smoky place with a lead-heavy alligator. The Spaniard turning his back with his voluminous coat-tails sailing, and his feet off the ground, floating bird-like up into the pin-point distance. The Spaniard with his finger on the page of a book, looking over his shoulder, as did the framed Sibyl on the wall in his father's study—no! then, it was old Miss Eckhart's 'studio'" (408). *The Golden Apples* never resolves the question of just how many pictures Miss Eckhart had on the walls of her studio, much less what their meanings are. In effect, Welty has Miss Eckhart's walls contain a double image—pairing both Perseus and Medusa and Medusa and the Sibyl. This crucial sibyl reference, moreover, was added in revision to the "Music from Spain" typescript.

It turns out that Domenichino's famous portraits of sibyls may have indeed inspired Welty's portraits of sibylline rather than Medusan powers. It is no absurdity that a music teacher in rural Mississippi might have a picture of a sibyl by Domenichino on the wall of her studio, perhaps next to her Perseus and the Medusa by Cellini. Domenichino's sibyls strike the exact pose that Eugene remembers, looking over a shoulder while laying a finger on the page of a book. By Domenichino's time, however, this pose was often transferred directly to portraits of St. Cecilia, the patron saint of music. Domenichino's Borghese sibyl has indeed been known both as a St. Cecilia portrait and as a Cumaean sibyl. Apparently, the Cumaean sibyl's indelible association with "prophetic song" in Virgil's Fourth Eclogue caused her to become associated with other kinds of music, and eventually with St. Cecilia. Miss Eckhart's sibyl, fittingly, represents not merely the teaching and performance of music so much as a sibylline scene of instruction—the creation and transmission of a new text for women's heroism.

—Peter Schmidt, *The Heart of the Story: Eudora Welty's Short Fiction* (Jackson: University Press of Mississippi, 1991), 246, 248–51

SARA McALPIN

In *Losing Battles* talking, like remembering, also appears as a basic and vital aspect of staying alive. In this novel, even more than in *Delta Wedding*, talk is incessant. Consistent with her expressed desire "to *show* everything and not as an author enter the character's mind and say 'He was thinking so-and-so'," Welty presents the entire novel from outside her characters, allowing them to reveal everything we learn about them only through their conversation and action. Talking, however, like remembering, serves the family as a device for hiding or ignoring certain aspects of reality, and often reinforces the impression that family exerts a restrictive and negative influence. For all their talk and ostensible sharing with each other, for example, there is very little sense in the novel that individuals succeed in genuinely communicating with each other.

The one exception to this generalization occurs with Jack and Gloria. Although they do not view reality in precisely the same way, they *are* able to share their differing perspectives. While Jack sees all his actions in terms of "family duty," Gloria persistently reminds him of her opposing framework: ". . . we're going to get clear away from *everybody*, move to ourselves." Although they are clearly caught in the ambivalence of "being pulled two ways," they are thus far able only to express conflicting views; they do not yet fully understand the truth of Miss Beulah's summary of that inevitable dimension of human experience: "Life's given to tricks like that . . . You just have to be equal to the pulling."

While Gloria and Jack are able in their conversation to move toward some tentative mutual understanding of reality as it is, the more characteristic result of the cascade of talk throughout *Losing Battles* is to mold reality according to the speakers' desires. As Louis Rubin has commented, the people in this novel "do not talk *to*, they talk *at*. Part of the reason that they talk is to communicate, but part of the reason is to dissemble, to mask, to hide. They converse obliquely, chattering away all the time but never entirely revealing themselves or saying what they think; and the barrier, the mystery that results, lies at the center of the high art of Eudora Welty."

The same kind of oblique, masking talk pervades *Delta Wedding*. Like the Vaughn-Beecham-Renfro family, the Fairchild family has its own devices for ordering reality as it chooses, occasionally contributing to negative consequences for individual members. In *Delta Wedding*, however, primarily because the narrator has access to several minds and is not limited to dramatic presentation as in *Losing Battles*, the distortions of reality occasionally appear somewhat more subtle. Typically, though not exclusively, in *Delta Wedding* it is through the private reflections of a single character, rather than in overt conversations or actions, that we learn how the family functions to limit or alter reality. ⟨. . .⟩

While it is clear in her rich creation of characters in both *Delta Wedding* and *Losing Battles* that no single life is unworthy of Welty's careful attention, however, in these two novels her primary focus remains on individuals within a group: her focus is on the family. "At all times," she says, "I'm interested in individuals . . . and in personal relationships, which to me are the things that matter; personal relationships matter more than any kind of generalizations about the world at large." Even more specifically, she declares, "Family relationships are the basis for all other relationships."

In her concentration on family relationships in *Delta Wedding* and *Losing Battles*, Welty implicitly juxtaposes herself to Willa Cather who, writes Welty admiringly, "*contended* for the life of the individual . . . This contending was the essence of her stories." In her own two novels, I think, Welty *contends* for the family. For her, as for numerous other southern authors, the family, linked by inseverable bonds, is the arbiter of behavior and action. Under the family the individual is to a large extent subsumed; what any individual ultimately does is chiefly determined by the collective authority of family.

Ambivalently wrapped like a bulb in "layers of violence and tenderness," then, the family functions in *Delta Wedding* and *Losing Battles* both to nurture and to suppress its individual members. As a force within each novel the family provides the source not just for viewing and ordering reality, but finally for *shaping* reality. Functioning with considerable ambivalence, which underscores the mystery of both the individuals within the family and the group itself, the family in each novel twists, trims, and expands reality sufficiently to understand it, cope with it, live with it, survive it.

"We come to terms as well as we can with our lifelong exposure to the world," wrote Welty in "One Time, One Place," in 1971, "and we use whatever devices we may need to survive." In *Delta Wedding* and *Losing Battles*, she vividly asserts that one of the devices we need most, with all its limitations and imperfections, is family.

—Sara McAlpin, "Family in Eudora Welty's Fiction," *The Critical Response to Eudora Welty's Fiction*, ed. Laurie Champion (Westport, CT: Greenwood Press, 1994), 306–7, 311

DANIELLE FULLER

In the worlds of Welty's novels, as in the white Western masculine tradition, marriage sanctions and "normalises" heterosexual sex whilst the family and community regulate the terms in which marriages are made: the social class and geographical origin of those involved, their material wealth and their conformance to the values and moral codes which are in operation. Welty's focus on and examination of the relationship between women, their families and their community, constantly reveals (and critiques) these social codes that seek to publicly "police" women's sexuality and subjectivity. The communities and families which Welty depicts are variously located both in time and space, and whilst some are rooted in rural areas, others, like the inhabitants of Morgana, are centred in small towns. These varied circumstances account for differences in the ways that this "policing" operates and a number of strategies are employed across Welty's fictional communities. Hence, the communally held views in Morgana are quick to name the behaviour of Miss Eckhart and Virgie Rainey in *The Golden Apples* as "other" and deviant, but despite some similarities between the value systems of the Morgana ladies and the Fairchild aunts, the contexts in which their attitudes are played out differ in important ways. Shellmound (in *Delta Wedding*) is situated in the Mississippi Delta, where, as Robbie Reid observes, "the land belonged to the women" and consequently it is "the women of the Fairchilds who since the Civil War, or—who knew?—since the Indian times, ran the household and had everything at their fingertips—not the men." It is from within the "shell" of this woman-dominated home place that the codes for sexual and marital relations emanate. That the apparent matriarchal tradition of Shellmound's Delta location does not guarantee its young women freedom from censure is clear in the attitudes of Aunts Mac, Tempe and Shannon towards Dabney's choice of Troy as a husband, and indeed, in Ellen's ambivalent feelings towards the lower-class Robbie Reid. It is rather that, for the Fairchild men and women, as Welty wrote of Jane Austen's world, "family relationships are the natural basis of all other relationships" and hence the class, race, and history of the Fairchild family necessarily inform the standards by which its members judge each other as well as outsiders ("The Radiance of Jane Austen," in *The Eye of the Story: Selected Essays and Reviews* (New York, Random House, 1977), 3–13).

Furthermore, whilst the women own the land, their control over the household does not appear to extend much beyond the borders of Ellen's garden. In the fields, where the crops which ensure the economic future of Shellmound are grown, it is the Fairchild men and their white overseer, Troy Flavin, who organise and supervise the black labourers. As Elizabeth Fox-Genovese has elaborated at length in her study of slave-holding women, the plantation household was inescapably dominated by the "massa" and the racial and gender hierarchy that his headship represented (*Within the Plantation Household: Black and White Women of the Old South* (Chapel Hill: University of North Carolina Press, 1988)). Hence, although, as Ann Romines points out, Welty has a "near-mythic view of the Delta" as a matriarchy, I would suggest that it is a matriarchy surrounded by and embedded in—both literally and metaphorically—a "plantation discourse" that confirms the social and economic power of white males of the middle and upper classes (*The Home Place: Women, Writing and Domestic Ritual* (Amherst: University of Massachusetts Press,

1992), 212). The attention and service that the Fairchild women demand of their men only serves to reaffirm the legacy of nineteenth-century Southern codes which posited men as the protectors of a lady's honour. Even as the women look to George and the dead Denis as heroes whose difference from the Fairchild family character ensures a never-ending source of love and protection, so they perpetuate and re-enact the gendered divisions and hierarchy of their white, middle-class world. Those like Robbie Reid who threaten this order are constantly reminded by the women who "belong" to Shellmound that their behaviour is deemed inappropriate or antagonistic to family harmony.

Intimacy and the choice of a partner on the basis of sexual desire is thus severely constrained for women, and Welty's female characters often find themselves caught in relationships in which they must struggle to renegotiate the terms upon which the partnership is founded. These negotiations are complicated by the practical difficulties for women, married and unmarried alike, of demonstrating their sexual desire outside the public gaze. Furthermore, any desire on the part of women to please and be pleased places them in a vulnerable position in regard to masculine constructions of their female sexuality as unempowered and available for male pleasure.

Through incidents such as George's rape of the "bayou girl," Welty encircles the main narrative event of the Delta wedding—the marriage of Ellen's daughter Dabney to the overseer Troy—with experiences that question and complicate its meaning. The multi-voiced narrative of *Delta Wedding* makes it impossible to ignore the parallels and echoes between the journeys towards selfhood of Laura, Shelley, Robbie, and Dabney. Their rites of passage and growing awareness of their sexuality are not simply feelings of wholeness and separateness, of self-knowledge, but are shown to be inevitably bound up in and defined by issues of power and gender. The constant shifts between narrators of three different age groups, several of whom are "outsiders" (Ellen, Robbie, and Laura), result in both alignments and contradictions of points of view. In this way, the women's differing perspectives on the function and behaviour of the Fairchild men, marriage, and family represent an ongoing critique of the social codes and structures within which they live. By entering her character's consciousness and by providing Shelley with a diary, a private space where she can articulate some of these contradictions, Welty's narrative and her portrayal of female sexuality avoid resolution. Shelley's growing doubts about her sister's forthcoming marriage, for instance, seem to be confirmed yet complicated by her dramatic confrontation with white masculine authority in Troy's office.

When she runs to fetch Troy for the wedding rehearsal, Shelley has already rejected marriage as a possibility for herself (p. 136). Encountering Dr.

Murdoch in the village graveyard, Shelley and her cousin Laura are appalled at his depiction of the eternal cycle of marriage, motherhood and death: "'You'll marry in a year and probably start a houseful like your mother!'" (p. 135), he predicts, gleefully imagining how they will all fit into the Fairchild plot. In fact Ellen herself embodies a warning to the younger Shellmound women. The pragmatic demands of her role as "the mother of them all" (p. 10) restrict her own pleasures in her garden and in her relationship with Battle and threaten to overwhelm her. Aware of her mother's fatigue, Shelley blames her father, Battle, for "getting Mama in this predicament—again and again" (p. 229). Then, when she hears the story of her birth narrated as a comedy, Shelley flees the room as if to escape the inevitability of her own biology (p. 216). Shelley herself sees only pain and anguish in her mother's first childbed. Her desire to escape the patterns of life and the roles assigned to women by Delta tradition is echoed by Laura, who knows that she will leave the blind protection of Shellmound to go back to a more solitary and unpredictable life with her father in Jackson (p. 237). (Laura, it seems, senses the insularity of the "matriarchal" Shellmound, where Ellen pays attention to the girl's physical, "feminine" appearance.)

However, it is only when she arrives at the overseer's office and walks "into the point of a knife" that the complexity of male power fully confronts Shelley (p. 195). She stumbles on a tableau in which four black field hands face Troy, who meets the threat of Root M'Hook's icepick with his gun. The black men are subject to the white man's gun and his power to judge the terms of their dispute. By shooting at Root's shaking hand, Troy commits an act that maintains and marks his position as a white, working-class male within the hierarchy of the plantation. In terms of the plantation discourse supporting this hierarchy, Troy acts to protect the Fairchild land from the threat which the black community appears to pose to it. By doing so, he reinscribes his position within a system and a discourse that engenders that land as female, pure yet fertile, and available for possession. Shelley finds herself witnessing something which has been previously kept hidden from the female gaze and Troy is quick to push her behind his chair, as if it is her honour that he is protecting. In this episode Shelley's "honour" as a white Fairchild woman appears to be equated with ownership and mastery of the land, but Shelley herself is allowed no active role in an interaction that seeks to define her place in the social order, and, like the black field hands, she is subject to white, male power. Gender, race, and class thus intersect in Welty's narrative in ways which reveal the many layers of male power and the marginalisation of both white women and the black community in the dominant discourse of the 1920s Delta community.

The power games that are played out in this scene are complicated still further by the linking of male violence to female sexuality. The dispute between the field hands has arisen over Pinchy's sexuality: "'Pinchy cause trouble comin' through'" (p. 195). Pinchy, a black female servant in the Fairchild household, spends the majority of the novel mysteriously but insistently "seeking" and "trying to come through" (p. 32). As Barbara Ladd has argued, her behaviour and final emergence from her seeking suggest a passage of initiation into womanhood ⟨"'Coming Through': The Black Initiate in *Delta Wedding*," *Mississippi Quarterly* 41 (Fall 1988): 541–52⟩. In this confrontation, Pinchy becomes an objectified but desired absence whose sexuality the black men seek to control and possess. Their violence is matched and challenged by the violent assertion of a white man's power, which is in turn linked to a masculine construction of white female sexuality. The eruption of violence in Troy's office foregrounds and problematises racial and gender oppression, ominously suggesting that masculine constructions of female sexuality are complicit with violence.

Welty's narrative critiques this complicity by entering Shelley's consciousness. Jumping through the blood on Troy's doorstep, Shelley begins to realise her difference and alienation from the behaviour she has witnessed. This knowledge causes a "sharp, panicky triumph" since she has seen "the reason why Dabney's wedding should be prevented." The imitative nature of men and the consequent fixity of the social order has been revealed to her through Troy's "performance" as "an overseer born and bred" (p. 196):

> She felt again, but differently, that men were no better than little
> children. . . . Women, she was glad to think, did know a little better.
> (p. 196)

Yet her knowledge about gender difference, sexuality and power and the fear that she experiences "for life itself" (p. 197) as a consequence of this knowledge can only be given expression in the private space of her diary. Shelley sees her sister stepping straight into the arena of oppression which she has just left, yet is unable to warn her about it (p. 85). Although Troy may not mark out his power over Dabney with violence, he has already prescribed for her a role as the mother of his children (p. 113).

Is it possible, then, for women to express their sexuality and identity within marriage without submitting to masculine definitions of desire which place women in the position of the unempowered? Welty continually problematises this dilemma, and, in doing so, she both resists and reworks the representations of female sexuality that are a part of the Southern women's literary tradition. The association of women with plants and nature found, for example, in the works of Ellen Glasgow, is transformed from the level of symbolic beauty with hints of a gentle sensuality, to a blatantly sexualised rendering of the landscape as fecund. Furthermore, Welty's landscape may contain mystery, but it is bereft of the dark shame which seems to haunt Faulkner's ambivalent descriptions of the land. In the passages that describe Dabney's morning ride, nature reflects and embodies her desires, and, as she moves through the fields and woods of Shellmound, she alone is in possession of her sexuality. When she parts the vines "as thick as legs" to look into the whirlpool that is full of eyes and snake heads "horridly sticking up," Dabney is described as "feasting her fear on the dark, vaguely stirring water" (p. 123). Welty's description of the "churning" waters encapsulates the ambiguity of this moment in which the virgin bride Dabney appears both to enjoy and to become mesmerised by the whirlpool. Initially struck by vertigo when she first looks at the whirlpool, Dabney gradually feels herself "leaning, leaning" towards its darkness, its history of drownings and its water thick with roots and hair (p. 123). Welty's imagery both entrances and repulses her reader, suggesting both allurement and fear, celebration and enchantment. It is as if Dabney were paying homage at a shrine to female sexuality but one which encapsulates the difficulties and complexities facing women who wish to play out their sexual desires in heterosexual relationships.

—Danielle Fuller, "'Making a Scene': Some Thoughts on Female Sexuality and Marriage in Eudora Welty's *Delta Wedding* and *The Optimist's Daughter*," *The Mississippi Quarterly* 48, no. 2 (Spring 1995): 291

BIBLIOGRAPHY

A Curtain of Green. 1941.
The Robber Bridegroom. 1942.
The Wide Net and Other Stories. 1943.
Delta Wedding. 1946.
The Golden Apples. 1949.
The Ponder Heart. 1954.
The Bride of Innisfallen and Other Stories. 1955.
The Shoe Bird. 1964.
Losing Battles. 1970.
One Time, One Place: Mississippi in the Depression: A Snapshot Album. 1971.
The Optimist's Daughter. 1972.

The Eye of the Story: Selected Essays and Reviews. 1978.
The Collected Stories of Eudora Welty. 1980.
One Writer's Beginnings. 1984.
Photographs. 1989.

EDITH WHARTON
1862-1937

EDITH WHARTON was born Edith Newbold Jones on January 24, 1862. She was educated privately in New York and Europe. Edith Wharton's upper-class childhood in "old New York" provides the setting for her best fiction, which presents scathing critiques of a society hostile to women's intellectual and artistic aspirations. A female intellectual at a time when women were considered more or less ornamental, Wharton once said of herself that she was considered too intellectual to be fashionable in New York, and too fashionable to be considered intellectual in Boston. This witticism has a serious side that may help to explain why she spent most of her adult life in France, returning only once, in 1923, to receive an honorary degree from Yale, the first woman ever so honored.

In 1885, she married Teddy Wharton, a man more interested in hunting and fishing than in art and ideas. The marriage was not a happy one, due in part to Teddy Wharton's bouts of depression. Teddy also embezzled money from Edith's estate (using some of the money to purchase a house for his mistress in Boston). In 1913, they were divorced, two years after Edith's passionate affair with a journalist named Morton Fullerton, an affair begun in response to Teddy's infidelities and emotional distance. After her divorce, Wharton never remarried.

Her life was filled with writing and writers. She had a long-time friendship with Henry James that began when he suggested that Wharton "do New York," which she did with great success in *The House of Mirth* (1905), her second novel. The novel charts the destruction of Lily Bart at the hands of a mercenary society, a formula reversed in *The Custom of the Country* (1913), in which Undine Spragg spares no one in her quest for material gain. Although in most Wharton novels society is seen as a repressive, highly codified environment in which those who do not conform are punished, Wharton rarely presents any alternatives for her characters. We see this most clearly in her most well-known novel, *The Age of Innocence* (1920), in which the conventions of society win out over the passion between Ellen Olenska and Newland Archer. It is for this novel that Wharton was awarded the Pulitzer Prize for fiction in 1921. She was the first woman to receive the award.

Wharton was also the first woman writer to be awarded a gold medal for "special distinction in literature" by the American Academy of Arts and Letters, and she was the first American woman to be made Chevalier of the Legion of Honor, in France, for her war-relief efforts. During World War I, Wharton raised thousands of dollars and established a network of hostels for refugees, organized welfare committees to care for children, and sponsored fund-raising efforts among the artists, writers, and musicians of Europe. After the war, Wharton returned to writing full time. Her short stories and serialized novels often appeared in popular magazines, and during the 1920s she was one of the highest-paid American writers.

Her keen eye for social criticism and her elegant prose style have made Wharton an enduring figure in American literature. In addition to her short stories and novels, she wrote nonfiction works, including essays and articles on travel, architecture, and decorating. She died of complications from a stroke on August 11, 1937, at the age of seventy-five.

CRITICAL EXTRACTS

ELIZABETH AMMONS

The manuscript of *The Reef* explicitly refers to the fairy tale. In the finished novel, Anna Leath and George Darrow, betrothed, spend together at the château de Givré a "perfect" afternoon and evening, during which they discover on the estate "a little old deserted house, fantastically carved and chimneyed, which lay in a moat under the shade of ancient trees." That pleasure house, in an earlier version of the passage, has a name: "the Sleeping Beauty's lodge." Revisions in Edith Wharton's manuscripts often reveal her wish to avoid the symbolically obtrusive, especially in naming people and places; and *The Reef* is no exception. Her deletion of the direct reference to the Sleeping Beauty, as well as her substitution of the names Givré for "Blincourt" ("blin[d] court"[ship], hence "the reef") and Darrow for "Caringdon" (in addition to "don[e] caring," too close to "C[h]ar[m]ing Don"?), suggest that Wharton, far from abandoning the Sleeping Beauty motif, wanted to make it more subtle, lest she insult the reader's intelligence or mar the book's delicate weave of fairy-tale associations by including heavy-handed symbols. The published novel, stripped of obvious allusion (like a building that no longer needs scaf-folding), depends on inherent patterns of imagery and refined symbolism to communicate the fairy-tale motif and its thematic implications.

In her first husband, prior to the action of *The Reef*, Anna Summers thought she found her Prince Charming, her liberator and hero. She soon realized that the change in her name from Summers to Leath had contrary significance. The summers of her life were chillingly replaced by a lethean existence at his château de Givré: palace of rime, hoar-frost. The French château which "had called up to her youthful fancy a throng of romantic associations, poetic, pic-torial, and emotional," the château which was for Anna "a castle of dreams, evoker of fair images and romantic legend," turned into a chamber of horrors where "life, to Mr. Leath, was like a walk through a carefully classified museum. . . . [while] to his wife it was like groping about in a huge dark lumber-room where the exploring ray of curiosity lit up now some shape of breathing beauty and now a mummy's grin." Her husband's kiss, instead of awakening her passionate impulses and desires, "dropped on her like a cold smooth pebble." She and her stepson, Owen, "were like two prisoners who talk to each other by tapping on the wall." In effect, Anna found herself living in a gothicized fairy-tale world, complete with wicked mother-in-law and haunt-ing portrait of a dead first wife—the "exiled consort removed farther and far-ther from the throne." This was definitely the wrong fairy tale. Anna wanted to be awakened into "contact with the actual business of living"; she wanted to be freed, not imprisoned. ⟨. . .⟩

The structure of the novel charts the crash of the woman's romantic fan-tasy. In contrast to the gloomy weather and dingy urban settings of Book I, Anna's idyllic world of latent animation at the château in Book II does seem a fairy-tale world coming to life. However, the harder she clings to her dream in the face of realities it cannot accommodate, the more inhospitable and enclosed the atmosphere becomes. In Book III she has "the eerie feeling of having been overswept by a shadow which there had been no cloud to cast . . ." (Wharton's ellipsis). The day turns rainy and its two main events are Anna's visit to an injured child and Darrow's secret meeting with Sophy in a decaying summer-house. In Book IV Anna does not leave Givré, where her dream of perfect love is attenuated as she learns the truth about Darrow's char-acter. The dream dissolves altogether in Book V, which, like Book I, takes place mainly in Paris. The atmosphere grows stormy and dark, the action con-sists of frantic journeys and conferences in hotel rooms, and Anna last appears not at the château but in the bedroom of a strange woman in a shabby Parisian hotel. This last scene is upsetting, even cruel, as critics remark. But it is so for a purpose. Although Anna can no longer delude herself about marrying Darrow, she still clings to her hope of being saved by someone other than her-self. She decides "it was Sophy Viner only who could save her—Sophy Viner only who could give her back her lost serenity. She would seek the girl out and tell her that she had given Darrow up; and that step once taken there would be no retracing it, and she would perforce have to go forward alone." If successful, the plan will reanimate her dream: Darrow and Sophy's careless affair will be transformed into a beautiful love-marriage, and Anna will be transfigured into a self-sacrificing heroine. Wharton does not let Anna find Sophy and therefore be saved by her. She has her find herself among strangers in a tawdry hotel love-nest, and there all illusion about fairy-tale love explodes. In the person of the slovenly Mrs. McTarvie-Birch at the Hôtel Chicago we finally ⟨ see the embodiment of Anna's earlier image of the woman in love as "a slave, and a goddess, and a girl in her teens": a prostitute who is bought and owned like a slave, enthroned on her bed like a goddess, and distracted by her pet poodle like a girl in her teens. That Anna mistakes this woman and her pimp for husband and wife serves as one last grotesque indication of how naive she is about the whole subject of love, sex, and marriage.

Edith Wharton, I want to emphasize, does not mock Anna in *The Reef*. (To be sure, the final scene is ironic; but the irony is sobering, not amusing or contemptuous.) Rather, she develops Anna's story to confute a fairy-tale fantasy cherished by many women because they are taught to believe in it. The target of criticism in *The Reef* is not women but the culture which represses them and encourages them to believe that love and marriage will someday release them into reality. Love and marriage are not a release. Anna's dream cannot even withstand an engagement, let alone marriage which, as her first union demonstrated and her relationship with Darrow suggests, simply delivers a woman from one subservient life into another.

—Elizabeth Ammons, "Fairy-Tale Love and *The Reef*," *American Literature* 47, no. 4 (January 1976), excerpted in *Modern Critical Views: Edith Wharton*, ed. Harold Bloom (New York: Chelsea House Publishers, 1986), 41, 45–46

CYNTHIA GRIFFIN WOLFF

Ethan Frome was an important book to Edith Wharton. In 1936 when Owen and Donald Davis did a dramatization of the novel, Wharton took the unusual step of writing a short preface. "My poor little group of hungry, lonely New England villagers will live again for a while on their stony hillside before finally joining their forebears under the village headstones," she says. "I should like to think that this good fortune may be theirs, for I lived among them in fact and in imagination, ten years [her ten years of residence at Lenox], and their strained starved faces are still near to me." Wharton was seventy-four when she wrote these words (just a little less than a year before her death), and there is a sense of insistent presence attached to the people of Starkfield that does not emerge when she refers to any other of her fictional creations. ⟨. . .⟩

An astounding discovery awaits us: the man whom we come to know as the young Ethan Frome is *no more than a figment of the narrator's imagination*. Wharton's method of exposition leaves no doubt. We are not permitted to believe that the narrator is recounting a history of something that actually happened; we are not given leave to speculate that he is passing along a confidence obtained in the dark intimacy of a cold winter's night. No: the "story" of Ethan Frome is introduced in unmistakable terms. "It was that night that I found the clue to Ethan Frome, and began *to put together this vision* of his story . . ." (emphasis mine). Our narrator is a teller of terrible tales, a seer into the realms of dementia. The "story" of Ethan Frome is nothing more than a dream vision, a brief glimpse into the most appalling recesses of the narrator's mind. The overriding question becomes then—not who is Ethan Frome, but who in the world is this ghastly guide to whom we must submit as we read the tale.

The structure demands that we take him into account. Certainly *he* demands it. It is *his* story, ultimately his "vision" of Ethan Frome, that we will get. His vision is as good as any other (so he glibly assures us at the beginning—for "each time it was a different story"), and therefore his story has as much claim to truth as any other. And yet, he is a nervous fellow. The speech pattern is totally unlike Wharton's own narrative style—short sentences, jagged prose rhythms, absolutely no sense of ironic control over the language, no distance from it. Yet, the fellow is nervous. He seems anxious about our reaction and excessively eager to reassure us that had *we* been situated as *he* was, catching a first horrified glimpse of Ethan Frome, we "must have asked who he was." Anyone would. Frome is no mere bit of local color. He is, for reasons that we do not yet understand, a force that compels examination; "the sight pulled me up sharp." (It would pull all of you up sharp, and all of you would have done as I did.)

Certain elements in Wharton's story are to be taken as "real" within the fictional context: Ethan Frome is badly crippled; he sustained his injuries in a sledding accident some twenty-four years ago; he has been in Starkfield for most of his life, excepting a short visit to Florida, living first with his parents and then with his querulous, sickly wife Zeena; there is a third member of the household, his wife's cousin, Miss Mattie Silver; she too was badly crippled in the same sledding accident that felled Ethan. To these facts the various members of the town will all attest—and to *nothing more*. Everything that the reader can accept as reliably true can be found in the narrative frame; everything else bears the imprint of the narrator's own interpretation—as indeed even the selection of events chronicled in the frame does—and while that interpretation *might* be as true as any other, we dare not accept it as having the same validity as the bare outline presented above. Even at the end of the narrator's

vision, in the concluding scene with Mrs. Hale, Wharton is scrupulously careful not to credit the vision by giving it independent confirmation.

—Cynthia Griffin Wolff, "*Ethan Frome*: 'This Vision of His Story'," *A Feast of Words: The Triumph
of Edith Wharton* (New York: Oxford University Press, 1977), excerpted in *Modern Critical
Views: Edith Wharton*, ed. Harold Bloom (New York: Chelsea House Publishers, 1986), 65,
70–71

ALLAN GARDNER SMITH

Edith Wharton's feminist contributions to the novel have been extensively
admired, to the point of inspiring an enthusiastic analysis by Josephine Jessup
in *The Faith of Our Feminists*. In the genre of the realist novel, however, Wharton
obeyed the constraints of the visible; she adhered, perforce, to what could be
seen by her society, to the areas of consensus—however critical—about the
"real" state of that society and its interpersonal relations. In the genre of the
ghost story, on the other hand, she was able to penetrate into the realm of the
unseen, that is, into the area that her society preferred to be unable to see, or
to construe defensively as super (i.e. not) natural. Schelling's definition of the
unheimlich or uncanny held it to be the "name for everything that ought to have
remained . . . hidden and secret and has become visible," a formulation which
drew Freud toward a sexual implication, but which seems to me to retain a
reservoir of unexplored content in the possibility of socially legitimated reti-
cence or ideological denial, beyond the repressions of an individual ego or
characteristic neurosis.

The most distinctive suppressed material (I use the term in distinction to
"repressed," which is by definition unconscious) is sexual: the description of
conduct which could not be acknowledged even in fiction. After the
researches of R. W. B. Lewis, who has published the pornographic fragment
"Beatrice Palmato" (which Wharton intended as background for a less explicit
and therefore publishable version of the story, to appear in a volume significantly titled *The Powers of Darkness*), we know that Wharton explored this field,
with a remarkable intensity. But I am concerned with material that is sexual not
in unsanctioned eroticism and explicitness so much as in the sense of a "sexual
pathology of everyday life," surfacing in stories of the invisible.

To disentangle this "sexual pathology of the everyday" from the erotic it
is useful to examine "All Souls'" (1937, the last story that Edith Wharton sent
to her publisher) which isn't, the narrator remarks, "exactly a ghost story"
because it contains a mystery but no apparitions. An elderly woman, left alone
in her house with an injured ankle, experiences a day that others claim did not
exist, finding that the electricity and telephone have been cut off, and the servants [are] mysteriously absent. The evening before, October 31st, she had

met an unknown woman on her way to the house to "visit one of the girls," but thought little about it after fracturing her ankle. The injury which makes her a prisoner, a sudden snowfall, and the size of her house intensify Mrs. Claymore's helplessness and fear as she stumbles from room to room, oppressed by silence that is "folded down on her like a pall" and that the presence of any other human, however secret, would have flawed "as a sheet of glass is flawed by a pebble thrown against it." The controlling, rational presence of the mistress of the house has to be inscribed on this flawless silence in the absence of her servants, who have apparently gone to join in an orgiastic coven (which, an epilogue suggests, will draw inexorably any who have entertained the remotest wish to assist at it and will thereafter make them move heaven and earth to take part again). The crippled intellect stumbling in its empty house carries sexual implications which are confirmed by the location of Mrs. Claymore's profoundest source of fear, a man's voice, speaking in low, emphatic tones in the "back premises," specifically, the kitchen, which normally belongs to the servants. The peripeteia which occurs at this point replaces sexual threat with the bathos of absence; the voice, in a foreign language unknown to her, proceeds from a portable radio, and she faints in shock.

Several lines of thought are suggested by this story. The first is that "All Souls'" can be read as a parable of frustration: Mrs. Claymore, delirious after the fall that damaged her ankle, fantasizes a situation which expresses her sexual desires in suitably censored and transformed version. This is the sort of reading suggested by the perceptive remark of R. M. Lovett, who noted as early as 1925 (before "All Souls'" was written) that "the wellings-up from the turbid depths of the subconscious she prefers to treat by the symbolism of the supernatural, and to draw the obscure creatures of the depths into the light of day as apparitions." Passing over the emotive coloration of Lovett's dictum, this seems to me an accurate proposition which, applied to "All Souls,'" shows how Mrs. Claymore's "illicit" desires are projected onto the servants but kept offstage and by this absence are intensified in suggestiveness, becoming an unspeakable witches' coven.

The next line of thought qualifies this reading without denying it, in suggesting that "All Souls'" dramatizes the psychic deformations entailed by Mrs. Claymore's inheritance of an authoritarian male position in relation to the house and servants. Since the death of her husband she has maintained an almost compulsive control over the household, dressing for dinner, and ruling her five retainers with an "authoritative character" so that the house is always immaculate, even down to the empty servants' rooms. Her terror of something going wrong in this regime acknowledges the irrationality and instability of her financial and class-determined position beneath the rationality or common sense of her acceptance of it. The servants are as much a threat as a comfort, especially the faithful Agnes, who has been with her mistress for so long without revealing her affinity with the inconceivable "fetch" who calls for her. Mrs. Claymore, masquerading as male, inherits with her costume the terror of the female that suggests, as in earlier periods, the accusation of witchcraft.

The aggressive modernity of the portable radio in "All Souls'" enshrines Edith Wharton's contention in the Preface to Ghosts, her 1937 collection of stories, that, contra Osbert Sitwell, ghosts did not go out when electricity came in, because she could imagine them "more wistfully haunting a mean house in a dull street than the battlemented castle with its boring stage properties," and it documents her interest in the haunting by absence in everyday life rather than by presence in an extraordinary one. Mrs. Claymore's unacknowledged terrors and longings take on pathos in a confrontation with the absent male, foreign (revolutionary?) voice, which expresses a hollowness even at the center of threat, paralleling the emptiness of the snow outside, the silence within the house, or the emptiness and silence within herself.

In these respects "All Souls'" can be paired with "The Looking Glass," published two years before, in 1935, which explores the pitiable emptiness of a woman clinging to her beauty after it has gone, and to the memory of a distant encounter, in which no words were spoken. Duped by a version of what those words might have been, she leaves a considerable inheritance to the woman who misled her, a masseuse. Yet here Edith Wharton raises the possibility that the Word has been spoken: the young man employed by the masseuse for verisimilitude in her communications from "beyond" dies, leaving a last letter, which is the only communication to convince, but remains unseen both by the reader and the charlatan. Thus the absence within the text becomes a possible reproach to the materialism of the masseuse's heavily processed first-person account. An irony of the story is, however, that the most significantly unspoken (i.e. unseen, unacknowledged) element within the story is precisely the full extent of that materialism: the masseuse believes that she saved her patient from the "foul people" who might have exploited her belief in spirits, whereas she has done exactly that herself.

Taken together, these two stories illustrate Edith Wharton's complexity of approach to such issues as the unease of women in male roles, mistrust between women and the distortions of the master/servant, employer/employee situations, in which the unspoken, suppressed issue of status and suborned affection return in terror or the attribution of occult powers, and the servant/employee is perceived as a witch or spiritualist with access to psychic forces denied to the ostensibly superior woman.

—Allan Gardner Smith, "Edith Wharton and the Ghost Story," Gender and Literary Voice, Women and Literature, vol. 1 (New York: Holmes and Meier Publishers, 1980), excerpted in Modern Critical Views: Edith Wharton, ed. Harold Bloom (New York: Chelsea House Publishers, 1986), 89–92

JUDITH FRYER

We know that Wharton knew a great deal about cultural anthropology; one learns from *A Backward Glance* that she had been reading Darwin, Huxley, Spencer, "and various popular exponents of the great evolutionary movement." She made skillful use particularly of *The Golden Bough* in analyzing her own former world in tribal terms and in dramatizing its rituals, from the performance of the Old New York audience attending the Opera, with which the novel opens, to the final scene where Newland Archer waits beneath Ellen Olenska's windows until the lights go on, and "as if it had been the signal he waited for"—as if the play were over—he "got up slowly and walked back alone to his hotel." The repetitive rituals of *The Age of Innocence* are the signs of a female society—but a female society in decline, with frozen rituals. Old New York may once have been ruled by the matriarchal Grandmother Mingott, with her "strength of will and hardness of heart, and a kind of haughty effrontery"; but by 1870 "Catherine the Great," as she is called, is fat and immobile: an "immense accretion of flesh" has changed her from an active woman into "something as vast and august as a natural phenomenon." Because of the burden of her flesh, she can no longer go up and down stairs, and all the family come to her, where with "moral courage" she still suggests the disorder of the "inaccessible wilderness near the Central Park," startling and fascinating her visitors with her ground-floor arrangement of sitting-room giving onto an unexpected vista of bedroom, recalling "scenes in French fiction, and architectural incentives to immorality such as the simple American had never dreamed of." It is, however, only "a stage-setting of adultery," as Newland Archer reflects when he goes with May, a Mingott granddaughter, to receive their betrothal blessings—like the stage-setting for the other scenes in the novel; in it old Catherine leads a blameless life. Her empty place in the family opera box signifies her diminishing importance; it is filled with the younger representatives of the female order, among them her daughter Augusta Welland and Augusta's daughter May, a young girl in white with fair braids who lowers her eyes now and then to her bouquet of lilies-of-the-valley (which Newland has sent her and will send every day until their wedding), touching the flowers softly with her white-gloved fingertips. There is one exception to the "abysmal purity" of this box, and that is another Mingott granddaughter, the Countess Ellen Olenska, who shocks the Old New York audience by her offense against "Taste" in wearing a simple dress which has no tucker and slopes away from her shoulders; her grandmother will later say that Ellen is the only one of the family like her.

Wharton gives here two simultaneous performances. Onstage, the performers follow the "unalterable and unquestioned law of the musical world [which] required that the German text of French operas sung by Swedish artists should be translated into Italian for the clearer understanding of

English-speaking audiences." It is significant that the opera is *Faust* and that the first person we meet in *The Age of Innocence* is Christine Nilsson, the opera singer of whom Henry James had written, "What a pity she is not the heroine of a tale, and that I didn't make her!" James probably meant by this that Madame Nilsson seemed to him even more vital, more energetic, larger, and bolder than someone like his own actress Miriam Rooth of *The Tragic Muse*. Christine Nilsson was no innocent Marguerite or Gretchen, but a woman of charm and experience who has *chosen* to play this part, and plays it with deliberation and genius. The contrast between Madame Nilsson's power and the repeated ritual of performance—at the end of the novel the same people will gather again to see "the same large blonde victim . . . succumbing to the same small brown seducer"—must have been striking to Wharton; knowing her Goethe, she was certainly aware that Part II begins with Faust's invocation to "The Mothers," dangerous powers of darkness. But for the audience the Opera is an occasion for another sort of performance, an ongoing ceremony which is taken for reality itself, with laws unalterable and unquestioned: the pre-Opera dinner; the arrival in Brown coupes—late because "in metropolises it was 'not the thing' to arrive early . . . and what was or was not 'the thing' played a part as important in Newland Archer's New York as the inscrutable totem terrors that had ruled the destinies of his forefathers thousands of years ago"; the costumes of the audience, as prescribed and as elegant as those of the actors; and the visiting back and forth from one box to another. All of this seems as natural to Newland "as all the other conventions on which his life was moulded: such as the duty of using two silver-backed brushes with his monogram in blue enamel to part his hair, and of never appearing in society without a flower (preferably a gardenia) in his buttonhole."

All of these details of the social ritual of Old New York have little to do with Newland Archer's profession as a lawyer, or with his thinking self—for despite his dilettantish qualities he reads a great deal in his own library (in fact he reads the same books as Wharton, in *A Backward Glance*, admits to reading); but they have a great deal to do with his day-to-day behavior, for after his brandy, cigars, and conversation with the men, he must always return to the drawing-room world of the women. He values that world, and he even wishes to protect and preserve it, just because of the sense of continuity and stability it offers. When he turns his eyes to the Mingott box, therefore, his first response to the observation of something that offends against "Taste" is to rush to the box to persuade May to announce their engagement early, adding the strength of his family to that of hers to affirm their respectability—or reinforce their boundaries—in face of what he perceives as disorder.

—Judith Fryer, "Purity and Power in *The Age of Innocence*," *American Literary Realism 1870–1910* 17, no. 2 (Autumn 1984), excerpted in *Modern Critical Views: Edith Wharton*, ed. Harold Bloom (New York: Chelsea House Publishers, 1986), 106–8

WAI-CHEE DIMOCK

The most brutal moment in *The House of Mirth* dramatizes not so much the centrality of sex as the centrality of exchange. Sexual favors are what Gus Trenor wants, but his demands are steeped in—and legitimated by—the language of the marketplace, the language of traded benefits and reciprocal obligations. Odious as it may seem, Trenor's speech merely asserts what everyone assumes. "Investments" and "returns," "interests" and "payments": these words animate and possess Wharton's characters, even in their world of conspicuous leisure. The power of the marketplace, then, resides not in its presence, which is only marginal in *The House of Mirth*, but in its ability to reproduce itself, in its ability to assimilate everything else into its domain. As a controlling logic, a mode of human conduct and human association, the marketplace is everywhere and nowhere, ubiquitous and invisible. Under its shadow even the most private affairs take on the essence of business transactions, for the realm of human relations is fully contained within an all-encompassing business ethic. Some characters—Trenor and Rosedale, for instance—obviously speak the voice of the marketplace, but even those who hold themselves aloof (as Lawrence Selden does) turn out to be more susceptible than they think.

Of all the characters, Lily Bart has the most puzzling and contradictory relation to the marketplace. A self-acknowledged "human merchandise," she is busy marketing herself throughout most of the book, worried only about the price she would fetch. She tries to induce Percy Gryce to purchase her, and if she had succeeded she would have been "to him what his Americana had hitherto been, the one possession in which he took sufficient pride to spend money on it." Much later, as she forces herself to accept Rosedale's attentions, she consoles herself by calculating "the price he would have to pay." Lily is clearly caught up in the ethos of exchange. And yet her repeated and sometimes intentional failure to find a buyer, her ultimate refusal to realize her "asset"—as her mother designates her beauty—makes her something of a rebel. She is not much of a rebel, of course, and that is precisely the point. For Lily's "rebellion," in its very feebleness and limitation, attests to the frightening power of the marketplace. It attests as well to Wharton's own politics, to her bleakness of vision in the face of a totalizing system she finds at once detestable and inevitable.

The persistent talk of "cost" and "payment" in *The House of Mirth* raises the question of *currency*. How does one compute the "cost" of an action, what constitutes a "debt," and in what form must "payments" be made? Money, the standard medium of exchange, is not the only currency in circulation. Trenor clearly does not wish to be paid back with a check. In fact, "payment in kind" is never expected in transactions in the social marketplace, and this unspoken rule makes for a plethora of business opportunities. A "society" dinner, for instance, is worth its weight in gold. Since the likes of Rosedale habitually "giv[e] away a half-a-million tip for a dinner," Jack Stepney regularly "pay[s] his debts in dinner invitations." Others—even those who protest—eventually follow Stepney's example, for the simple reason that Rosedale is "placing Wall Street under obligations which only Fifth Avenue could repay." There are other expenses, other debts, and other means of payment as well. Lily's visit to Selden's bachelor apartment is a "luxury" that is "going to cost her rather more than she could afford." Still she might have "purchased [Rosedale's] silence" if she had only allowed him to take her to the train station, since "to be seen walking down the platform at the crowded afternoon hour in the company of Miss Lily Bart would have been money in his pocket." Business, in the social world, operates by what we might call the commodification of social intercourse. Everything has a price, must be paid for, just as—on the opposite end—everything can be made to "count as" money, to be dealt out and accepted in lieu of cash. Dispensed in this manner, social gestures lose their initial character and figure only as exchange values: the dinner invitations, for Stepney and Rosedale, presumably have no meaning except as surrogate cash payments. A social world predicated on business ethics is an essentially reductive world, and the power of money lies not so much in its pristine form as in its claim as a model, in its ability to define other things in its own image. The fluidity of currencies in *The House of Mirth*, the apparently endless business possibilities, attests to the reduction of human experiences to abstract equivalents for exchange.

The principle of exchange, the idea that one has to "pay" for what one gets, lays claim to a kind of quid pro quo justice, and it is this justice, this "fair play," that Trenor demands from Lily. What he does not (or chooses not to) recognize is that what he calls "fair" is by no means self-evident and certainly not computable on an absolute scale. The problem stems, of course, from the rate of exchange, from the way prices are fixed. After all, why should a single dinner cost Rosedale a tip worth half a million (why not a quarter of a million, or a million)? And, for that matter, why should a ride in the park *not* be sufficient "payment" for the money Lily owes Trenor? In both instances, the "price" for the received benefit could easily have been otherwise, since the rate of exchange is altogether variable, altogether an artificial stipulation. In other words, two items might be yoked in one equation, pronounced of equal worth, but their "equality" will always remain imputed rather than inherent. Prices will remain arbitrary as long as the exchange rests on a negotiated parity between the exchange items—negotiated according to the bargaining powers of the contracting parties. Not everyone pays a half million dollars for a dinner invitation. Some pay nothing at all. The manipulatable rate of exchange makes it a treacherous model for "fair play." Lily "owes" Trenor the payment that he now demands only according to his rate of exchange—not hers—and his ability to set the rate and impose it on Lily says nothing about fairness, only something about power.

Power in *The House of Mirth*, many critics have suggested, is patriarchical. They are right, no doubt, about the basis for power, insofar as power is economic and insofar as money making is a male prerogative, but the actual wielders of power in the book are often not men but women. On the whole, Wharton is interested less in the etiology of power than in the way power comports itself, in the mode and manner of its workings. She is most interested, that is to say, in the mediated and socialized forms of power, power that women do enjoy and that they use skillfully and sometimes brutally. Within the orbits of exchange, power resides in the ability to define the terms of exchange, to make one thing "equal" to another. That privilege belongs, obviously, to only one of the partners, and this intrinsic inequity gives the lie to Trenor's notion of fairness. A presumed model of justice and mutuality, exchange really grows out of an imbalance of power, which it in turn reconstitutes. Its "fair play" is in fact a fiction masking a deeper reality of unfairness, for the rate of exchange is no more than a tautological reflection of the inequity that is the condition as well as the result of its operations.

—Wai-Chee Dimock, "Debasing Exchange: Edith Wharton's *The House of Mirth*," PMLA 100, no. 5 (October 1985), excerpted in *Modern Critical Views: Edith Wharton*, ed. Harold Bloom (New York: Chelsea House Publishers, 1985), 123–26

ELAINE SHOWALTER

Telling the history of women past thirty was part of the challenge Wharton faced as a writer looking to the twentieth century. The threshold of thirty established for women by nineteenth-century conventions of "girlhood" and marriageability continued in the twentieth century as a psychological observation about the formation of feminine identity. While Wharton's ideas about personality were shaped by Darwinian rather than by Freudian determinants, she shared Freud's pessimism about the difficulties of change for women. In his essay "Femininity," for example, Freud lamented the way that women's psyches and personalities became fixed by the time they were thirty. While a thirty-year-old man "strikes us as a youthful, somewhat unformed individual, whom we expect to make powerful use of the possibilities for development opened up to him by analysis," Freud wrote, a woman of thirty "often frightens us by her psychical rigidity and unchangeability. Her libido has taken up fixed positions and seems incapable of exchanging them for others." From Wharton's perspective Lily Bart is locked into fixed positions that are social and economic as well as products of the libido. Her inability to exchange these positions for others constitutes an impasse in the age as well as the individual.

Wharton situates Lily Bart's crisis of adulthood in the contexts of a larger historical shift. We meet her first in Grand Central Station, "in the act of transition between one and another of the country houses that disputed her presence at the close of the Newport season," and indeed *The House of Mirth* is a pivotal text in the historical transition from one house of American women's fiction to another, from the homosocial women's culture and literature of the nineteenth century to the heterosexual fiction of modernism. Like Edna Pontellier, Lily is stranded between two worlds of female experience: the intense female friendships and mother-daughter bonds characteristic of nineteenth-century American women's culture, which Carroll Smith-Rosenberg has called "the female world of love and ritual," and the dissolution of these single-sex relationships in the interests of more intimate friendships between women and men that was part of the gender crisis of the turn of the century. Between 1880 and 1910, patterns of gender behavior and relationship were being redefined. As early as the 1880s, relationships between mothers and daughters became strained as daughters pressed for education, work, mobility, sexual autonomy, and power outside the female sphere. Heroines sought friendship from male classmates and companions as well as within their single-sex communities.

These historical and social changes in women's roles had effects on women's writing as well. Pre-Civil War American women's fiction, variously described as "woman's fiction," "literary domesticity," or "the sentimental novel," celebrated female solidarity and revised patriarchal institutions, especially Christianity, in feminist and matriarchal terms. Its plots were characterized by warmth, intense sisterly feeling, and a sacramental view of motherhood. As these "bonds of womanhood," in Nancy Cott's term, were being dissolved by cultural pressures toward heterosexual relationships, women's plots changed as well. In 1851, for example, Susan Warner's best-selling novel *The Wide, Wide World* tearfully recounted the history of a girl painfully separated from her mother. But in 1882, in Warner's artistically superior but less-celebrated *Diana*, we are given an astringent and startling modern analysis of the psychological warfare between mother and daughter and the mother's fierce efforts to thwart her daughter's romance. As women's culture came under attack, so too its survivors clung desperately to the past, seeing men as the interlopers in their idyllic community. While some women writers of this generation championed the New Woman, others of the older generation grieved for the passing of the "lost Paradise" of women's culture. In their fiction, male invaders are met with hostility, and the struggle between female generations is sometimes murderous. By the century's end, as Josephine Donovan explains, "the woman-centered, matriarchal world of the Victorians is in its last throes. The preindustrial values of that world, female identified and ecologically holistic, are going down to defeat before the imperialism of masculine technology and patriarchal institutions."

The writers and feminist thinkers of Wharton's transitional generation, Elizabeth Ammons has noted, wrote "about troubled and troubling young women who were not always loved by their American readers." This literature, Ammons points out, "consistently focused on two issues: marriage and work." Seeing marriage as a form of work, a woman's job, it also raises the question of work and especially of creativity. The fiction of this transitional phase in women's history and women's writing is characterized by unhappy endings, as novelists struggled with the problem of going beyond the allowable limits and breaking through the available histories and stories for women.

Unlike some other heroines of the fiction of this transitional phase, Lily Bart is neither the educated, socially conscious, rebellious New Woman, nor the androgynous artist who finds meaning for her life in solitude and creativity, nor the old woman fiercely clinging to the past whom we so often see as the heroine of the post–Civil War local colorists. Her skills and morality are those of the Perfect Lady. In every crisis she rises magnificently to the occasion, as we see when Bertha insults her, her aunt disinherits her, Rosedale rejects her. Lawrence Selden, the would-be New Man to whom she turns for friendship and faith, criticizes Lily for being "'perfect to everyone'"; but he demands an even further moral perfection that she can finally only satisfy by dying. Lily's uniqueness, the emphasis Wharton gives to her lonely pursuit of ladylike manners in the midst of vulgarity, boorishness, and malice, makes us feel that she is somehow the *last* lady in New York, what Louis Auchincloss calls the "lone and solitary" survivor of a bygone age.

I would argue, however, that Wharton refuses to sentimentalize Lily's position but rather, through associating it with her own limitations as the Perfect Lady Novelist, makes us aware of the cramped possibilities of the lady whose creative roles are defined and controlled by men. Lily's plight has a parallel in Wharton's career as the elegant scribe of upper-class New York society, the novelist of manners and decor. Cynthia Griffin Wolff calls *The House of Mirth* Wharton's "first Kunstlerroman," and in important ways, I would agree, Wharton's *House of Mirth* is also a fictional house of birth for the woman artist. Wolff points out that *The House of Mirth* is both a critique of the artistic representation of women—the transformation of women into beautiful objects of male aesthetic appreciation—and a satiric analysis of the artistic traditions that "had evolved no conventions designed to render a woman as the maker of beauty, no language of feminine growth and mastery." In her powerful analysis of Lily Bart's disintegration, Wharton "could turn her fury upon a world which had enjoined women to spend their artistic inclinations entirely upon a display of self. Not the woman as productive artist, but the woman as self-creating artistic object—that is the significance of the brilliant and complex characterization of Lily Bart." In deciding that a Lily cannot survive, that the lady must die to make way for the modern woman who will work, love, and give birth, Wharton was also signaling her own rebirth as the artist who would describe the sensual worlds of *The Reef, Summer,* and *The Age of Innocence* and who would create the language of feminine growth and mastery in her own work.

—Elaine Showalter, "The Death of the Lady (Novelist): Wharton's *House of Mirth,*" *Representations* 9 (Winter 1985), excerpted in *Modern Critical Views: Edith Wharton,* ed. Harold Bloom (New York: Chelsea House Publishers, 1986), 140–42

DONNA M. CAMPBELL

Edith Wharton's impatience with what she called the "rose and lavender pages" of the New England local color "authoresses" reverberates throughout her autobiography and informs such novels as *Ethan Frome* and *Summer*. In *A Backward Glance* she explains that *Ethan Frome* arose from her desire "to draw life as it really was in the derelict mountain villages of New England, a life . . . utterly unlike that seen through the rose-coloured spectacles of my predecessors, Mary Wilkins and Sarah Orne Jewett." The genre of women's local color fiction that Wharton thus disdained was in one sense, as Josephine Donovan has suggested ⟨in *Local Color: A Woman's Tradition* (New York: Felix Ungar, 1983) and *After the Fall: The Demeter-Persephone Myth in Wharton, Cather, and Glasgow* (University Park, PA: Pennsylvania State University Press, 1988)⟩, the culmination of a coherent feminine literary tradition whose practitioners had effectively seized the margins of realistic discourse and, within their self-imposed limitations of form and subject, transformed their position into one of strength. Wharton, however, was determined to expose the genre's weaknesses rather than to capitalize upon its strengths. At the outset of her career, the 1890s backlash against local color and "genteel" fiction showed Wharton that to be taken seriously, she would have to repudiate the local colorists.

What needs to be recognized is the degree to which Wharton, as an ambitious woman writer responding to the 1890s transition between local color and naturalism, effected this repudiation very early in her career, well before challenging the tradition in regional novels such as *Ethan Frome* and *Summer* or assuming the persona of the secure literary grande dame of *A Backward Glance*. In both "Mrs. Manstey's View," her first published story (Scribner's Magazine, 1891), and "Bunner Sisters" (written circa 1891; published 1916 in *Xingu*), Wharton interfuses the city landscapes of naturalism with the potent iconography and themes of local color, providing a chilling commentary upon the limitations of local color fiction in a naturalistic world that encroaches upon and threatens its ideals. ⟨. . .⟩

From the comic misunderstandings of romance, "Bunner Sisters" descends into melodrama and, finally, into the naturalistic world of the streets. Stories of unpleasant reality replace the pleasantly melodramatic stories of Miss Mellins: surrounded at Tiffany's by ticking clocks suggestive of her time-dominated post-lapsarian state, Ann Eliza learns of Mr. Ramy's drug problem; returning to the shop after her marriage, Evelina "pile[s] up, detail by detail, her dreary narrative" (p. 251) after her child's birth and death, of Ramy's abuse and abandonment, and of begging in the streets, a tale quite unlike the uneventful happenings she used to report. Like the naturalistic "brute" who crushes Mrs. Manstey's magnolia blossom underfoot, Mr. Ramy is thus identified as a disruptive, threatening emissary from the world of naturalism, and Evelina has moved from her sister's local color world to a naturalistic one. This dose of unpleasant reality ironically turns Ann Eliza back into a storyteller, this time as a creator of false rather than true stories. Miss Mellins had invented lurid stories of the city and brought some controlled excitement into their safe environment; now Ann Eliza must invent stories of safety to conceal the terrifying reality of their plight. Knowing at last the "truth" of life as it is lived outside the shop, she must use her fictive arts to conceal Evelina's situation, just as she had once used similar arts to conceal the breach between her feelings and her actions when Evelina fell in love with Mr. Ramy.

The concluding sections of "Bunner Sisters" emphasize the completeness of the sisters' assimilation into the naturalistic world of "real life" and the utter hopelessness of their plight. As Evelina reveals her final betrayal—conversion to Roman Catholicism—Ann Eliza barely protests, for the faith that had early caused her to kneel in fervent prayer has given way to the belief that "if he was not good he was not God, and there was only a black abyss above the roof of Bunner Sisters" (p. 254). The dissociation of time from faith that had begun when Ann Eliza gauged time by the nickel clock instead of the church tower is completed when she denies that either time or faith has a place in her life: she saw "the church tower with the dial that had marked the hours for the sisters before [she] had bought the nickel clock. She looked at it all as though it had been the scene of some unknown life" (p. 262). Her refusal is ironic, however, for she has moved into the clock-metered biological time of naturalistic fiction, where the natural processes of decay chip away at the advantages of youth and strength. Having lost her savings, her shop, her faith, and her sister, she plunges into the indifferent "great thoroughfare" of the city and asks about a position as a saleslady, only to be told that the stores "want a bright girl . . . not over thirty, anyhow; and nice-looking" (p. 263). Like Mrs. Manstey, whose movement beyond the "frame" of her bow window costs her her life, Ann Eliza, bereft of the safe "frame" of her shop window, faces the dangers of the city alone. She looks for a replacement refuge, "another shop window with a sign in it," in much the same way that Carrie Meeber and Susan Lenox were to do. But unlike Carrie and Susan, she is neither eighteen years old nor beautiful; in a world that favors those who are young, male, prosperous, and well-connected, she remains a local color heroine—old, female, poor, and alone. It reverses the happy ending of the heroine starting fresh, marking instead, as Edmund Wilson comments ⟨in "Justice to Edith Wharton," *The Wound and the Bow* (Cambridge: Riverside Press, 1941), 204⟩, "the grimmest moment of Edith Wharton's darkest years."

"Bunner Sisters," like "Mrs. Manstey's View," calls into question some of the most seriously held beliefs of local color fiction: the critique of limited perspective and subject matter in "Mrs. Manstey's View" gives way here to a persistent attempt to refute the power of renunciation. Ann Eliza sacrifices everything for her sister, giving up Mr. Ramy, her savings, her shop, and her relationship with Evelina itself. Her reward for all this is Evelina's self-pity, selfishness, simpering vanity, and peevish demands for yet more sacrifice, for Ann Eliza, like Ethan Frome, is "tied to an inferior partner." ⟨Blake Nevius, *Edith Wharton: A Study of Her Fiction* (Berkeley: University of California Press, 1961), 126⟩. In addition, she must face the possibility that she is, as Evelina hints, somehow to blame; after all, she did bring the clock home and help the courtship along. Part of Ann Eliza's education is learning to confront, as she now does, that Howellsian dilemma, "the awful problem of the inutility of self-sacrifice":

> Hitherto she had never thought of questioning the inherited
> principles which had guided her life. Self-effacement for the good
> of others had always seemed to her both natural and necessary; but
> then she had taken it for granted that it implied the securing of that
> good. Now she perceived that to refuse the gifts of life does not
> ensure their transmission to those for whom they have been
> surrendered; and her familiar heaven was unpeopled. (p. 254)

⟨Elizabeth⟩ Ammons ⟨in *Edith Wharton's Argument with America* (Athens: University of Georgia Press, 1980), 13⟩ objects that "there have been no 'gifts of life' to surrender, much less transmit," but if one can accept the local color notion that the "silvery twilight hue which sometimes ends a day of storm" (p. 188) or, less poetically, the small daily pleasures of the sisters represent a satisfying life, then Ann Eliza's turn of phrase must be accepted as legitimate. Both Mrs. Manstey and Ann Eliza make tremendous sacrifices to preserve something they value, and in neither case does the action have any meaning. Both risk everything they have, and lose.

The evidence of Wharton's repudiation of, and by extension her deep engagement with, local color and naturalism can be found in many of her writings. It underlies the irritated references to naturalism in her correspondence, and it exists in the earnest and atypical explanations of her work that she offers in the Introduction to *Ethan Frome* and in *A Backward Glance*. Even more convincing is the fictional representation of this struggle for autonomy. "Mrs. Manstey's View" offers a picture of a woman artist so hampered by the limitations of her art, and so dependent upon others for preserving its conditions, that she can ultimately maintain her sense of artistic integrity only through a violent action that leads to her death. The story suggests both Wharton's fear of entrapment within an unnecessarily limited tradition and her apprehension that a radical break could destroy her promising career; as Wharton probably recognized, the familiar local color elements of "Mrs. Manstey's View" may have helped this first story of hers to be published.

"Bunner Sisters," Wharton's most overt exploration of naturalism and local color fiction, deserves to be better known than it is, not only because of its considerable literary merit, but because it provides in miniature an account of the literary shift from local color to naturalism from the standpoint of a woman writer who prepared herself to meet the challenge. Versed in the self-sacrificing ethos of local color fiction, Ann Eliza Bunner interprets the world with a deadly innocence and a willful insistence on what Wharton saw as its rosy light of romance, and she pays for her misreading in her naturalistically conceived fate. Wharton's strategy, in these early works as in *Ethan Frome* and *Summer*, was to engage, transform, and finally dismiss both genres within her own highly conscious fiction. Determined not to emulate her hapless creature Ann Eliza Bunner, Wharton took care not to be stuck in what she saw as the airless, timeless, self-sacrificing confines of local color fiction until changing literary fashions should figuratively throw her out onto the littered naturalistic streets.

> —Donna M. Campbell, "Edith Wharton and the 'Authoresses': The Critique of Local Color in Wharton's Early Fiction," *Studies in American Fiction* 22, no. 2 (Autumn 1994): 169

JULIER OLIN-AMMENTORP

Wharton's initial reaction to ⟨World War I⟩ epitomizes the mixture of emotions with which she would view the war as a whole, and which would shape much of her writing about the war. Writing to Bernard Berenson ten days after the mobilization of France on Aug. 1, 1914, Wharton remarked:

> It is all thrillingly interesting, but very sad to see one's friends going to the slaughter.
> There is so much to say that I won't begin now—but, oh, think of this time last year! Hasn't it shaken all the foundations of reality for

you? ⟨*The Letters of Edith Wharton*, ed. R. W. B. Lewis and Nancy Lewis (New York: Scribner's, 1988), 357⟩ ⟨. . .⟩

The tension between romanticization and realism, fascination and horror is mirrored further in Wharton's attitude toward her trips to the front. Although Wharton shies away from the horrors of war, she often expresses a desire to witness, even experience, the war first-hand. The "reprisals too hideous to picture," the events "one dare not picture," did not deter Wharton from traveling as close to the front as she could and from glorying in such travel. In one letter, Wharton refers to her travels to the front as "eight days of wonderful adventures" —an enthusiasm one would expect more from a jaunt through Italy than from close views of the war. ⟨*Letters*, 356⟩ Further, Wharton seems to have had a constant, almost nagging fear of missing out on some kind of "real" or "genuine" experience of the war. Charles Bowen in *The Custom of the Country* remarks that American women miss out on "the real business of life" in America, that is, money and financial affairs. For Wharton, the "real business of war" seems to be the front lines, and her war writings reflect her fear that, as a woman and a civilian, she may be missing out on the "real" experience of war. Wharton's war writing, both fiction and nonfiction, is haunted by this sense, despite the fact that she describes herself repeatedly as the exception to the rule that women and civilians must keep away from the front. In one letter to Henry James she temporarily forgets her civilian status, boasting that she is going "off again to see other military scenes inaccessible to the civilian" ⟨*Letters*, 356⟩. In another, she notes that she is going "to see a little corner of reconquered Alsace, which no one has been allowed to visit as yet" ⟨*Letters*, 356⟩. She is thrilled at being told at Verdun, "Vous etes la premiere femme qui soit venue a Verdun" ("You are the first woman to have come to Verdun") ⟨*Letters*, 350⟩. Wharton's thrill in these situations demonstrates her fear of missing "the real business" of war—that is, she is thrilled to find herself such an exception because it means that she is not, in fact, missing the "real thing." Just as she once referred to herself as "him"—part of the privileged sex—in a letter ⟨*Letters*, 398⟩, so here she has unconsciously turned herself into part of the military she seems to long for as she goes off to "military scenes inaccessible to the civilian."

In spite of such unusual access to scenes of the war, Wharton's fiction reflects a fear that, in the end, she did miss "the real thing." Her war stories are, as she acknowledges, not typical war stories: they are not stories of action and heroism or even tedious hours in the trenches, but rather stories "suggested by the war"—stories suggested by Wharton's experiences, observations, and reflections on the war and on the home front culture that the war produced. ⟨. . .⟩

Many critics have noted that, with the exception of *The Age of Innocence* (1920), Wharton's fiction declines in quality in the post-war period. Although some of the later novels, particularly *The Children* (1928) and *The Mother's Recompense* (1925), have redeeming qualities, it is hard to argue that any of them except *Summer*, written during the war, and *The Age of Innocence* match the quality of her best prewar fiction: *The House of Mirth, Ethan Frome, The Custom of the Country*. The war seems to have shaken both Wharton and her writing profoundly. Her early question to Berenson—"hasn't it shaken all the foundations of reality for you?"—may have predicted a shake-up from which Wharton never fully recovered.

Her remarks in *A Backward Glance* seem to confirm this. The thirteenth chapter of her memoir is "The War"; the fourteenth and final, "And After"—as if everything after the war (which concluded nearly twenty years before her death) were merely an aftermath. "My chief feeling, I confess, was that I was tired—oh, so tired!" she says of the war's end; she lists those close to her who died in and during the war, including four war casualties—Ronald Simmons, her young cousin Newbold Rhinelander, and two French friends—and three who died of old age during the war: Henry James, Egerton Winthrop, and Howard Sturgis. She even speculated, she says, on whether she would write any more:

> After "A Son at the Front" I intended to take a long holiday—perhaps to cease from writing altogether. It was growing more and more evident that the world I had grown up in and been formed by had been destroyed in 1914, and I felt myself incapable of transmuting the raw material of the after-war world into a work of art. Gardening, reading and travel seemed the only solace left. ⟨*A Backward Glance* (New York: Scribner's 1961), 369–70⟩

The remaining pages of her memoir are devoted to travel reminiscences and to memories of friends; the final paragraphs are undeniably melancholy. The "after-war world" was not a place where Wharton felt at home, nor a place "transmute[d]" easily into the art she had learned. The war, so "thrillingly interesting" at its outset, became a far larger and more crushing part of her life than she could ever have imagined. The short stories "suggested by the war" illustrate Wharton's attempt to come to terms, literarily, with the war; the fiction after the war suggests how difficult that task would be.

—Julier Olin-Ammentorp, "'Not Precisely War Stories': Edith Wharton's Short Fiction from the Great War," *Studies in American Fiction* 23, no. 2 (Autumn 1995): 153

KATHY GRAFTON

In Edith Wharton's 1917 novel *Summer* the relationship between the heroine, Charity Royall, and her lover, Lucius Harney, depicts a kind of feminine sexual awakening that is profoundly original in literature. As Cynthia Griffin Wolff notes in her introduction to the book, "*Summer* is not the first Bildungsroman to focus on this awakening to maturity as it occurs in a woman's life; however, it is the first to deal explicitly with sexual passion as an essential component of that process." (x) The precise way in which this sexual relationship is entered into by these young people has significant psychoanalytical ramifications. Specifically, Harney's need for a certain degradation of Charity to occur before he can find her sexually accessible, his subconscious need to separate feelings of sexual desire and attraction from feelings of genuine tenderness and high esteem, and Charity's own need to experience her sexuality as a forbidden pleasure, constitute driving forces in the revelation of their relationship within the novel. Freud's 1912 essay "The Most Prevalent Form of Degradation in Erotic Life" proves insightful in a close analysis of the relationship between Charity and Harney—particularly with regard to the factors that contribute to Harney's perspective and involvement. ⟨. . .⟩

Freud claims that the most prevalent way in which the male then copes with his divided feelings is to create two love objects—one to love, the other to desire. He then degrades the desired love object in some way in order that his desire for her become acceptable to himself:

> The principal means of protection used by men against this complaint consists in lowering the sexual object in their own estimation, while reserving for the incestuous object and for those who represent it the overestimation normally felt for the sexual object. As soon as the sexual object fulfills the condition of being degraded, sensual feeling can have free play, considerable sexual capacity and a high degree of pleasure can be developed. ⟨Sigmund Freud, "The Most Prevalent Form of Degradation in Erotic Life" (1912) in *Collected Papers* (New York: Basic, 1959), 208⟩

Although Harney does not himself degrade Charity, she suffers degradation in his eyes due to Mr. Royall's outburst. Harney also does not understand why this outburst makes her suddenly seem more sexually accessible to him in comparison to Annabel Balch, his well-brought-up fiancee. Freud also addresses this problem:

> The man almost always feels his sexual activity hampered by his respect for the woman and only develops full sexual potency when he finds himself in the presence of a lower type of sexual object; and this

again is partly conditioned by the circumstance that his sexual aims include those of perverse sexual components which with his well-brought-up wife, for instance, he does not venture to do. ⟨Freud 210⟩
⟨. . .⟩

In drawing a correlation between Harney's need for degradation and Charity's need for forbiddenness, we must consider the standards of the society in which they lived and the ways in which they were educated by this society. In fact, Freud posits this cultural education concerning sexuality as the main catalyst for these tendencies in men and women. His sociosexual typology, dependent on Vienna, successfully maintains its validity when translated to Nettleton in that Wharton, in accord with Freud, perceives "the excessive self-denial that respectable middle-class society imposed on the sexual needs of ordinary humans" (Gay 338).

Indeed, Wharton had ample occasion to experience these excessive restrictions in her own life. For example, she "did not find out where babies came from until several weeks after her marriage" ⟨Cynthia Griffin Wolff, A Feast of Words: The Triumph of Edith Wharton (New York: Oxford University Press, 1977), 40⟩. Though she pleaded with her mother a few days before her marriage to explain the "facts of life" to her, Wharton met only with "icy disapproval" and the impatient reply, "You've seen enough pictures and statues in your life. Haven't you noticed that men are—made differently from women? . . . Then for heaven's sake don't ask me any more silly questions. You can't be as stupid as you pretend!" (Wolff 40). Wharton is, unquestionably, a perfect example of the kind of woman Freud is speaking of in his essay. Thus it is not surprising that Wharton's descriptions of the social milieu of Nettleton readily correspond to Freud's descriptions of the social late-nineteenth-early-twentieth-century Vienna, where "court preciosity found an equivalent in every bourgeois household, where girls were so sheltered from the facts of sexuality that many marriages foundered in frigidity"—indeed, where "[in] sex-starved young women, neuroses were commonplace" (Johnson 240). In short, Wharton seems to agree with Freud that "the unconscious . . . cannot escape culture" (Gay 338). ⟨. . .⟩

The fact that Charity is degraded in Harney's eyes allows him to lower his estimation of her; she thus becomes sexually desirable for him. However, his fiancee, Annabel Balch, remains untainted in his mind. Although she is portrayed as sexually repressed, Harney's esteem for her remains high as he reserves for her the feelings of tenderness and regard he theoretically reserves for his mother and/or sister. Because Harney is unable to feel sexual desire for Annabel, he needs Charity.

On the other hand, Charity has been educated to understand her own sexual desires as something that must remain unacknowledged and stifled because of society's expectations. She specifically learns this through the fate of Julia Hawes. Yet she chooses to break the rules, and the knowledge that she is doing so greatly contributes to her excitement. Because her sexual relationship with Harvey is taboo in the eyes of her society, an inevitable link is formed in her mind between the fulfillment of sexual desires and forbiddenness. The application of Freud's essay to the story of Charity Royall helps us to uncover and clarify many of the underlying factors and potent forces that are the catalysts for the sexual awakening that she and Lucius Harney experience.

It is interesting, finally, that Charity and Harney's relationship does not completely fit Freud's pattern. Specifically, Harney is not at a loss for tender feelings toward Charity, as Freud's male is for his desired object. Neither does the need for forbiddenness continue to dominate Charity's sexuality, making her ultimately frigid. Instead, Harney displays a combination of tenderness and degradation in his actions toward Charity, and Charity develops an understanding of her own sexuality and affirms herself, no longer relying on forbiddenness, when she chooses to have her baby, believe in the love that she and Harney shared, and marry Mr. Royall. She becomes a powerful source of life in the end rather than the frigid woman exemplified by Freud's model.

—Kathy Grafton, "Degradation and Forbidden Love in Edith Wharton's *Summer*," *Twentieth Century Literature* 41, no. 4 (Winter 1995): 350

JOHN CLUBBE

No American author has written with more understanding and artistry about the interplay among character, social history, and domestic esthetics than has Edith Wharton. In 1897 she established herself as an authority on interiors with *The Decoration of Houses*, written with the noted Gilded Age designer Ogden Codman, Jr. From that time forward Wharton's fine-tuned readings of interior space became a signature aspect of her writings. Edmund Wilson ⟨in "Justice to Edith Wharton," reprinted in *Edith Wharton: A Collection of Critical Essays*, ed. Irving Howe (Englewood Cliffs, NJ: Prentice-Hall, 1962), 23⟩ once called her, rightly, "not only one of the great pioneers, but also the poet, of interior decoration." It is in *The House of Mirth* (1905) that her genius in this area is most compelling. Part of the triumph of *The House of Mirth* results from the pains Wharton took to correlate the character of the clearly beautiful and clearly flawed Lily Bart to her environment, an environment that consists chiefly of a sequence of interiors.

The House of Mirth chronicles the efforts of Lily Bart, single, poor, and twenty-nine, to move from the interiors that constrict her to the ideal but unfocused interior that haunts her dreams. That over the novel's course she fails to realize a lastingly viable interior for herself or to find herself truly at home in any interior space may seem the result of her background, financial status, and the limited scope offered women of her acquaintance, but Wharton makes it abundantly clear that in spite of it all Lily has numerous chances to take charge of her life. An analysis of Lily in relation to interior space lends support to the position that Wharton's presentation of her heroine is not unrelievedly deterministic, as many contemporary feminist critics have argued, but many-faceted, subtle, and richly ambivalent. ⟨. . .⟩

Of primary importance in Wharton's portrayal of Lily's opportunities to make different choices in her life are two flats—relatively new kinds of interior space in the early twentieth-century urban scene. The first belongs to Lawrence Selden, where the novel opens with a charming and, we realize later, prescient interchange between Selden and Lily. "'Even women,' he said, 'have been known to enjoy the privileges of a flat'" (p. 9). He has invited Lily, whom he has encountered at Grand Central Station, to tea. Lily replies, "'Oh, governesses—or widows. But not girls—not poor, miserable, marriageable girls!'" But Selden knows "a girl who lives in a flat," his rather plain cousin Gerty Farish. To this seeming exception Lily ripostes: "But I said *marriageable*—and besides, she has a horrid little place . . . I should hate that, you know" (p. 10). Comfortable in Selden's domain, Lily recalls her previous discomfiture in Gerty Farish's flat, an interior in which she will later be offered affection as well as hospitality. Her initially negative response to Gerty's flat becomes more negative as the novel proceeds, but it turns out uncannily prophetic of her inability generally to "read" interiors except from the standards of her imagined "good taste." Lily never penetrates beyond surface signs, never seeks out the deeper and ever-changing meanings of personal settings. One of Wharton's essential lessons is that failure to understand interiors in relation to those who inhabit them augurs other kinds of failure. Responding meaningfully to place is intimately tied to conceptualizing and working realistically toward a better fate for oneself: both require an imagination vigorously alive to otherness. But throughout most of the novel Lily's imagination remains passively narcissistic.

We need to consider Wharton's portrayal of Lily in terms of Selden's and Gerty's flats within the context of early twentieth-century architectural/sociological history. Flats were still at this time a relatively new phenomenon in New York as in other large American cities. Though Manhattan experienced a flurry of apartment house construction while Wharton worked on *The House of Mirth*, its first apartment building dated only from 1869 and its most famous— still its most famous—the grand Dakota overlooking Central Park, went up only in 1884. The idea of flats came from France, and in America as in England flats long carried connotations of dubious French mores. The middle-class and wealthy thought living horizontally in flats slightly immoral. Did not proper people live vertically in houses? In *The Age of Innocence* (1920) Wharton records society's shock in the 1870s when the wealthy Mrs. Manson Mingott, a venerable society dowager, instead of living on the several floors of her New York townhouse, decided to live exclusively on the ground level. Guests in her sitting-room had "the unexpected vista of a bedroom." Living on one floor creates what Wharton, tongue-in-cheek but accurately in terms of contemporary opinion, called "the stage-setting for adultery."

By 1905, when she published *The House of Mirth*, many families as well as single men lived in flats. Still, when a single woman—at least a *"marriageable"* single woman—took a flat by herself, she risked societal disapproval. Even an independently-minded, unattached woman like Lily Bart deems it slightly improper for a woman to have her own flat. Given "the moral code of bachelors' flat-houses" (p. 20), Lily dares much even visiting Selden in his. But if she dares much, ultimately perhaps—so the overall perspective of *The House of Mirth* may imply—she does not dare enough.

—John Clubbe, "Interiors and the Interior Life in Edith Wharton's *The House of Mirth*," *Studies in the Novel* 28, no. 4 (Winter 1996): 543, 545–46

BIBLIOGRAPHY

The Decoration of Houses (with Ogden Codman Jr.). 1897.
The Greater Inclination. 1899.
The Touchstone. 1900.
Crucial Instances. 1901.
The Valley of Decision. 1902.
Sanctuary. 1903.
The Descent of Man and Other Stories. 1904.
Italian Villas and Their Gardens. 1904.
Italian Backgrounds. 1905.
The House of Mirth. 1905.
Madame de Treymes. 1907.
The Fruit of the Tree. 1907.
A Motor-Flight Through France. 1908.
The Hermit and the Wild Woman and Other Stories. 1908.
Artemis to Actaeon and Other Verses. 1909.
Tales of Men and Ghosts. 1910.
Ethan Frome. 1911.

The Reef. 1912.

The Custom of the Country. 1913.

Fighting France, from Dunkerque to Belfort. 1915.

Xingu and Other Stories. 1916.

The Book of the Homeless (editor). 1916.

Summer. 1917.

The Marne. 1918.

French Ways and Their Meaning. 1919.

The Age of Innocence. 1920.

In Morocco. 1920.

The Glimpses of the Moon. 1922.

A Son at the Front. 1923.

Old New York: False Dawn, The Old Maid, The Spark, New Year's Day. 1924.

The Mother's Recompense. 1925.

Writing of Fiction. 1925.

Here and Beyond. 1926.

Twelve Poems. 1926.

Twilight Sleep. 1927.

The Children. 1928.

Hudson River Bracketed. 1929.

Certain People. 1930.

The Gods Arrive. 1932.

Human Nature. 1933.

A Backward Glance. 1934.

The World Over. 1936.

Ghosts. 1937.

The Buccaneers (incomplete). 1938.

I Π Ð Ϲ X